M

MI5'S FIRST SPYMASTER

ABOUT THE AUTHOR

Andrew Cook worked for many years as a foreign affairs and defence specialist, and the contacts he made enabled him to navigate and gain access to classified intelligence services archives. He is only the fifth historian to be given special permission under the 1992 'Waldegrave Initiative' by the Cabinet Office to examine closed MI5 documents that will never be released. He is author of critically acclaimed *Ace of Spies: The True Story of Sidney Reilly*, *To Kill Rasputin: The Life and Death of Grigori Rasputin* and *Prince Eddy: The King Britain Never Had*, all published by Tempus. He was the historical consultant for the recent BBC *Timewatch* documentary on Rasputin, and was presenter and historical consultant for the Channel 4 documentary about the life of Prince Albert Victor. He is a regular contributor on espionage history to *The Guardian*, *The Times* and *History Today*. He lives in Bedfordshire.

MI5'S FIRST SPYMASTER

ANDREW COOK

TEMPUS

Paperback edition first published 2006

Tempus Publishing Limited
The Mill, Brimscombe Port,
Stroud, Gloucestershire, GL5 2QG
www.tempus-publishing.com

British Library Cataloguing in Publication Data.
A catalogue record for this book is available from the British Library.

ISBN 0 7524 3949 9

Typesetting and origination by Tempus Publishing Limited
Printed in Great Britain

Contents

ACKNOWLEDGEMENTS

I am greatly indebted to all those who have assisted me at the various stages of this project.

In particular, my thanks go to the Melville family, both in Ireland and New Zealand, and to HM Government. As a result of an approach to the Cabinet Office, the Government agreed to provide me with a briefing based on the records of William Melville's service with the War Office for the purpose of this book. I am equally indebted to Lindsay Clutterbuck, Steve Earl, Tom Oakley and John Ross of the London Metropolitan Police for their assistance with New Scotland Yard records and archival material.

I am also grateful to the following individuals who have helped me at various stages of my research: Michel Ameuw (France), Dr Michael Attias (UK), Jordan Auslander (USA), Dmitri Belanovskii (Russia), Marc Bernstein (USA), Jackie and Teresa Cahill (Kenmare), Dan Downing (*Sneem Parish News*), John Fitzpatrick (Sneem), Michael Gasson (BP Archive), David Humphries (PRO), Rajesh Kalyan (UK), Carol Leadenham (Hoover Institution, Stanford, California), Ken Linge (DABS Forensic Ltd), Aisling Lockhart (Trinity College, Dublin), Dr Sylvia Moehle (Germany), Danny Moriarty (Kenmare), Mary Morrigan (Dublin), Father Patrick Murphy (Parish Priest, Sneem), Stephen Parker (UK), Elizabeth Parkes (New Zealand), Joanna Quill (National Army Museum), Caroline Quirke (Assistant Registrar, Killarney), Rachel Sampson (BP Archive), Laura Scannell (Bar Council Archive), Graham Salt (UK) and Mark Tami MP.

I would like to thank those who have previously written on this and related subject matters for speaking or corresponding with me – Professor Christopher Andrew (Corpus Christi College, Cambridge), Gill Bennett (Chief Foreign Office Historian), Christy Campbell, Dr Nicholas Hiley (University of Kent), Alan Judd, Nick McCarty and Tom Wood.

The help and co-operation of the families of those who played a role in Melville's story has been greatly appreciated, as has the assistance of Francis & Francis (private and commercial investigators) who helped in tracing them.

A special thank you also goes to Caroline Beach, Sophie Bradshaw, Jo De Vries, Elaine Enstone, Monica Finch, Ingrid Lock, Carolyn Jardine, Patrick Ooi, Janie New, Hannah Renier, Bob Sheth and Chris Williamson for their hard work at various stages of this project. Also to RP Translate Ltd for their sterling work in translating source material from Russian, German and French into English and to my publisher Jonathan Reeve for his support and advice.

PREFACE

Shortly after her retirement as Director-General of the Security Service (MI5), Dame Stella Rimington paid tribute to the founding fathers of the Service and publicly acknowledged the role of William Melville, the man 'who came to be known as M'. At the start of the twentieth century, when London fogs – pea-soupers – blanketed the city, it was Melville who, from a small secret office in London's Victoria Street, determinedly lobbied the Government to create an effective counter-intelligence service. Today, MI5, the organisation he strove to create, is a household name and one of the world's leading intelligence agencies.

Melville talked to kings and murderers, con men and wily diplomats; he had a way of getting what he wanted from them all. In his day he was a master of detection. He had a devious mind and a bleakly humorous view of humanity, and because he understood the motive of the criminal or the desperate, he was able to pioneer methods and tactics that still work – today, methods improved by advanced technology.

Melville was the son of a publican in rural Ireland. Guileful and single-minded, he came to London when it was the hub of the Empire and worked his way through the ranks of the Metropolitan Police. As the most famous detective in England and head of Scotland Yard's Special Branch, he retired at the start of the new century and disappeared from public view. The enduring achievement of his life lay ahead: to transfer the ethos and practices of detection to the War Office, its spies and agents all over the world.

He died in 1918, and eighty years passed before his true significance as MI5's first spymaster became apparent with the release of early Secret Service documents to the Public Record Office. Very little further documentation about Melville and his career has come into the public domain since. To piece together an accurate picture of his extraordinary life, I have drawn on as many primary sources as possible. Melville's family and the descendants of those who played key roles in his story have been tracked down and interviewed; they have been invaluable in illuminating a life's work that pitted Melville against Jack the Ripper, Irish terrorists, anarchist assassins and German spy rings.

Now, with the help of recently declassified records, family accounts and documents that still await official release, the full story of his incredible career can finally be told for the first time.

Principal Characters

Sir Robert Anderson

Assistant Commissioner in charge of CID, Metropolitan Police 1888–1901. Engaged by Home Office on secret Irish work 1868; ran entrapment operations against Irish Nationalists.

Arthur Balfour

Nephew of Lord Salisbury, Conservative MP 1874–22. Prime Minister (1902–05), Foreign Secretary 1916–19).

Sir Edward Bradford

Chief Commissioner, Metropolitan Police, from 1890 following the resignation of James Monro.

William Burrell

Divisional Detective Inspector, CID, Metropolitan Police, from 1888. Special Staff, MI5, from 1914.

Vladimir Burtsev

Russian Revolutionary journalist and émigré. Arrested and tried for incitement to murder the Tsar in 1898.

Hector Bywater

Agent, Secret Service Bureau, from 1910.

Auguste Coulon

French anarchist and police informer. Suspected *agent provocateur* in 1891 Walsall bomb case.

Sir Henry Curtis-Bennett

Barrister; defence counsel at German espionage trials in First World War. Agent, MI5, from 1916.

Sir Mansfield Cumming	Head of Foreign Department, Secret Service Bureau, from 1909. Director of Secret Intelligence-Service (MI6) until 1923.
Major James Edmonds	Head of Section H, Intelligence Department, War Office, from outbreak of Boer War. Head of special section, Directorate of Military Operation. Led initiative resulting in creation of Secret Service Bureau, October 1909.
Herbert Fitch	Inspector, Special Branch. Resigned from Metropolitan Police January 1924.
Major Nicholas Gosselin	Deputy to Edward Jenkinson, Assistant Under-Secretary, Police and Crime in Ireland, from 1884.
Arthur Hailstone	Inspector, Special Branch, Metropolitan Police, from 1891. Secret Service Bureau from 1911.
Sir William Harcourt	Anti-imperialist Liberal MP 1868–1904. Home Secretary (1880–85).
Sir Edward Henry	Assistant Commissioner in charge of the CID, Metropolitan Police (May 1901–March 1903). Chief Commissioner (1903–18).
Edward Jenkinson	Pro-Home Ruler; Assistant Under-Secretary, police and crime in Ireland, from 1882. Recruited own spy ring and adopted covert role at Home Office.
Sir Vernon Kell	German intelligence analyst, War Office from 1902. Head of Home Department, Secret Service Bureau, from 1909. Director General, MI5, until 1940.

William Knox D'Arcy	Solicitor who purchased concession to prospect for oil in Persia 1901. Secured backing of British Government and Burmah Oil 1905, struck oil 1908 to form company now known as BP.
Chf. Inspector John Littlechild	Inspector, Special Irish Branch. Head of Special Branch (1887–1903).
Henry Dale Long	Agent, 'W. Morgan Investigation Bureau', from 1903. Secret Service Bureau from 1909.
Sir Melville MacNaghten	Assistant Commissioner in charge of CID, 1903–13.
Sir Henry Matthews	Home Secretary 1886–90. Attracted severe criticism over failure to apprehend Jack the Ripper.
Det. Sergeant Patrick McIntyre	Founder member, Special Irish Branch, 1882. Head of Special Branch; reduced to ranks after disciplinary action.
General F.F. Millen	Double agent. Member, Fenian Brotherhood and Clan-na-Gael; took part in unsuccessful Irish coup 1865. Named by James Monro as instigator of 1887 Jubilee Plot.
James Monro	Assistant Commissioner in charge of CID, Metropolitan Police, 1884–88. Chief Commissioner until 1890.
Joseph Moroney	Alias: Joseph Melville. Member, Clan-na-Gael. Involved in 1887 Jubilee Plot.
Charles Parnell	Irish Nationalist MP 1875–90; Irish Leader, House of Commons 1878. Political career ruined by divorce case.
Jacob Peters	Latvian revolutionary arrested for murder after Houndsditch shootings. member, Bolshevik Party; Deputy Chairman, Cheka, from 1917.

| Patrick Quinn | Founder member, Special Irish Branch. Superintendent and Head of Special Branch 1903–18. |

Sidney Reilly — Born Sigmund Rosenblum. Special Branch informer from 1896. Agent, Secret Intelligence Service (1918–22); executed by Russian secret police 1925.

Gustav Steinhauer — Chief of German Secret Service; established spy network in Britain before First World War. Bodyguard to Kaiser, worked with Melville, to thwart assassination attempt on Wilhelm II.

Richard Tinsley — Agent, Secret Service Bureau; provided intelligence on suspected German spies heading for Britain via Belgium.

Sir James Trotter — Head of Secret Section 13, War Office. Recruited Melville 1903 to take responsibility for agent recruitment and co-ordination.

Howard Vincent — Founder and first Head of Criminal Investigation Department, Metropolitan Police. Assistant Commissioner in charge of CID 1878–84.

Sir Charles Warren — Chief Commissioner, Metropolitan Police 1886–88; resigned in wake of police failure to apprehend 'Jack the Ripper'.

Adolphus 'Dolly' Williamson — First Head of Detective Department and Head of Special Irish Branch 1882–87. Deputy to James Monro from 1887.

ONE

THE MAN FROM KERRY

A secret is no longer a secret once it is revealed.

This self-evident truth is difficult for most people to grasp. William Melville, M of the British Secret Service, had no problem with it. In the last months of his life he was persuaded to commit a brief account of his career to paper. He had, after all, been known as *Le Vile Melville* to revolutionaries from St Petersburg to New York; men had been jailed for conspiring to kill him. This being known, a less revelatory memoir would be hard to imagine.[1]

It did, however, confirm suspicion that he had not, as the public thought, retired in 1903, but instead had worked in some secret capacity at a time when MI5, according to official histories, did not yet exist.

His life's work depended upon discretion. So did his reputation, which was the foundation of his family's prosperity, and he was never such a fool as to threaten that. There were skeletons in Melville's cupboard that he never expected to emerge.

Concluding his short memoir, he offered mild advice to those who proposed to embark upon a career in counter-espionage.

> Above all, the mysterious manner should be avoided. It only engenders distrust. A frank and apparently open style generally gains confidence... people as a rule are not averse to seeing you again. One can joke and humbug much in a jovial manner; one can talk a great deal and say nothing.

The genial mask concealed a ruthless operator.

Melville came out of the back of beyond, but the present inhabitants of his home town would thank no one for saying so. Sneem in County Kerry is a thriving tourist centre and one of the prettiest little places in the west of Ireland, its gaily painted houses set around an old stone bridge over a tumbling stream amid greensward surrounded by hills. But at a longitude of nearly 10 degrees west of Greenwich, it is further out in the Atlantic than almost anywhere else in Europe.[2]

Sneem suffered badly in the famine of the 1840s. From good beginnings as the hub of many outlying cabins and cottages, with a couple of schools, a penny post to Kenmare, seven markets a year and a post of constabulary, by 1850 – when Melville was born there – Sneem had declined into no more than a sad huddle of grey houses and listless people: 'a poor, dirty village' in the words of one traveller.

William was the son of James and Catherine Melville. As far as we know he was their first child. Family legend[3] has it that Catherine (*née* Connor) gave birth to him at a place called Direenaclaurig Cross (a junction of two roads) on the shore side of Kenmare Road, which leads east. The road itself had been officially called into existence some twenty years before. Until then, west of Kenmare towards Sneem and the ocean there had been no more than a track, impassable in bad weather.

Sneem in 1850 had a population of 360 living in about sixty dwellings, from the poorest one-roomed mud cabins with rags stuffing the windows to those slate-roofed, mortar-covered houses, mostly terraced, which survive today set around two triangular greens.

Having been born on 25 April 1850, William was baptised into the Roman Catholic Church the following day. There was no Irish civil registration until 1864. The baptismal record we owe to the often erratic attention of the parish priest. Father Walsh, the inspiration for Father O'Flynn in a popular song of that name, was priest in Sneem from 1829 until his death in 1866. He rarely preached a sermon from one year's end to another and was a notorious backslider when it came to record-keeping. Speaking English and Irish, he kept the books, when he bothered, in dog Latin. He devoted himself to hunting, being the proud owner of six or seven greyhounds even during the famine ('though nobody could tell how he was even able to feed himself'), as well as a collection of jackdaws and hawks; his usual garb was a battered hat and hairy suit made of buffalo skin and he and the local doctor once caused an explosion while concocting home-made gunpowder.[4] We must, in the circumstances, be grateful for what little information we have.

The very poorest of the native Irish at this time lived in medieval conditions, in earth-floored dwellings having only one or two rooms. They burned turf for cooking and warmth and would share their roof with the animals overnight in winter. They had to live at subsistence level off whatever they could grow, and the animals they could keep, on any strip of land rented from English landlords. Getting cash depended on employment by these landlords on their land or at the nearest Big House. Otherwise farming and fishing, a little discreet smuggling of brandy, wine or tobacco by sea, or a skilled trade were the only options short of emigration to America or England.

Perhaps because the well-off Anglo-Irish around Sneem intermarried with each other over generations and generally put down roots, thus supporting the economy and the smuggling to a greater extent than elsewhere, the village was not entirely deserted like so many during the famine; most unusually for this time and place, the population actually increased in the ten years before William was born.

James Melville is recorded as a tenant, apparently a farmer, in the land valuation records of 1852, and in the next few years he and Catherine got enough money together to start a business in the middle of the village. They kept a bakery and also sold liquor. The traditional Irish pub with a shop at one end of the counter is still familiar.[5] Quite how many children they had is uncertain. Two girls, Catherine and Mary, and three boys, survived to be baptised, and these at long intervals.[6] After William came Richard in 1859, who was enrolled at the village school when he was five, and George in 1868, who does not appear on the school rolls until 1875. Unlike his brothers, William's school attendance would appear to have been somewhat erratic to say the least, tailing off during his last year to virtual non-attendance. As the eldest, his duties in the bakery would almost certainly have come before schooling.[7]

He would have learned the practical skills of rural life. Almost every family, even the tradespeople, kept a few chickens and grew vegetables, and James Melville as baker and liquor-seller kept a pony and cart for haulage and would have expected his sons to help out. As his parents ran a cash business the boy was probably acute enough about figures.

With Father Walsh to offer pastoral care, and the town's Roman Catholic chapel being left to crumble, religion is unlikely to have played a major part. Sneem's Catholic community was not to be allowed to slide into non-observance, however. In 1855 the Earl of Dunraven took a holiday home locally, and converted to Catholicism. When he saw the leaky old earth-floored shack of a chapel in Sneem he determined to donate something better, and commissioned no less a man than Philip Hardwicke, the distinguished London architect, to design a new church. As is usual in such matters, construction hit a snag. The local builder, Mr Murphy, died. But the new church had found a practical saviour in his son, who, at nineteen, was just six years older than William Melville. Murphy managed to get the church completed on time and its consecration in 1863 was followed by a bonfire and festivities, which continued until dawn. So well did the young Murphy, another Sneem boy made good, profit from building Sneem's church that he went on to found the multi-national construction company that still bears his name.

William Melville would have been a familiar figure to everybody in that village of only three or four hundred people. We gather that he did not leave home until his later teens, because he was known locally as a great hurley player.[8]

In the Melville family it is said that as he grew up, William used to take the pony and cart each Wednesday to Killarney Station to collect supplies. One Wednesday he did not return. A

search was mounted and the pony was found, patiently waiting
at the station. William had taken the train to Dublin.[9]

Whether he stopped for days, or years, in Dublin, Liverpool or
anywhere else, is impossible to say. He could have left Sneem at
seventeen or at twenty-one; we do not know for sure. Reports
he wrote later in life demonstrate a high degree of literacy, so
he may have done as many ambitious young English men did
and attended evening classes after a day's work in a shop. Self-
help – social and financial advancement through hard work,
good books and respectable living – was in vogue in these mid-
Victorian years, and as he would have known from personal
observation, money spent on drink – money that he may have
wanted to send home – would be wasted. The first record so far
discovered of Melville's presence in England is his acceptance
into London's police in 1872; yet it doesn't seem likely that what
Dubliners are pleased to call a bog-trotter, however bright and
adaptable, could have crossed from Sneem to London and within
months acquired the basic worldly wisdom required of even the
greenest police constable. William probably spent a few years in
a big city after he left home.

London was at this time the largest conurbation on earth,
with a population approaching four million and growing
fast.[10] Lambeth, comprising the parts of London immediately
south of the Thames, which is where Melville was working when he applied to join the police force, was decidedly
mixed. Along the riverbank, Waterloo was the haunt of prostitutes, cheap music halls and the usual con men and hus-
tlers who congregate around railway stations; Vauxhall was
blighted by terrible poverty and the dirt and smell of dockside
workshops, potteries and distilleries; and in both districts the
roar and steam of the railways were ever present. Behind them
lay Kennington, a central suburb where many of the stately
Georgian houses were now in multiple occupation. In winter,
a noxious cloud of river fog and coal dust would descend upon
the entire area for days at a time.

When Melville joined the Metropolitan Police at the age of twenty-two, he is said to have been a baker in the employ of James Macaulay at 99 Kennington Road, Lambeth.[11] No.99 is gone now, but it was one of a row of houses backing onto the grounds of Bedlam, the Bethlehem Hospital for the insane. James Macaulay the baker is shown living there, with his wife and six children and a middle-aged lodger, in the 1871 census.[12] Upstairs was the home of the secretary of a religious society and his family. Kennington was quite respectable.

Maybe it was the sight of new police accommodation being built just along Kennington Road at No.47 that sparked Melville's idea of becoming a London policeman. Irishmen quite often did; they comprised around six per cent of the force at a time when the Irish in Ireland had good reason to consider themselves oppressed by an imperial power. Indeed, Irish-American agitators, having failed in a half-hearted bid to promote an uprising in Dublin, had settled for terrorism in mainland Britain. There had been a devastating Fenian attack on the Middlesex House of Correction in Clerkenwell in 1868, with twelve people killed, though mercifully few signs of violent insurrection since.

Melville, although he was Irish and proud of it, had no truck with that sort of thing. He was sober and intelligent with a strong constitution and the social skills necessary to deal with the public. Metropolitan Police officers must be at least five feet eight inches tall. This was above the average. At five feet eight and a half, Melville got in.

And promptly got out again. Having been admitted as PC 310 to the register of E Division (Bow Street and Holborn) on 16 September 1872, he was one of over a hundred officers dismissed for insubordination on 20 November.

In a way the problem went back to the Clerkenwell bombing. It had been after this that the Government, threatened with further terrorism, realised that effective defence required a better-informed, more astute body of police. At the time there were 8,000 men in the Metropolitan Police and according to the Home Secretary just three of them were 'educated'.[13] On 'Irish duty' (that is, watching known Fenians), they were already routinely armed. Beat officers were not respected by their superiors, yet a job as demanding and responsible as this must attract men of high calibre. This meant better pay and a less militaristic approach. But the Government took a long time to draw up new pay scales, and some senior policemen took even longer to change their authoritarian attitudes towards the rank and file.

When Melville joined in 1872 nothing had been done. The proposed pay increases were almost insultingly stingy, and at a meeting at the Cannon Street Hotel, all those present elected PC Henry Goodchild to be secretary of a Pay and Conditions Negotiating Committee to represent them. They specifically ruled out strike action; they had simply set up the machinery for collective bargaining.

This alone was enough to alarm the Home Office. It immediately made a better offer, to the great satisfaction of Sir Edward Henderson, the Commissioner. Unfortunately, Assistant Commissioner Labalmondière and the Superintendents, many of whom had a military background, saw things differently. The Superintendents demanded that Goodchild give them details, in writing, of all the men who had been at the meeting, or meetings, where the Pay and Conditions Committee had been voted into existence. He refused. They told him he was going to be transferred; he saw this for the punishment it was, and asked to have the charges against him read out. The Assistant Commissioner sacked him on the spot for insubordination.

Goodchild quickly canvassed his supporters. The Commissioner's enquiry stated that on Saturday evening, 16 November:

At Kensington, 43 men of T Division, when paraded by their Inspector for night duty at 9.45 p.m., refused to move off to their beats. Of these, four men, on the appeal of the Superintendent, at once went on duty. The remaining 39 men persisted in their refusal until 12.45 p.m.

At Bow Street a similar course was pursued by 71 men of E Division, who refused to go on duty until 11.30 p.m.

At Molyneux Street, 65 men of D Division, when ordered to move off, at first refused, but on the Superintendent's appeal at once went on duty.[14]

All the offenders in E Division, and 39 from T division, were dismissed. Nearly all were reinstated a week later, dropping a 'class'. Melville had not far to fall, and after this hiccup his upward progress in the force recommenced on 29 November. The future trajectory of Goodchild, a brave man, is not recorded.

Melville was based during his first six months at Bow Street; this was Metropolitan HQ, Scotland Yard not yet having been built. As a constable, Melville would carry a truncheon and a whistle and, accompanied by a more experienced officer, patrol E Division from Covent Garden to Holborn.

The ideology of the 1870s was proudly bourgeois, with a social conscience. There was a sense that government brought responsibilities, as well as rights. So, although Gustave Doré had illustrated the smoke-laden, overcrowded nightmare of central London as recently as 1869, the squalor in which the poorest people lived was slowly lessening. In the last decade or so investment in a new sewage system had made the Thames cleaner and connected private houses to efficient main drains. The London Underground railway was expanding, allowing better-paid workers access to the suburbs. As business grew there were more clerical jobs and, with universal education, more people capable of doing them. Public hangings had stopped (one of the Clerkenwell culprits was the last man hanged in public). The filth and cruelty of Smithfield's livestock market had been replaced by a properly organised meat market. Cock-fighting and prize-fighting were not the socially acceptable pastimes they used to be. And Shaftesbury Avenue would soon be driven through the notorious rookeries of St Giles where policemen dared not go.

The West End may have been tidied up, but the Bow Street force must have smirked at Sir Edward Henderson's diktat of the previous year. Alarmed by a spate of thefts from washing lines, the Commissioner had earnestly instructed all constables 'to call at the houses of all persons on their beats having wet linen in their gardens, and caution them of the risk they run in having them stolen'.

E Division was rough, and policing it a twenty-four-hour job. It contained not only St Giles, but a major railway station at Charing Cross, the sinister black arches of the Adelphi along the river – full of rough sleepers, and the Strand, with its theatres and restaurants attracting gullible provincials and sophisticated Londoners alike. Opposite Bow Street, a gas-lit Covent Garden market began trading in fruit, vegetables and flowers long before dawn; the pubs were always open, fights commonplace, and prostitutes never off the streets. Behind the great thoroughfares, above the warren of lanes strewn with horse dung and rotten vegetables, in cold and threadbare rooms there slept, and worked, a motley band of fly-by-night purveyors of abortifacients and dubious publications by mail order. E Division was a good place to start if you wanted an overview of human life at its most desperate.

In April of 1873 PC Melville was transferred to L Division, Lambeth and Walworth, where he occupied police accommodation at 47 Kennington Road just off the Westminster Bridge Road. Some of the faces would have been familiar, for many of the prostitutes who lodged around Waterloo crossed the bridges in the evenings to pick up customers along the Strand and bring them back to York Road or other streets within walking distance of the river.

That there was a huge gulf between the behaviour of the indigent and streetwise of London and the new 'respectable' classes is demonstrated by the first case of Constable Melville's that we know about, from *The Times* in 1876.[15] The complainant was one Kate Beadle, a young woman who had for several years been housekeeper to a Mr Crisp and his family at Islington. She said that her gold watch, diamond rings and earrings, to a total value of about £30, had been stolen from her by Henry Levy, aged thirty-nine, 'a betting man'. Hers was a sad tale of a maid gone wrong. In August of 1876 she went to Brighton Races with Miss Crisp. Upon leaving they became separated. Two well-dressed men reassured her that they had seen Miss Crisp and she wasn't far away; she would soon turn up. Miss Beadle went with them to a nearby public house. They bought her a glass of what she thought was 'lemonade and claret'. She must have 'got stupid'. The next thing she knew she woke up next morning sitting on a doorstep and noticed to her dismay that her diamond ring, valued at £24, was gone.

She tottered off towards Brighton, and along the way a working man told her she could find a bed for the day – presumably to sleep off the effects of that single, devastating lemonade and claret – at a house near the town. She found the place and was relating her woes to the landlady when a young man who overheard said she could come to his house instead.

So – the court did not enquire too deeply here – she stayed with him for three or four days. Then they went to London together and took lodgings in Hercules Buildings, Westminster Bridge Road. He was a gentlemanly fellow, and single, but unfortunately in the habit of taking everything she put down. Jewels and earrings just vanished into thin air. Distraught, Miss Beadle made discreet enquiries and was told that if she were truly contrite she could return to her work at Mr Crisp's. This she decided to do; but when she announced her intention Henry, who had a persuasive way with him, swore that if she did he would send daily letters and wait outside the house. So – with unprecedented cunning – she pretended she would stay, but went to visit the Crisps at Islington anyway. When she came back he had taken all her clothes.

At this point we may assume that she approached the kind policeman of Kennington Road and Mr Henry Levy's fate was sealed. Detective Melville followed him all the way to Muswell

Hill and took him into custody at the Alexandra Races. The accused allegedly said 'I know all about it. I wish I'd never seen her. I've lost more than I've gained by her.' Pawn tickets were found. He claimed that all the goods had been taken with Miss Beadle's consent. He had a wife and children, and according to another detective who gave evidence in court, was 'a rogue and a vagabond, well known at racecourses'.

In this stratified society, women of all but the very highest and lowest class were treated like children, and in consequence they were as naïve as children.

The Times already referred to Melville as a detective. He was not a member of the central Detective Branch, which was quite small and had been in existence since 1842. He was probably relieved not to be, because neither its effectiveness nor its probity were held in great esteem. Each division used officers as detectives, but they were occasional, plain-clothes 'winter patrols' of two working on a monthly shift system in the divisions.[16] So Melville would have been a detective for part of the time and pounding the beat in uniform for the rest.

The next case of his to be reported in *The Times*[17] showed him in contact with a much rougher type, and off duty. As he was in plain clothes, he was probably rather useful. Two couples living at Tennison Street, York Road, were followed late one dark afternoon in November 1877 by Detective Sergeant Ranger and Sergeant Walsh. Off-duty Constable Melville was also following. At Brixton, the two couples were joined by a man named Smith. The police suspected all three men of a series of burglaries in South London, and when Detective Sergeant Ranger and the others approached, one of the women was found to be concealing a jemmy and skeleton keys. At the station they were all charged with loitering with intent in possession of housebreaking implements, and the men were accused of burglary. The police bungled here, as possession of jemmies and skeleton keys was evidently less serious at 6.00 p.m., when they were taken in, than it would have been had the police waited until 9.00 p.m. The chairman of the Surrey Sessions, regretting this

anomaly in the English law, awarded Melville £1 for his trouble
anyway. This kind of gratuity by results was at the discretion of
the magistrates and was common. The result in this case was
crime prevention.

The burglars probably came to the knowledge of the police
through an informer. This was perfectly obvious and yet it was
not mentioned. Unless an informer (a criminal associate) or
informant (an uninvolved observer) is known to bear a grudge
against a person who is innocent, or otherwise stands to gain
from a conviction in court, there is no point in the defence raising the matter. To this day informers are usually invisible: detectives 'act on information received' and no questions are asked.
In the 1870s the use of informers was particularly problematic.
The most senior policemen had not risen through the ranks,
and did not approve of their officers consorting with criminals
and spending time in pubs. Quite apart from the risks of collusion and alcohol dependency, they believed (rightly) that this
gave detectives a bad name. Further, because detectives had to
advance money out of their own pockets for information, and
could not claim the money back unless a crime was attempted
and someone convicted, their evidence was always suspect.[18]
This was never acknowledged in court either.

In February 1879[19] Melville appeared in the witness box at
Southwark court with his right hand in a sling. The week before
he and 'another detective' called Beale had followed a couple
of ticket-of-leave convicts (men released on parole). They saw
them enter 1 Windmill Street, and emerge having changed their
clothes. They followed the men to a window of Sarah Bennett's
shop at 30 Blackfriars Road where one fellow surreptitiously
cut a pane out of the window, seized two boxes of cigars, and
passed his booty to the other. Constable Melville raced across
the road but the pair had begun to run; he grabbed the one with
the cigars and in the ensuing struggle his hand was severely cut
with glass before he overcame the offender. Added to the charge
of theft was that of cutting and wounding Constable Melville
of L Division.

Melville was plainly well suited to this kind of work. He gave evidence confidently and stated no assumptions that could provide an opening for an astute cross-examiner. He liked to see without being seen and, with the policeman's towering helmet off, he had the detective's required ability to melt into a crowd: he was an open-faced young man, ordinary in every way.

It so happened that the central Detective Branch was being reformed after a scandal that emerged in 1877. A Madame de Goncourt had been swindled out of £30,000 and two men associated with horse-racing fraud, Benson and Kerr, were wanted to answer charges. Benson was in custody in Amsterdam and the Superintendent of the Detective Branch, Adolphus 'Dolly' Williamson, sent a smart, multi-lingual Chief Inspector Druscovitch to Holland to collect him. Bringing him back to London seemed unusually difficult. At home, Sergeant Littlechild and a couple of other officers were on the track of Kerr, but he too kept slipping through their fingers. No sooner did they find out where he was staying than he had moved on. Littlechild was getting suspicious by now, and he was not the only one. Finally they caught up with him in Edinburgh. Kerr tried to make a run for it; Littlechild raced after him and the man pulled a gun. 'For Heaven's sake, don't make a fool of yourself, it means murder!' cried Littlechild.[20] Kerr submitted, and the story began to unravel.

For the past four years – between 1873 and 1877 – a Detective Inspector Meiklejohn had been in Kerr's pay – hence the tip-offs. And Meiklejohn, who knew that Druscovitch was worried by his brother's debts, had offered Druscovitch the opportunity to earn backhanders from Kerr as well. A chief inspector called Palmer was also implicated. Palmer, Druscovitch and Meiklejohn (who later went into business as a private detective) were jailed for a couple of years and the scandal tainted 'Dolly' Williamson's career. He was not corrupt, but his supervisory skills were called into question. An enquiry was set up and an opinionated young barrister and journalist called Howard Vincent saw his chance: this was a golden opportunity for him to make a strong representation to the enquiry, and to come in as a new broom who would lead the detective force.

Charles Howard Vincent was not yet thirty. After Westminster School, where as a frail, undistinguished scholar he had failed to shine, he had served in the Army for five years and in the Territorials; he had lived in Paris and Dresden, Moscow and Constantinople; he was war correspondent to the *Daily Telegraph*. As a barrister he was ambitious and hard-working but lacked professional focus, and therefore preferment in the law. But he knew English politicians and senior civil servants, and had enough contacts in Paris to put his plan into action.

He travelled to Paris and with the help of a *préfet* in the Sûreté wrote a précis of the way the French criminal investigation system worked, with recommendations for its adaptation to English use. This he refined, according to his biography, eighteen times.[21] The result was short, readable and incisive. The service required re-structuring. The central Detective Branch should be enlarged and divisional detective patrols should liaise with it, the whole thing forming a criminal investigation department.

The enquiry committee were impressed; everyone admired the French system, and here it was, on paper ready to be implemented. Vincent moved on to the next step: to gather support for himself as holder of the Head of CID post that would necessarily be created if his recommendations were adopted. He concentrated attention upon his legal experience – there were quite enough ex-soldiers in the police already and they seemed to be part of the problem – and his four languages, and attracted the backing of the Attorney General and several members of the committee including Sir William Hardman, the Chairman of Surrey Sessions (who had coincidentally given Constable Melville his £1 reward). Sir Richard Cross, the Tory Home Secretary, was pleased to offer him a job. Vincent's salary, at his own suggestion, was set at that of an assistant *commissaire* – £1,100 pa. His title was to be Director of Criminal Intelligence. His position was at first anomalous, for he was both subordinate to the Commissioner and independent; in charge, but with no power of enforcing directives to staff.[22]

Despite press scepticism, Vincent created the job through trial and error without experience, thanks largely to guidance from Sir Adolphus Liddell, a senior civil servant at the Home Office. Vincent, who was friendly with M. Lepine of the Sûreté, grasped from the start the international scope of crime, but had to create a frame within which everyone could work. A letter from the Home Secretary dated 14 September 1878 gently chides the new Director on the political niceties:

> while direct communication between yourself and foreign police authorities for the *purposes of information* is unobjectionable, all demands for arrest, whether by telegram or otherwise, must be made through the diplomatic channel and the Foreign Office, and all demands for arrest on the part of the English police must be sent to the Secretary of State for transmission to the competent authorities abroad through the Foreign Office.[23]

There was always pressure from abroad about London's refugees, and anarchists especially. Vincent was relaxed about social-democratic clubs, and thought they posed no threat whatsoever. And at first the Fenians were of no particular concern, for he discovered that there was a shadowy character called Anderson at the Home Office who monitored their activities. But anarchists were different. The anarchist movement was of course opposed to authority, but beyond that it split. While some simply wanted the freedom to do as they wished and expected that if everyone did so capitalism would just crumble away, others believed that this process would take too long unless given a helping hand. This 'helping hand' was propaganda by deed; in other words, showing just how great life could be if you summarily got rid of the symbols of repressive order. Kings, seats of government, expensive restaurants and police headquarters were favourite targets chosen on the basis that 'scum rises to the top'.

Vincent was aware that royal lives could be in danger from assassins, and also that continental governments believed the English dealt much too lightly with openly anarchist refugees.

Certainly revolutionaries could meet and publish in London in a way they were not free to do anywhere else. It always irritated foreign countries when their home-grown anarchists fled across the Channel, wrote rallying cries to violent action, printed them and sent them home.

It was also politically awkward, as the Foreign Office for its own reasons would not, and would not be seen to, bow to political pressure to deal with foreign revolutionaries. Further, the British ruling classes claimed that a fundamental difference in political philosophy was involved: they claimed that the 'safety valve' of social clubs, freedom of speech and movement and peaceful demonstration functioned well. Their relative liberality allowed them to keep an eye on potential troublemakers and defused revolutionary intentions in a cloud of hot air. So, with M. Lepine and others demanding action, and the Home Office and Foreign Office refusing to act, 'Vincent... lived under a constant cross-fire of alternating censure'.[24] All he could do was visit socialist and anarchist clubs on the quiet, in disguise (which, according to his biographer, he did[25]), and make sure that there was strong but unobtrusive security around visitors like the Kaiser, who made a State visit in 1879. He also employed a single Scotland Yard inspector, Von Tornow, who quietly kept an eye on political insurgents from continental Europe.[26]

The police force had some difficulty in accommodating itself to the new CID set-up. From the start in 1878 the uniformed men resented having a permanent plain-clothes branch in every division; they were seen as having a financial advantage, as one tradition carried over from the old detective force was that of rewarding them out of treasury funds. Over the years it had become a bounty system in all but name. They were not particularly well paid but could double their income if a senior officer recommended rewards by results in big cases.[27] Also, since there were fewer of them, they had the career advantage of being more noticeable in work, which by its nature required initiative.

Melville at least must have felt quite sanguine about his prospects in the force. Just seventeen days after his appearance at Southwark

Magistrates' Court with his arm in a sling, on 20 February 1879 he got married. His bride was an Irish girl, Kate Reilly from a village in County Mayo, far north of Kerry but also way out along the west coast. She worked at Barratt's the drapers on the Westminster Bridge Road and they married just around the corner – in Southwark but still within a hundred yards of the Lambeth police accommodation – at St George's Roman Catholic Church.

Melville's confidence was justified. Four months after the wedding he was promoted from Constable to Detective Sergeant in the CID. He was now stationed in P Division, which abuts L Division and includes Camberwell, Walworth and Peckham, districts slightly further south of the river. He was still dealing with straightforward crime of the kind that is motivated by greed or jealousy rather than ideals, and still ending up in street brawls for his pains, according to *The Times*.[28] An account of a case at Marylebone Police Court shows him making a difficult arrest in Clerkenwell.

A Mr Tufts, of Westbourne Park near Paddington, was first into the witness box, and described how he and his wife had gone out the previous Saturday evening at 7.00 p.m. and returned around midnight. They were still up at 1.00 a.m. when they heard a lot of noise upstairs and their two servants (who had been with them for years) rushed down terrified. The police were called. They found the attic skylight open and all in confusion, and a thousand pounds' worth of gold, jewellery and clothing gone from three bedrooms over two floors.

Melville explained to the court how the following Tuesday evening at 5.00 p.m. he, along with Inspector Peel and two sergeants of G Division, went to Clerkenwell and waited two hours for one of the suspected men, a twenty-seven-year-old 'general dealer' called Armstrong, to come out of his house in Bowling Green Lane. He made the arrest, but Armstrong refused to go quietly and put up a furious fight. Quite a crowd gathered. It was probably not a crowd supportive of the police. Melville, by his own account (one detects an underlying bitterness) had just about reached the limit of his endurance when Inspector Peel finally broke it up.

At the police station, and at the houses of Armstrong and his co-accused, cash, revolvers, cartridges, diamonds and skeleton keys were discovered. One of the men was seen by Melville surreptitiously passing his ill-gotten gains to the wife of the other and, as in the earlier Lambeth case, both couples were charged. Detectives like Melville were aware of the usefulness not only of informants (for this arrest clearly depended upon information received) but of burglars' womenfolk to the breaking-and-entering trade. Women wore such a lot of clothes. At dead of night, a woman wearing a bonnet and cape over a voluminous dress could conceal the booty about her person and depart innocently arm in arm with her lover from the scene of the crime. If the fellow had to make a run for it, the police would pass her by and even if they didn't, they couldn't search her without taking her to the police station; there were no women police.

While stationed at P Division Melville probably worked out of Walworth Road Police Station. No.44 Liverpool Street, the house where he and Kate and their eighteen-month-old baby Margaret were living at the time of the 1881 census, would have been conveniently close. The street name was later changed to Liverpool Grove but the house is still there, one of a pretty, three-storey terrace with Gothic windows opposite a leafy churchyard. It was a tranquil backwater, convenient for East Street market and omnibuses to the Elephant and Castle just half a mile away.

The Elephant and Castle was the major commercial centre for inner South London and its huge department store, Tarn's. At six storeys high with associated factories and accommodation for nearly three hundred staff, Tarn's was a magnet for eager ladies from nearby Blackheath and Dulwich, Clapham and Stockwell who could not resist – straight from Paris! – its parasols, hats, furs, dress materials ('New Shades in French Beiges, Summer Serges, Indian Cachemires, and Merinos, Alpacas and Russell Cords'[29]), bedsteads, Davenports and Canterburies, overmantels and dressing sets, bamboo whatnots, and on, and on. No doubt Kate Melville spent a few rapturous hours gazing into its plate glass windows.

One woman who was quite a lot richer was also distracted by the delights of the Elephant and Castle in August of 1880. She took £400 in cash from her bank there: three £100 notes, one £50, four £10 notes and the rest in gold and silver. She put the cash in a purse inside a bag before setting off for an absorbing shopping trip with her little girl and her sister-in-law. When at last they caught a tramcar home to Clapham, she asked her sister-in-law for the money and was told the little girl had it; but the bag was open and the money gone. She asked the conductor urgently to stop the tram, insisting that she must return to the bank and get the notes stopped. He ignored her and rang the bell, but she grabbed her skirts, jumped off and hurried to the bank as her sister-in-law and daughter rode away.

Within weeks, Detective Sergeant Melville had traced some of the notes. The tram conductor had ordered a new suit from a Clapham tailor and changed a £10 note to pay for a gold watch and chain for his girlfriend. At Lambeth Police Court he was remanded week after week, but continued to insist that he had not only 'found' the original cash, but 'thrown away' the other £280. To help him remember where he had thrown it, he was remanded until November; and there *The Times*, infuriatingly, ends its tale.[30]

In January of 1882 Melville's name appeared again when he was one of the officers investigating a couple of shoplifters;[31] and at the end of that year, he bore witness against a light-fingered, twenty-four-year-old assistant to a milk roundsman, who was accused of stealing from funds received, which he was supposed to deposit twice daily. He had been employed by the roundsman for four months. 'Detective Melville in answer to the magistrate said he believed the prisoner had been living at a rather high rate, and on Sunday week had entertained some sixteen persons at dinner.'[32]

Melville had now been a policeman for over a decade. The little family was growing. This year Kate had given birth to a baby girl also called Kate. Perhaps Melville expected to carry on indefinitely outwitting the burglars and embezzlers of South London until he retired; but the opportunity soon arose to become part of something altogether more exciting.

TWO

DYNAMITE CAMPAIGN

In March of 1883, when Kate was six months pregnant with their third child, Melville was offered a position within a new covert branch of the CID based at Scotland Yard. Headed by Superintendent 'Dolly' Williamson, it would be called the Special Irish Branch (SIB).

Although the Special Irish Branch was new, its approach was not. It had developed out of existing efforts to contain Irish discontent. It was established in response to a Fenian bombing campaign which had begun in 1881 and was causing increasing alarm.

Since the Clerkenwell bomb of 1867 (an attempt to blow up the Middlesex House of Detention to release a Fenian prisoner), the British Government had employed Robert Anderson, an Anglo-Irish barrister, on Irish matters – that is, spying and counter-terrorism. At first he worked out of Dublin Castle where his brother occupied a senior position. The Dublin Metropolitan Police (DMP) relied on a network of clandestine agents all over Ireland (publicans, butchers, ordinary people in ordinary towns) to warn them of anti-British feeling. In other words they operated as an internal Secret Service. In England, this pro-active attitude to detection even of ordinary criminal cases had been considered too morally reprehensible to acknowledge as a police tactic until Howard Vincent took over the CID in 1877 and legitimised such cunning continental ways for use in criminal cases.

From 1868 onwards Robert Anderson was based at the Home Office in Whitehall, but he was not associated with the police. His position was anomalous for the next decade or so. From the start his most important agent was Henri Le Caron. Le Caron had been born Thomas Miller Beach in Suffolk. After four years working in Paris, at the age of twenty-one he emigrated to

America and served in the Civil War, adopting a new French name and rising to become a Major. Afterwards he studied medicine. His contacts with Fenians during the war intrigued Anderson and on a visit to England in the autumn of 1867, they met at 50 Harley Street, where Le Caron – as he put it – 'entered British service'. He would faithfully report the mood and intentions of those Irishmen in America who busied themselves raising money to drive the British out of Ireland.[1]

In 1870, therefore, Anderson was able to take credit for gathering the evidence against Michael Davitt. Davitt, a Lancashire man originally from County Mayo who spent time in America and later became a Member of Parliament, was jailed for running guns into Ireland. And yet, Anderson fumed forty years later in his autobiography 'this very time was chosen by the War Office to sell off stores of discarded rifles'.[2] Departments of state did not communicate with each other about security. The armed services had not yet confronted the realities of espionage, counter-espionage or terrorism. But if the success of a counter-terrorist effort is to be judged by the ability of a populace to go about its business unafraid, then Anderson and Le Caron between them successfully kept any Fenian threat largely out of the public's sight and mind throughout the 1870s. In this they were assisted by the Irish Americans' incompetence, in-fighting and dishonesty – as well as by betrayal from within.

In 1880 there was a change of Government and the Liberals came in. Anderson went on a six-month holiday, and had barely returned when Fenian intelligence spectacularly failed. In January of 1881 the United Irishmen of America blew a hole in Salford Infantry Barracks and their bomb killed the garrison butcher's seven-year-old son. In the Queen's Speech a few days later, Victoria declared her Government's intention to pass a Coercion Act for Ireland. Gladstone, now Prime Minister, had been drawn into this against his will. In Anderson's view, stated in his biography of 1910, a Coercion Act – which if passed would permit detention without trial, trial *in camera* or without a jury, curfews and other essential weapons of a police state – was entirely necessary in London as in Ireland; neither place could be governed without one.[3]

Sir William Vernon Harcourt, the new Home Secretary, was already reviewing security. The three perceived threats were assassination, bombs and published incitements to violence of the kind printed in America's *United Irishman*. Harcourt was under pressure on all sides. Queen Victoria leant on him from above. She sat at the head of a pan-European royal clan, devoured newspapers and letters in several languages and kept a keen eye on 'revolutionists'. In the course of her reign she had been subject to several assassination attacks, and in recent years the King of Italy had been set upon by a man with a dagger, and the Tsar, the Kaiser and the King of Spain had all been shot at least twice.

In Parliament, arguments were being made in favour of removing the Metropolitan force from the Home Secretary's remit and transferring it to local control, probably by Watch Committees of the type that prevailed in every other city. Harcourt was fully aware of Anderson's view that at any moment the Irish-Americans might begin a violent campaign in Britain. He was certain that such outrages could not be dealt with by policemen subject to the picayune demands and strategic ignorance of local committees. Harcourt knew that the Home Office must be in charge. If anything happened he would be blamed, but so be it.

Something did happen. The Irish outrage at Salford in January of 1881 was followed by the discovery of other bombs in Liverpool, Chester and Manchester. On 23 January Harcourt told Howard Vincent of the CID to devote the next month of his time to the Fenian outrages and nothing else. The Fenian Office became a department within CID at Scotland Yard. It was at the heart of communication between Vincent, Anderson, Sir Edward Henderson the Police Commissioner, the regional police, the DMP, the Royal Irish Constabulary (RIC) and Colonel Majendie, an explosives specialist based, like Anderson, at the Home Office. Between them this crowd, reporting to the Home Secretary, saw off any remaining reservations that senior

Metropolitan officers may have had about running the CID as a pro-active detective force.

In May of 1881 Tsar Alexander II was assassinated and the German Government protested that a German socialist paper from London called *Freiheit* had celebrated the event and encouraged repeat performances. The Queen's links with Germany, and her alarm, could not be ignored. In July *Freiheit*'s editor Johann Most was tried for incitement to murder and imprisoned for eighteen months. In America, President Garfield was assassinated.

In the summer of 1881 Harcourt was in no great panic over threats from continental revolutionaries because he had taken action. In the light of Garfield's assassination, royal protection was stepped up. Howard Vincent was to have foreign communist and social-democratic groups and publications watched from now on. Importantly, the Most trial had calmed foreign diplomatic concerns about British firmness.

But Anderson was still coming up with intelligence about Irish-American threats. Michael Davitt, who had been released from Dartmoor in 1877, was arrested within three weeks of the Salford bomb and found guilty of incitement to insurrection. Although he was detained in Portland prison for over a year, in Ireland the Land League (which he had inspired) did not wither away. There was strong support for land reform, and rent strikes and boycotting were used as a means to coerce the less stalwart supporters of the principle. Where an Irish tenant refused to withhold rent, the local community would boycott (that is, not trade with) him. Evictions and serious hardship followed from this, making Ireland's political problems worse and increasing support in England for the League's aims, which were promoted in Parliament by the charismatic Member for Meath, Charles Parnell.

Anderson knew Parnell's thinking, as he had heard his spy Le Caron's account of a meeting with Parnell in London in the spring of 1881. Thanks to a larger Secret Service grant Anderson was also making contacts within rank-and-file London activists. 'What grand copy it would have been for the newspapers of that time if, in describing the Fenian procession… they could have added that the band instruments had been taken out of pawn with money supplied by the Home Office!'[4] Certain people in power still had reservations about the wisdom of employing agents. Gladstone, knowing this, preferred to remain unaware of the details of secret intelligence and Harcourt had to take the full weight of threats against the state upon his own shoulders. For decades the conventional view had been that by paying informers, one encouraged them to act as *agents provocateurs*. Anderson, a deeply religious man, was poker-faced.

> I warned the leaders who were in my pay that if outrages occurred
> I should possibly denounce them and certainly stop their stipends.
> I use the word 'stipend' advisedly. In work of this kind payment
> by results may operate as a positive incitement to crime, whereas
> the regular payment of a fixed amount has a marvellous influence
> on the recipient.

Le Caron certainly had no problem with it. In Chicago in the August of 1881 he was a delegate to what he called the 'Grand Dynamite Convention' of Clan-na-Gael. (The Fenian Brotherhood and Irish Revolutionary Brotherhood had re-invented themselves as Clan-na-Gael in 1867). The majority of those present in the large, smoke-filled hotel meeting room – according to Le Caron they were predominantly lawyers – decided upon direct action in mainland Britain. Afterwards a small group of militants discussed strategy for a future terror offensive. They would leave the Royal family alone, but any other British institution was fair game.

Home Secretary Harcourt, a volatile character and still, in this summer of 1881, in a sanguine mood, dismissed threats of a London bombing campaign as 'a Fenian scare of the old clumsy kind.'[5] But nothing focuses the mind so much as a double assassination, and when in May of 1882 the Chief Secretary for Ireland and his Permanent Under-Secretary were stabbed to death as they walked across Phoenix Park in Dublin, security flew to the top of the agenda. The well-informed wondered whether the Land League and its supporters in Parliament would break decisively with the Fenian group from across the Atlantic over this; if they did, they predicted,[6] there would be no brake on Fenian violence whatsoever. What in fact happened was that the Land League treasurer moved to Paris, from which city he could quietly divert funds to Clan-na-Gael activities upon request.[7]

Chief Inspector Littlechild of the CID spent five months in Dublin after the Phoenix Park murders working with the Irish police. 'I assisted the Dublin police by posing as a certain character, and staying in low hotels in the city, in which it was thought that information might be gained of the perpetrators of the deed.'[8] In response to a plea from Earl Spencer, the Lord Lieutenant, the Cabinet set up an extremely well-funded anti-Fenian department there under a Colonel Brackenbury. Brackenbury's view, partly informed by Spencer, was trenchant: for a variety of reasons, the RIC and the DMP were an inadequate defence against Fenian plotters. A small, separate investigative branch with wide powers must be created to deal with them. Brackenbury personally did not want to be at the head of it. He did not want this Irish posting and never had; he wanted to fight with the British Army in Egypt.

Fortunately for him Earl Spencer had a private secretary called Jenkinson who was only too pleased to assume Brackenbury's position. Edward Jenkinson had liberal views about Ireland. He was a Home Ruler, believing that the grievances of the Irish were genuine and must be addressed. He was opposed to Irish-American terrorism because he believed that it would harden British attitudes while creating Irish martyrs. He had been a divisional commissioner in India and like most ex-colonial officers he was accustomed to the principle and practice of infiltrating spies into the civilian and/or criminal population. He had no background in international espionage. But he seized the opportunity, for which Brackenbury had prepared the ground, to create an Irish-American intelligence network. At Dublin Castle he had Anderson's brother Samuel to assist him, but Jenkinson was no collaborator; he respected only his own intellect. But he revelled in the work. Within months he was convinced that nothing other than a multi-tentacled secret police initiative covering Europe, North America and the whole of Great Britain could be truly effective; and he was the man to run it.

Irishmen, not Irish Americans, were arrested for the Phoenix Park murders. Five were hanged, eight were jailed, and five got away to France or America. Terrorist attacks worsened. In Glasgow in January of 1883 bombs were left at a railway station and an aqueduct and a large gas-holder was dynamited to smithereens. But it was London that faced the major threat to public institutions and transport. It was far larger and more anonymous than other cities and held the most important targets. On the night of Thursday 15 March a bomb went off at Printing House Square, home of *The Times*; on 16 March another exploded behind the Home Office.

Superintendent Williamson instituted the new Special Irish Branch on St Patrick's Day, Saturday 17 March; its base was a first-floor office in an alley with a dog-leg bend called Whitehall Place. Howard Vincent was based at Scotland Yard, less than a hundred yards away, and retained overall control of the CID, which included the SIB. Williamson was to liaise with Vincent and Anderson and to report matters of immediate significance directly to the Home Secretary.

At 10.00 a.m. on Tuesday 20 March his hand-picked force of twelve detectives, to be directed in operational matters by Chief Inspector Littlechild, gathered in the corner office overlooking the Rising Sun pub for the pep talk and induction session. 'Dolly' Williamson, an equable character with a dry sense of humour who liked to stroll around London in a floppy hat with a flower in his buttonhole, began with two advantages. One was his own experience. For some time he had been deployed by Vincent to investigate political matters. The other was that his new force had the London bombings fresh in their mind.

Explosions gave the public a shudder of horror, outrage and sympathy; but a detective's work can be tedious. One of

Melville's reports, written on 4 April 1883 a fortnight after the
first meeting of the SIB, describes a typical day.

> PC Enright and PC McIntyre report that at 12.30 p.m. 3rd inst.
> O'Connor left Pond Place and proceeded by Piccadilly to Brewer
> Street, Soho, but did not call at any house there; then to the
> American Reading Rooms, 14 Strand, where he left at 4.15 p.m.
> and then proceeded to the Embankment over Westminster Bridge
> and down the Albert Embankment by St Thomas' Hospital. Here
> he leant on the parapet of the embankment, took out a paper
> and appeared to be surveying the Houses of Parliament and at
> the same time was making notes onto the paper. He proceeded
> onto Lambeth Bridge from which he seemed to be surveying
> the Archbishop of Canterbury's palace (Lambeth Palace) and also
> making notes on the paper. He then went along the Wandsworth
> Road and thence to 2, Ponton Terrace, Nine Elms Lane, occupied
> by Mr Enright, which he entered at 7.00 p.m.
>
> P.Sgts Melville & Regan report continuing the observation at
> above address, and at 11.00 p.m. saw O'Connor and Enright leave
> there, the two proceeding very slowly and apparently in earnest
> conversation to Battersea Bridge [Chelsea Bridge] where they
> parted, Enright turning towards his home as above. We followed
> O'Connor via Sloane Square to his home at Pond Place, which
> he entered at 11.30 p.m.[9]

One imagines Melville quietly giving Regan the wink and
taking a right turn at Sloane Square, rather than a left towards
Pond Place, and skiving off to get the last train home from
Victoria. Who were they following and why? O'Connor certainly seems to have had the profile of a plotter, spending the
day reading the papers and designing the downfall of the state
and the evening over a bite and a jar discussing it. Quite who
he was, and why Enright and PC Enright shared the same name,
is lost to us, although a clue may lie in the list of detectives
gathered at Scotland Yard for that first meeting on 17 March.

Littlechild's twelve apostles were Inspectors Hope and Ahern, Sergeants Jenkins, Melville and Regan, Constables O'Sullivan, Walsh, McIntyre, Foy, Thorpe and *two* Enrights.

O'Connor, whoever he was, was probably being drawn into some sting inspired by a London informer of Anderson or Jenkinson. None of this matters except in serving to illustrate the many frustrations and red herrings of the job. The foot-slogging underling can only follow orders, which sometimes prove to have been futile in intent.

Melville wrote his report on a Wednesday. Having spent Tuesday evening hanging about waiting for his mark to emerge from 2 Ponton Terrace, by Friday he was putting in his overtime in a comfy room in Bloomsbury; a fact that would emerge when *The Times* reported the Dynamite Conspiracy[10] trial at Bow Street with Harry Poland prosecuting. (Court cases were theatre, and at this time well-known barristers attracted an audience.)

Jenkinson's intelligence was said to be behind the Dynamite Conspiracy arrests. A florid character called Gallagher, well financed by American Fenians, had recced the House of Commons and planned to blow it up with explosives made in Birmingham. Birmingham detectives had followed a trail that led from manufacturer to bomb-makers and had picked up some of the gang involved. The rest were taken into custody in London. Among their effects were orders for admission to the House of Commons last November, clothes bearing heavy traces of nitro-glycerine, maps including maps of London, and other evidence which appeared incriminating.

In the dock were Gallagher and a brother of his, and their alleged co-conspirators Whitehead, Dalton, Wilson, Curtin (also known as Kent) and Ansburgh.

Curtin, an American, had come to London on 5 April, a Thursday; he was charged with 'conspiring with others to take possession of explosives in order to commit a felony'. Chief Inspector Littlechild explained that upon his arrival Curtin had been followed to a modest hotel at 11 Upper Woburn Place, Bloomsbury. Melville gave evidence that in the evening of Friday

6 April he had, acting under instructions, booked a room at this hotel, and on Saturday morning he had breakfasted with Mr Curtin. He had engaged the fellow in conversation: it was difficult to know what to do with yourself in London when you don't know anybody, he had remarked, and Curtin agreed, saying that he had only arrived the day before yesterday and would leave tomorrow. When Curtin left the hotel Melville and another officer followed him. Curtin was seen to stand outside the post office, Lower Strand, for fifteen or twenty minutes watching the Charing Cross Hotel. Then he went to a pawn shop.

Inspector Littlechild said that on Saturday 7 April he and Sergeant Melville and other police officers took Curtin into custody (without explanation) in Euston Square as he made his way towards the station. They all took a four-wheeler to Scotland Yard.

When they got there Superintendent Williamson asked Curtin for his story. He claimed to be living at 11 Upper Woburn Place, and to have come from New York where he lived at 301 East 59th Street. He had crossed the Atlantic to Queenstown, then travelled to Glasgow where he had worked at a shipyard; he had arrived in London the Thursday before.

He was taken to Bow Street and charged, and proved to have money in pounds and dollars. He denied knowing any of the others. He was shown a letter with his signature on it addressed to one of the Gallagher brothers; the letter had been taken from Gallagher's room at the Charing Cross Hotel. (Littlechild asserted that when they met, Curtin and Gallagher shook hands in mutual recognition.) While Curtin was interviewed at Scotland Yard Melville returned to the hotel in Upper Woburn Place and searched Curtin's room. In a portmanteau he found a couple of shirts labelled 'Kent'.

The case continued at the Old Bailey in June. All the big guns were there: the Lord Chief Justice, the Attorney General, Colonel Majendie ('Her Majesty's Inspector of Explosives') and representatives of the Royal Irish Constabulary, among others. The prisoners were 'taken from and brought to the court under a strong guard of mounted police'. The stage was set. Against this sombre background, it would have been hard to convince a jury of their innocence.

A man Curtin had worked with in Glasgow confirmed the story that he had worked there in a shipyard.

Ansburgh was brought before the court and Littlechild described his arrest at Savage's Hotel, 38 Blackfriars Road. The accused – Ansburgh – cross-examined Melville. Hadn't Melville told him (Ansburgh) that if he turned Queen's evidence he would get off, and pick up a £500 reward into the bargain? Melville denied it strongly. It would never occur to him to say such a thing. Ansburgh said 'You are a notorious liar.'

Melville was making a reputation, of a kind. All the same, Ansburgh was acquitted and so was Gallagher's brother.

Within a few weeks Melville and Kate would suffer a tragedy all too common in late Victorian England.

They had moved to Brixton. It was a more convenient commute than the house in Liverpool Street, Walworth. They were living – with a toddler of three, a one-year-old baby and another due at the end of June – in Tunstall Road. It was only a hundred yards from the railway station and a good train service to Victoria and Scotland Yard, and conveniently for Kate it was next door to the Bon Marché, another South London emporium.

When Kate Melville was due to have her baby they arranged for Margaret Gertie, who was nearly four, to go and stay with relatives in East London near the Royal Victoria Docks. Whether, as seems likely, they made this decision because with two tiny children at home already Kate would otherwise have too many to handle, or whether it was because Margaret Gertie had suspected scarlet fever and must be removed on medical advice, is unknown. But by the end of June scarlet fever had taken hold and the little girl was living at 31 Barnwood Road, Plaistow, in the O'Halloran household. Mr O'Halloran was her uncle, presumably the husband of Kate's sister.[11] Scarlet fever is an infection which was in those days untreatable, although most children recovered from it. It usually meant a throat infection, and always a fever and a nasty skin rash. It could take hold and reach a peak within a week. In Brixton on 3 July, Kate gave birth to William John, and Margaret died on the same day.

In the spring, Edward Jenkinson had been brought to London for a short stay to co-ordinate anti-Fenian activities from a temporary office in the Admiralty. He kept one eye on his key informer from New York, a binge drinker called 'Red Jim' McDermott, whose cover would be blown in the course of the summer and who would narrowly escape being shot by an Irish assassin. McDermott had been sent to England to initiate bogus bomb plots financed by money from Earl Spencer's fund, administered by Jenkinson.[12]

Jenkinson was never happier than when dreaming up entrapment operations of this kind. He was not impressed by the Yard men and still less by Anderson, and treated all of them with disdain. He profited from his moment of glory following the Dynamite Conspiracy arrests to insist that Fenian intelligence could not be adequately handled by disparate agencies. It needed one man (himself) to whom all would report, and who would have full control.

Harcourt knew that it would be politically unacceptable to put an official secret police chief in charge. Instead, by the end of the summer Jenkinson had become controller of Irish counter-terrorism in America, Ireland and continental Europe. On his recommendation Major Nicholas Gosselin looked after the same thing in cities like Birmingham and Manchester.

Jenkinson was a figure from an earlier age; a Machiavellian courtier, loyal mainly to Earl Spencer but essentially unsubtle. From his arrival in London onwards, Spencer and Harcourt received conspiratorial memos, often along lines suggesting that Jenkinson knew even more than he could possibly say but to reveal it just yet would mean certain death to his agents. Typical is this, to Spencer about P. J. Sheridan: 'as Y.E. [Your Excellency] knows I have a little game going on with him in America and any false step here might spoil the game…'[13] In Glasgow, where six months before, bombs had been left at a station and an aqueduct and a large gas-holder dynamited,

Jenkinson urged Harcourt (in July 1883) that Gosselin be dissuaded from making a move until Jenkinson's own scheme for trapping the culprits had come to fruition. Everything depended on his personal retention of 'the threads', as he called them, of Fenian plotting.

In London, Superintendent Williamson was supposed – in Jenkinson's view – to report to Major Gosselin. He seems to have kept on talking to Vincent, though. Jenkinson despaired of this unwillingness to sideline Scotland Yard, although thanks to Jenkinson's sniping and manoeuvring Anderson, at least, was fast fading out of the picture. The former spymaster was still working at the Home Office, but with less and less to do. His only advantage was Le Caron in America. Just as Jenkinson refused to reveal who his sources were, so did Anderson.

Jenkinson returned to Ireland late in the year. He had given Harcourt to understand that while Anderson had one source in America who might occasionally come up with the goods, he had few agents of value in England. Harcourt grew impatient and Anderson often had to submit to his 'dynamite moods'. He would be summoned to visit the Home Secretary at 7 Grafton Street only to be confronted with an outburst of frustration.[14]

Intelligence was still unreliable. At the end of October 1883 a bomb on a London Underground train at Paddington injured seventy-two people. This was followed by an explosion in a tunnel on the District Line at Westminster. Jenkinson was convinced that he had uncovered a plot to attack the Houses of Parliament. Nobody knew who or what to believe. Typical of this time is a note from Harcourt to Sir Henry Ponsonby, the Queen's Private Secretary, who had just accompanied Her Majesty safely to Windsor by royal train:

> I had one of the usual scares last night about your journey. Williamson at 12.30 a.m. came in with a letter fresh from the US describing the machine with which and the manner in which you were to be blown up on your way from Balmoral. As Hartington and the Attorney General were sitting with me we consulted what to do on this agreeable intelligence but as you were already

supposed to be half way through your journey it was not easy to know what course to take…[15]

In February of 1884 a series of railway-station bombs in London proved only too real. Out of office hours, telegrams like this one from Colonel Pearson came straight to Harcourt's home:

A serious explosion took place at nine this morning at the parcels office Victoria Station [–] porters injured. Cause at present unknown. [I cannot] say, but from what I can see I do not think gas is the cause. I have posted police all round until the arrival of Colonel Majendie to whom I have telegraphed. Nothing will be touched. Ticket office, parcels office and waiting room of the Brighton Line completely destroyed.[16]

In March the British Consul in Philadelphia wrote to the Foreign Office that his agent had it on excellent authority that this summer, unprecedented violence would be visited upon the English. O'Donovan Rossa himself, the voice of *United Irishman*, had read from a letter stamped and sent to New York by Royal Mail. He managed later to copy some choice extracts:

Can not give you the whole of it but if we had not been disturbed Birdcage Walk would have echoed and more than one stone would have tumbled… Pall Mall would have been shaken up more than Charles Street was. The fuse got detached from the cap and before we could make connection again we were spotted. You can look for something soon in either of these places…[17]

Sure enough, it would not be long before a bomb went off outside the Junior Carlton Club, just off Pall Mall. There were well-financed Irishmen in Antwerp, Bremen and London ready to dynamite the Queen, the Prime Minister, various other notables and all the bridges of London.[18] HM Consul in Florence communicated intelligence about American Fenians living in Old Compton Street and the Consul in Philadelphia spent some time chasing around American chemical works on Col. Majendie's instructions investigating the substance sold as 'Atlas Powder' he had found in a bomb.[19] Vernon Harcourt was overwhelmed by reports on 'Irish matters'. He recalled Jenkinson to London. Jenkinson arrived, still arguing about his terms and conditions of service, in March.

In April a man called Daly was arrested with bombs in Liverpool. Daly had been fitted up, although nobody knew that at the time. On 12 April Jenkinson wrote from England to Spencer about

...three hand bombs which came over about three days ago in the *City of Chester*...Our difficulty was to get the things passed to Daly and then to arrest him, with the things on him, without throwing suspicion on our own informant.[20]

But that was secret intelligence. For everyone else, the threat averted made the blood curdle just to think of it; and as if to prove the point, in May a police constable discovered dynamite at the base of Nelson's Column.

And then the Special Irish Branch blew up.

When it happened, on 30 May, Jenkinson had settled to work permanently out of Room 56 at the Home Office. He had insisted at first that the visit must be on his own terms.

The work in the 'ordinary' Crime Branch is now so entirely distinct and separate from that in the 'special' Crime Branch that without any confusion, or the necessity for any special arrangements, the work in the former Branch could be carried on by Mr Anderson while all papers belonging to the latter could be sent to me daily in London... Mr Anderson... dealing with all papers belonging to the Ordinary Branch. All reports either from Mr Anderson, Major Gosselin, Mr Williamson or from any of the local police authorities in Great Britain, all information and all despatches from the Foreign or other offices relating to Fenian organisations or the operations or movements of dynamiters would be sent to me...[21]

The man had no life. Besides retaining his current position in Ireland he still wanted 'a recognised official position in the Home Office'.[22] Harcourt had impressed Spencer that the English administration could not defend itself without him. Spencer sent him over but they remained in constant touch.

The Scotland Yard bomb went off at 8.40 p.m. in a cast-iron urinal beneath the Special Irish Branch's first-floor offices, on the corner opposite the Rising Sun. It blew the corner off the building: the corner office vacated at 8.00 p.m. by Chief Inspector Littlechild.[23] As the dust and paper settled it would have been out of character for Jenkinson to resist *Schadenfreude*. He wrote to Harcourt two days after the explosion:

> I did not find out till Saturday that there was a public urinal in Scotland Yard *under* the room in which the detectives sat. And the dynamite was no doubt placed in that urinal. Fancy their allowing the public to go in there at night, or indeed at any time, after the warnings they have received![24]

This was accompanied by a helpful diagram of the office, the urinal, and the pub, in which a bullseye marked the spot where the constable on watch *should* have been stationed, and X marked the spot where he actually was.

In the weeks that followed, heads rolled. Superintendent Williamson ('very slow and old-fashioned', according to Jenkinson in a note to Spencer[25]) was replaced by Chief Inspector Littlechild, whom Jenkinson knew from Dublin. The Assistant Commissioner in charge of CID, Howard Vincent, resigned. He had married a rich wife in 1882, and had since moved from Ebury Street (and his salon of notabilities *du jour* such as Charles Dilke) to the grandeur of Grosvenor Square and membership, sponsored by the Prince of Wales, of the Marlborough Club. Rightly anxious to protect the great and good, Vincent had of recent years initiated security arrangements that could seem intrusive. His biography, conceding this, quotes a fuming diary entry of Gladstone's from 1882 that describes the invasion of Hawarden by royal protection officers – 'Vincent's men', blundering oafs disguised as flunkeys, who lurked behind every bush in his garden, broke his china and mistook tea urns for bombs. While Vincent considered himself responsible for security in England (Sir Edward Henderson was not a hard-working Commissioner) and Anderson considered himself responsible for avoiding threats to that security from the Irish, everything passed off well enough – even though Anderson was always tight with information and Sir Edward showed no sign of making way for a younger man. But matters got a lot more complicated in 1883, the summer when Jenkinson blew into town for the first time. According to Vincent's biography he was ready to resign at the end of the year but 'on Home Office request' remained. In July of 1884, after the Scotland Yard blast, he left amid good humour from his officers and a strained relationship with Jenkinson. His position as Director of Criminal Intelligence was abolished in favour of a new job – the same job, working out of the same office in Scotland Yard, which by Act of Parliament would have a new title: Assistant Commissioner in charge of the CID. The post was offered to James Monro, a devout Christian with twenty years of service in Indian courts, where he had been a barrister, a magistrate and a District Judge. Jenkinson, in his arrogance seriously underestimating the newcomer, condescendingly remarked of Monro that he was 'a good man in his way'.[26]

Over in Whitehall Place the Special Irish Branch was expanding. Jenkinson already employed RIC men all over England, answerable directly to himself. But these dynamitards moved from country to country all the time. The French and American Governments would not lift a finger to help; to do so might lose them votes, especially in America. As soon as he got back to England in March, Jenkinson had begun to reorganise, insisting that there must be more men at all the ports, to watch comings and goings across the Atlantic.

This included the French Channel ports where men had been stationed for some time. As early as 1880, a letter in Foreign Office files requests permission to install English agents there to combat the trafficking, then common between England and

France, Holland and Belgium, of girl prostitutes. Maybe it was never granted. According to a Cherbourg police report written ten years later,[27] the English police presence in Cherbourg, Le Havre, Boulogne, Calais and Dieppe began in 1881 in reaction to suspicion that anarchists or nihilists might be crossing the Channel following the attempt on the Queen's life. The first such detective 'watching the Southampton line' at Cherbourg had been a German subject called Schmitt (*sic*) who was attached to Scotland Yard.

Since this initiative proved successful, the French report explained, the Yard later sent two more men to Le Havre and two to Calais. There had been several at Cherbourg since Schmitt and they worked happily alongside the French police – in fact, the foreign detectives were useful. Incidentally, the French policeman of 1894 pointed out, there had been a dramatic decline in petty thefts aboard cross-Channel passenger vessels since they arrived.

Monro had the happy knack of maintaining discipline while inspiring loyalty in his team. When he made changes, he explained why. Long before Vincent's time, detectives had been somewhat mistrusted because of the bounty system; everyone knew it was so, but they also knew that if the system were completely abolished pay would have to be improved. Monro understood that the CID must be held in respect or it would be ineffective. He supported a move away from the rewards-for-results system in every way he could. Rewards were more sparingly given, but serious crime decreased.

On the other hand, Jenkinson's influence was all-pervasive.

Every detective in the Special Irish Branch was a Metropolitan policeman through and through. Even if they were Irish – and most were – this was the case. If you were not stationed in London, most specifically in or around Scotland Yard, you didn't really know what was going on. You could never catch up. You were out of sight, and too far away for any hope of promotion. Go to the provinces, even to other parts of London, and you might never be seen again.

And yet when, in March of 1884, Jenkinson applied to have nine of Littlechild's original twelve men leave London and work with customs officers at the ports, Melville chose a posting as far as he could get from Scotland Yard. However ambitious he was, there is always a nagging question for a man with two children under the age of four who follows a dangerous occupation. Is he placing his wife under intolerable strain? Twice, now, police constables had found and defused bombs. He and Kate had survived the death of their child together. Was this daily confrontation with violence fair to her or the children?

Even if he gave no thought to ambition and did not feel endangered, he and Kate needed to make a new start after the bereavement of last summer. So Sergeant Melville and Kate, little Kate and the baby William packed their trunk, left the inspectors recruiting new men, and travelled to France to the first time: to the port city of Le Havre.

THREE

PLOT AND COUNTERPLOT

Le Havre extended along a windswept curve of coastline under a vast northern sky. Its docks, tucked into the north side of the wide estuary of the Seine, were the seat of its prosperity. In the eighteenth century, local dynasties had been founded on fortunes made from the triangular trade in sugar and slaves between Africa, France and the French Antilles, and Melville would have found out quickly enough that their names still carried weight in the town a hundred years later. Families like the Foaches and the Begouens once built ships, bankrolled the trade, even insured it and refined the sugar. Thanks to them Le Havre was endowed with a grand Hotel de Ville, a number of private mansions in the city centre, an imposing Palais de Justice and the deep Vauban Docks, based on those in the Port of London, that Melville would come to know well.

Nearly 300 metres of massive stone breakwater protected the port and people ashore would point out ships poised beyond the bar, awaiting pilots to bring them in. Since the first passenger steamships ploughed their way across the Atlantic in the 1830s, Le Havre had become more prosperous than ever, and now with mass emigration from the east, all Europe seemed to want to embark here for a new life in America. The steamship lines competed to offer something different. Some were technologically advanced, some more luxurious, some, like the Chargeurs Réunis, specialised in freight. Melville would have seen scores of ships of the Compagnie Générale Transatlantique and Messageries Maritimes.

It was a good place to bring up a family. Le Havre was a sort of cross between Brighton and Bristol: a station balnéaire and commercial port combined. Along the Boulevard Albert Premier facing the long beach, tall balconied hotels were springing up to

satisfy the new fashion for seaside holidays. Kate could wheel the
perambulator towards the Cap de la Hève which towered out of
the sea, or inland towards the old Priory on a hill overlooking the
bay. All this, after the smoke and grime of London: they would
have had no regrets. Melville was working with French customs
officers every day, and began to learn French.

The exact date of Melville's posting to France is uncertain. In
March of 1884 an English Port Policeman at Le Havre reported
two Irish-American suspects on the New York boat; we know
this from a letter from the Under-Secretary of State at the Home
Office to his opposite number at the Foreign Office.[1] That police-
man may have been Melville, who was the sergeant there along
with a PC Durham. By April, Monro was definitely employing
Inspector Maurice Moser on Irish duty in Paris.[2] The first proof of
Melville's presence at the coast is a letter from the Consul, Frederic
Bernal, to Jenkinson in London, in December of 1884.

Havre, December 16th 1884

Sir

Sergeant Melville called this morning at the Consulate General
and showed me a memorandum he had just received from London
with instructions to call on me for my intervention in the event of
his discovering the presence in this town of a certain individual. I
at once telegraphed you as follows. 'In case necessity arising could
do nothing without instructions from Foreign Office.'

You will remember a conversation I had with you some months
ago when I told you that the Foreign Office wished to know what
instructions the Home Office desired should be given me. I have
heard nothing more on the subject.

Were I to know that an individual who was on his way to commit,
or had committed, some attempt to blow up a place in England,

was here, it would be necessary for me 1st, to get the police to arrest him – provisionally, and 2nd, to formally apply to the *Procureur de la République* for his detention (that official would immediately ask for instructions from the Minister of Grace and Justice), but up to the moment I have no instructions which would justify my incurring such a [*sic*] responsibilities.[3]

Bernal sent a copy to the Foreign Office which was minuted by various hands. If this happened, who would deal with it? The Foreign Office decided that if Sergeant Melville or anyone else reported the presence of Irish dynamitards on French soil, they should inform the relevant British Consulate in America so that the men could be picked up there.

It is clear from Bernal's letter that after nearly eighteen months working directly to Harcourt, Jenkinson had not grasped the niceties of communication within departments of state in England, far less the diplomatic and legal complexities of enforcing his will abroad. He made people feel threatened. At the Foreign Office, in consulates abroad, and in Scotland Yard, people felt their authority undermined by his sweeping demands and force of character. Turf wars sprang up like brush fires.

In February of 1885, for instance, Jenkinson began to agitate for a sort of roving ambassador to tour consulates in every one of the United States and encourage them to… well, what? It depended how you read it. Maybe they were supposed just to keep their ears open, and maybe they were supposed to spend a little money (whether out of Foreign Office funds was unclear) employing agents, in which case they would become part of Jenkinson's empire at one remove. In a moment of carelessness, or weariness, Sir Julian Pauncefote at the Foreign Office allowed Jenkinson's emissary to go forth but his arrival did not always go down terribly well. There exists for instance an exasperated letter to London from Lord Sackville West at the Washington Legation; he personally had been begging for a dedicated employee to do this very job for some time. His requests had been ignored and now, it seemed, the Home Office was proposing to interfere in foreign affairs.[4]

As for Monro, he could get no co-operation from Jenkinson whatsoever. The CID was ignored. Jenkinson trusted only his RIC men, who were quietly operating in London as elsewhere in England entirely under his control, answerable to no one else. (He acknowledged that there were ten of them,[5] although later events would show that there were more.) Monro found this intolerable. Worse, Jenkinson would not share information; he insisted[6] that he was under no obligation to do so and could not work if he did. So Moser, in Paris in the summer of 1884, had found himself watching men who were working for Jenkinson. Nothing could be more futile. And the Special Irish Branch Port Police, leaving home at the crack of dawn on icy mornings for the docks, and prepared to do all they could to warn the authorities of the movements of suspects, needed something better to go on than a ship's manifest. How was Melville to investigate, or even identify, suspects on the New York boats if he had only a sketchy idea of who they were or why they were suspected? Jenkinson had proved dismissive of the SIB from the start and by the spring of 1885 matters were coming to a head.

In London there had been bombs at the Tower and the House of Commons. There was also social unrest which had nothing to do with Ireland, and following riots in Trafalgar Square, Commissioner Henderson resigned.

On 8 April James Monro and Edward Jenkinson, like a couple of recalcitrant schoolboys, sat down before the new Commissioner Sir Charles Warren. Warren was a military man. He settled the argument at once. When they departed he was entirely persuaded that Jenkinson's promise to communicate with him directly, cutting out Monro, would somehow ensure that Jenkinson volunteered information and that Monro would no longer concern himself with the work on which his detectives were engaged. Neither was remotely likely. Jenkinson on principle did not volunteer information. Monro remained rightly protective of his status and that of the Special Branch, and had been used to running his own show and letting Sir Edward Henderson as Commissioner do the PR and take the credit while he did the work. Now, in Warren, he was up against a man who was used to obedience from subordinates. As Assistant Commissioner in charge of CID, Monro was expected to take orders.

Six weeks later Home Secretary Harcourt called Jenkinson and Monro into his office in an attempt to mediate. He too failed. Monro was reasonable; all he wanted was to see the RIC off his patch and get some information to work with. Jenkinson was 'like a dog with a bone', Harcourt told him irritably, insisting 'It is monstrous that the London detectives should not know of these things.'[7]

Jenkinson had every reason to be wary. He had recently been approached, via the Consulate in Mexico and the Foreign Office, by a potentially invaluable spy, General F.F. Millen, who had been a leading Irish-American activist for twenty years (and had worked for the British in the 1860s on the recommendation of Lord Salisbury, who was keeping silent on the matter). He worked for the *New York Herald*, besides being a military man.

Millen would be risking his life and, in any case, expected a certain standard of living for his family. He would be a serious charge on the Secret Service budget.

Jenkinson dared not reveal Millen's identity. He thought Scotland Yard men were incompetent; thanks to them, his own name had already appeared in the newspapers. He insisted that he alone should be the judge of when to convey information to Monro, that Monro on the other hand should be under an obligation immediately to convey information to him, and that he should retain the RIC men. On the other hand Jenkinson had been made a fool of, recently, by 'the Burkham affair' in which bogus information was offered and largely paid for.[8]

By 17 June – at another, stormy tripartite confrontation – Harcourt had had enough.

> Sir W. Harcourt regretted to see that Mr Jenkinson manifested such a temper and frame of mind... and when Mr Jenkinson displayed such a state of mind in dealing with him, it gave rise to the impression in Sir W. Harcourt's mind that Mr Jenkinson might display the same feeling towards others, and that perhaps he had done so in dealing with Mr Monro...

Mr Jenkinson asked what was to become of the Royal Irish Constabulary.

Sir W. Harcourt observed that on the whole he thought the sooner they quitted London the better…

Mr Jenkinson observed that that being so, he did not see that there was much use in his appointment.

Sir W. Harcourt said that was a matter for him.[9]

Jenkinson, who was a little more subdued after this, spent the next few days producing a long memo setting out his case.[10] He was willing to concede almost nothing. At the end of June the Liberal Government fell, and would remain out of office for the next seven months. Harcourt went with it and departed in anger, as Jenkinson with characteristic arrogance had announced that Lord Spencer was coming over and would settle the dispute in his favour with the new Conservative Home Secretary, Sir Richard Assheton Cross.[11] Monro calmly wrote a note explaining why Jenkinson's scheme was not only operationally unsound, but unconstitutional.[12]

Cross, the incoming Secretary of State, was impatient with the whole thing. He met both men and scribbled a set of rules which he considered adequate to settle it. The rules could be partially interpreted, and were.

For the rest of 1885 Monro and Jenkinson were distracted by other matters. Jenkinson knew that a plot was being cooked up that would involve the Tsar in sponsoring Irishmen to drive the British out of Afghanistan, and possibly promote a Franco-Russian alliance against Germany. It was all a diversion. The Foreign Office was paying a senior Fenian called Carroll-Tevis in Paris and he, along with Jenkinson's man Casey, was deep in the plot. The English Government now had so many agents dotted about Paris, New York and London unknown to each other that they risked playing a double or treble game that would inevitably lead nowhere; this to a great extent was the case with the Russo-Irish plan.[13]

Nonetheless Jenkinson looked forward to Millen's arrival from America via Le Havre in November.[14] Before that a meeting of Irish revolutionaries would leave France by way of Le Havre in September.[15] It would be Melville's job to watch them; to watch them come in, and make sure they left; to watch Millen arrive. Jenkinson was still excluding the SIB from anything but mundane tasks, but Melville had plenty of routine work at the port, his French was fluent, and there was a new baby at home: in April, James Benjamin had been born.

There were no immediate bomb threats to London. In the lull that marked the second half of 1885 Jenkinson's urge to manipulate events became almost megalomaniac and his epistolary efforts more stupendous than ever. His eighteen-page *Memorandum on the present situation in Ireland* of 26 September set out an eloquent case for Home Rule which he sent to Lord Salisbury and selected members of the Cabinet. In his view, were Home Rule not conceded the violence would worsen; the reasonable majority of Parnellite Irish nationalists would be overwhelmed and outmanoeuvred by the violent extremists unless Parnell received support.

Salisbury dismissed this. Home Rule was out of the question from a Conservative government and he was perfectly prepared to confront an escalation of hostilities. Jenkinson bombarded his only sympathiser in Cabinet, Spencer's successor in Dublin Lord Carnarvon, with notes and memos; he even wrote about Home Rule to Gladstone, pointing out that only by keeping Parnell on side could violence (and implicitly a violent swing to the Tories) be prevented. Gladstone, who had always kept the Secret Service strictly at arm's length, sent the following somewhat deflating reply:

> I agree very emphatically – but these are not abstractions, they call
> for immediate action. I must ask in what capacity you address me
> – and what use I can make of your letter?[16]

1886 would be Melville's third year in Le Havre, and he was frustrated by a dangerous situation that nobody seemed to be doing anything about. There was a pretty little port called Honfleur set deep into the south side of the Seine estuary, and close to Honfleur was a dynamite factory. Ships laden with the stuff now sailed quite regularly away from Honfleur along the river mouth beyond Le Havre and out into the English Channel whence, it was claimed, they headed for the Baltic, their cargo apparently intended for use in the Russian mining industry. Melville would have been aware that the Irish-American dynamiters used materials bought in Europe. He could have a source of supply here under his nose, a short ferry ride away, and yet he had no intelligence with which to make further enquiries.

If he pointed this out in a report to his superiors in London, and we have no proof that he did, nothing came of it. Hostilities had re-opened in the New Year over, of all things, a threat to HRH the Prince of Wales. It came in a letter signed 'Magee', and under the mistaken impression that Mr Jenkinson was head of the Secret Police, the Prince of Wales passed it on to him. Rather than conveying the letter, or at the very least its contents, to Scotland Yard, Jenkinson organised a ludicrous sting operation.

> He sent a woman for the purpose of entrapping the writer of the threatening letter, entrusting to her a bag of farthings, supposed to represent sovereigns, in payment of the bribe demanded by the writer of the letter.[17]

This masterly ruse not only failed, but emerged into daylight when the Prince passed a subsequent letter directly to Scotland Yard. Dogged detective work by the SIB revealed that the woman had been one of many Irish people employed by a private agency off Piccadilly Circus which was supported by Mr Jenkinson's Secret Service funds and advertised for assistance in the public press.

As this case was followed up, the Tories were preparing for a fresh election. By February Gladstone and the other old faces were back. Hugh Childers was Home Secretary. In March Godfrey Lushington, Under-Secretary at the Home Office, declared that the endless squabbles were leading him to favour the loss of Jenkinson over the loss of Monro.

Unless the case is very carefully handled I believe Mr Monro would resign. And this would be a deplorable loss, very far exceeding any gain from Mr Jenkinson obtaining a free hand, if indeed that were possible.[18]

Nothing could be done to make these two work together. By May, Monro had gone on the offensive. He wanted Jenkinson out, and wrote a long memo listing every instance of the man's arrogant behaviour and more:

[and then]... the explosions at the Houses of Parliament and the Tower occurred. While investigating these cases, the manner in which my action as a police officer was interfered with is almost beyond belief. Not only was freedom of action denied to me, but in one instance illegal action was taken by Mr Jenkinson himself and suggestions involving illegal procedure were made to me by Mr Jenkinson which, had they been listened to, would undoubtedly have led to the failure of the case and involved the police in well-merited disgrace. I do not further allude to the matter here, but I am fully prepared to substantiate the accuracy of this statement.[19]

He concluded his note with a cool evaluation of Mr Jenkinson's usefulness.

I have already said that all the information regarding dangerous, or supposed dangerous, subjects in London was given to Mr Jenkinson by Scotland Yard... I have furnished to Sir Charles Warren a list of every file of information issued by Mr Jenkinson to me during the past year, and the result *qua* tangible information is absolutely *nil*. There have been many vague rumours communicated; the time of police has been frequently wasted on following up the intelligence of an (unintentionally no doubt) misleading character; but of real, practical, valuable information there has been a very decided absence.[20]

In June 1886, after just four months in office, the Liberal Government split over Home Rule. An election was called, and a coalition of Tories and Liberal Unionists took its place. Lord Salisbury returned as Prime Minister and Foreign Secretary, and for the first time a Roman Catholic, Henry Matthews, became the Home Secretary.

As for relevant information from overseas, in September of 1886 Monro was complaining that he seen not a single item of consular intelligence in a year.[21] Relevant documents from consulates went to the FO and thence to Jenkinson. But this is not to say Scotland Yard received no information from overseas. Some embassy intelligence certainly reached Monro, such as this hair-raising note on 10 July from the Secretary at the British Embassy in Paris:

> A man came to me this morning and said that he was convinced that some dynamite plot was being prepared by the Irish Americans who frequent Reynolds' Bar… He has overheard phrases like 'we shall have another earthquake ready soon'… He has twice seen suspicious looking bags at the Bar, which are taken charge of by the proprietor. My informant had an opportunity of touching one: he found it very heavy, and heard a ticking noise coming from it. He thinks it contains dynamite, which comes from Havre.[22]

The informant was sent direct to Scotland Yard and told Monro, in answer to questioning, that an Englishman had been seen hanging around Reynolds' Bar. Monro saw a means to expose one of Jenkinson's unacknowledged 'threads'. He knew that the man who ran the private agency off Piccadilly was called Winter, alias Dawson. He had long ago put the information before Childers and Jenkinson. Jenkinson tipped the man off; he fled to Paris; and it was he who was lurking around Reynolds' Bar. As Winter was a bigamist, Monro sent a man (either Melville or Moser) to Paris who arrested him and Monro asked Matthews to ask the Foreign Office for extradition. But Matthews agreed with Jenkinson that there was no need for that. The smoking gun – Monro's proof that Jenkinson was running a private detective outfit in London in parallel with the police – remained just out of sight.

The information about Reynolds' Bar had been followed by a tight-lipped little note from HM Consul Bernal in Le Havre itself on 26 July.

> I do not suppose the explosion of nearly two tons of dynamite which occurred here on Friday night, from which my house somewhat suffered, is of sufficient importance to Sir Julian Pauncefote, GCMG, to report officially, but I think it as well to mention that when the sloop came ashore she had on board 23 tons of dynamite from the factory at Ablon, near Honfleur; two and a half tons of gunpowder sent out to her from this port; &c. She was bound to St Petersburg, and the cargo was, I learn from one of the officials, for the Russian Government.[23]

Melville must have reported this event to London as well, for the following day the Commissioner, Sir Charles Warren, wrote to the Under-Secretary of State at the Home Office that 'I have reason to believe that explosives may be brought to this country by steamers plying between Russia and here' and asking for consular reports to be sent to him; for Port Police at Gravesend to be warned; and for crew lists to be obtained wherever possible. Known Irish dynamitards had visited St Petersburg that summer. This information was not of immediate concern to the police in charge of London, but it would have been useful background; even more useful had they known that plots involving Russia and Ireland were being cooked up by Jenkinson's men, apparently with Foreign Office connivance.[24]

Melville, conveniently located as he was, probably knew more about the provenance of dynamite than the Assistant Commissioner. Jenkinson was routinely holding onto key information from overseas which should go to the London police.

The Consul at Le Havre at least suspected that no one was paying attention.

> I don't know whether the authorities care to know that the Schooner *Little Vixen* of Plymouth sailed three days ago from

Honfleur for St Petersburg with ten tons of dynamite; 28 cases of fuse; and 2 cases of electric clocks.[25]

Relations between the English and French police at the ports were good. They helped each other. But what questions should be asked? Melville was not the only one whose effectiveness was diminished by lack of Irish intelligence from London. The Consul in St Petersburg pointed out:

> No information worth having can be obtained by HM Consuls without some clue. If you can furnish me this secretly, Russian police can give valuable assistance.[26]

But Jenkinson had gone too far. The 'threads', followed back to their source, became tangled. Lord Salisbury at least liked to feel he was in control and Jenkinson had never made any secret of his Home Rule sympathies; could he be trusted? It so happened that certain anti-Parnellite elements in London had been cooking up black propaganda against Parnell since the previous winter. One of them was a Captain Stephens, who had worked for Jenkinson until he was sacked for drunkenness. In September, at an audience with Matthews and Salisbury, Stephens asserted that there were letters in existence which proved Parnell approved and encouraged the dynamite faction. Jenkinson, he said, knew of these letters and suppressed them.[27]

On 11 December 1886 the stumbling block was at last removed. Home Secretary Matthews wrote to Jenkinson:

> I regret that today, after much anxious consideration, I have determined to relieve you from your present duties as speedily as possible and I fix the 10th January as a convenient day.[28]

Jenkinson burned his papers and left.

By February of 1887 Monro was in sole charge both of Irish intelligence as it concerned London, and of the Secret Service. Melville's career could truly begin.

FOUR

A Very Dangerous Game

1887: Jubilee Year. The crowned heads of Europe were invited to a fortnight-long celebration starting with a royal thanksgiving ceremony at St Paul's on 21 June. It would be a display of Imperial glory unprecedented in the fifty years since the coronation.

James Monro knew that if he could only bypass the Commissioner, he could bend Home Secretary Matthews to his will; and he managed it. He got Robert Anderson back into the Home Office and whisked day-to-day intelligence of international political crime out of Sir Charles Warren's hands altogether.

The Criminal Investigation Department was reorganised. 'Ordinary' serious crime would be dealt with by Section A. Superintendent Williamson would head Section B, a department about twenty-five strong dealing with Irish affairs in London as the old SIB had done. Section C would be the Port Police. All section heads would report to Warren.

Section D, an entirely new, very small and secret section called the Special Branch, would be financed separately from the Metropolitan Police; its money would come from the Treasury via the Home Office. It would consist of just four policemen but could draw on the resources of other CID sections if required. Chief Inspector Littlechild at its head would report to Monro, who (to Warren's annoyance) would report directly to Home Secretary Henry Matthews. Three inspectors would be answerable to Littlechild: Melville, Pope and Quinn. Their duties would take them outside London when necessary (Melville was still stationed in France), and would not be exclusively Irish. They would resurrect Von Tornow's old job, keeping a watchful eye on political agitators in general, and potentially murderous ones in particular. Information that came from Le Caron in America to Anderson would go to Monro directly. Occasional duties would include royal protection.

Jenkinson had retired to Buckinghamshire, yet his presence still hovered over the Secret Service. His plots had taken on a momentum of their own. More than once Monro would discover, long after he needed to know, that some allegedly dangerous Irishman was on the Secret Service payroll (like Casey or Millen or John Patrick Hayes) or in the pay of the Foreign Office like Carroll-Tevis. He was doing his job blindfold and did not know that Jenkinson had inspired an entrapment operation which even now was being put into action. Jenkinson had one idea: that the British must be shown that, unless Home Rule were granted, there would be a dynamite campaign.

Arthur Balfour, Salisbury's clever thirty-nine-year-old nephew, held the opposing view: the Irish required the smack of firm government. In March he became Secretary of State for Ireland and began to promote a Crimes Bill, which would outlaw organisations believed to be hostile to the Crown. There would be no collusion between the Tories and the Parnellites. *The Times* had come into possession of letters allegedly from Charles Stewart Parnell which revealed his sympathy with violent action. The newspaper ran a series of accusations against him while Anderson contributed concurrent articles about past, but quite recent, Fenian activities in America – anonymously.

By May the public was nervous. Scotland Yard was putting out press releases about a dangerous Clan-na-Gael man in Paris, Patrick Casey – Captain Stephens' cousin, who like him was in British service.

In Le Havre Melville was a new father again. Kate had given birth to Cecilia in 1886. The promotion to Inspector, with its increased pay, was welcome.

Monro expressed concern that explosives were on their way by a passenger ship of the French line from America via Le Havre for delivery to someone called Miller, or Muller, in Paris. He communicated a request, via the Foreign Office, for vigilance: 'I have a couple of officers at Le Havre and their services are very much at your disposal.' HM Consul Bernal reported that no explosives had arrived but if they did, Monro would be the first to know.

All the same, Melville had noticed an interesting individual passing through. A thin, middle-aged American called Muller wearing an astrakhan-collared coat had left New York on SS *Gascogne* of the Compagnie Générale Transatlantique on 18 April. He was on his way to the French capital. The explosives, if and when they arrived, might be destined for him.

Melville followed 'Muller' to Paris, to the Hotel du Palais in the Avenue cours la Reine, on the right bank overlooking the Seine near the Place de la Concorde, where the stranger signed in as General F.F. Millen. Melville installed himself nearby and kept a watchful eye on the slightly-built American, noticing that he wrote a lot of letters. No doubt enlisting the help of a concierge, he discovered that Millen's correspondents in London included a Colonel Farrer at the Oriental Club – probably his link to Jenkinson. There was also a certain Tevis who lived at a good address in Paris.

Monro, in London, literally didn't know the half of it, so if Melville ever got sight of the letters' contents Monro must have been mystified. Before he left Room 56 Jenkinson had burned the paperwork. There was no one (except the Foreign Office, and they were silent) to tell his successor that General F.F. Millen was working for the British. Or that General Carroll-Tevis, a soldier of fortune long resident in Paris who had risen high in the Fenian movement, and of whom Monro had never heard either, was a Foreign Office spy.

All that Monro, and by extension Melville, suspected was that somebody had engaged somebody else to ship the 'Greek Fire' as the explosive substance was said to be, to Millen who was supposed to organise 'a celebration of Mrs Brown's very good health'. The Queen was to be threatened with a Jubilee dynamite plot.

Melville reported from Paris that Millen was on his way back to the Channel coast, this time to Boulogne, and he followed. Nearly two weeks later, on 24 May, Millen's wife came from Dublin to join her husband at his hotel.

Melville and Monro perhaps expected some Irish-American emissary to arrive, but none did. And Millen made no sortie across the Channel. But Melville raised his eyebrows when a Scotland Yard inspector called Thomson, who had just retired, turned up with his own wife at the same hotel and the two couples made friends.

Melville had not been warned that Thomson and his wife would turn up. It is possible that Anderson, at the Home Office, had hired him and omitted to tell Monro. The Foreign Office's man in Paris, Carroll-Tevis, to whom Millen had only recently boasted that he had come to Europe to 'operate' during the Jubilee, had sent a female spy to Boulogne: later he told Michael Davitt so. After the event nobody wanted to say who had sent the Thomsons.

The Millens and the Thomsons moved together to a different hotel, the Hotel Poilly. Melville noticed with irritation that Millen was now posting his own letters. There was no longer any chance, as there had been in Paris, of getting a quick look at the addresses – unless the French police could be induced to let him have a look at whatever the postman took out of the box. They could not. He put the case before Monro: this would have to be done through official channels.

Monro passed on the request to the Foreign Office who got the heavy weight of Lord Salisbury's sanction behind them and informed the Ambassador as well as the Consul of the matter's importance.[1] At Boulogne, HM Consul Surplice engaged the assistance of the French police at once. At last Melville could legitimately read Millen's mail, which was shown to him by the French police when it was collected.

And now there arrived, to beard Millen in his lair, none other than Superintendent Williamson, who demanded that General Millen afford him 'absolute disclosure and abandonment of his mission'. Williamson believed that Millen's mission was to blow Queen Victoria to smithereens on behalf of Clan-na-Gael. 'Absolute disclosure' was a key request. Williamson, acting on Monro's orders, wanted to know who Millen was working for. Millen would neither confirm nor deny anything.

Melville took hold of the letters for long enough to read them and summarise passages. That is in part the reason why not only the ordinary French police, but also the Railway Police, attended a meeting between Surplice and Williamson on 15 June where the matter of Millen was discussed. They had his description – it would be known if he left Boulogne – but also it may be inferred that if items of mail were taken away to be read, they might have to be delivered separately to the mail train before it left, and the Railway Police would need to know.

Monro must find out who Millen was writing to. He had a very strong suspicion that Millen was one of Jenkinson's men even now. Lord Lyons, the Ambassador in Paris, confirmed that the French police would give every assistance in Paris as well as Boulogne; 'I trust however that there will be no relaxation of independent means of watchfulness on the part of the English police', he added pointedly.

Far from it. Whichever way you looked at it, the British Government had been keeping several so-called plotters, and an attendant cast of snoopers, in comfort at public expense. No entrapment could happen. It was a farce; there wasn't a genuine revolutionary among the lot of them. The Jubilee plot, which had seemed such a wizard wheeze, must be closed down.

Without any help from Millen it was rolling relentlessly on. Carroll-Tevis had engaged one Cassidy to ship the explosives and, unexpectedly, he did. They arrived unknown to Monro, in the form of dynamite powder, on the *City of Chester* in Liverpool on the very day of the Jubilee, along with two 'brothers' called Scott and a Mr Joseph 'Melville', whose real name was Moroney. Moroney, as Monro discovered, had been instructed in New York to complete the task in which Millen seemed to be failing. The three men also brought a couple of Smith and Wesson revolvers.

On 21 June, when hundreds of titled Europeans processed in open carriages through the streets of London to celebrate with Her Majesty at St Paul's, Millen at Boulogne 'had all his luggage packed and ready for flight and was evidently in a state of intense excitement'.[2] But nothing happened.

Monro now knew that General Millen was writing to Sullivan, the head of the Clan-na-Gael in America who knew perfectly well what Cassidy was up to, as well as to Tevis in Paris. Neither Millen nor Monro knew Tevis as anything but the agent of the Fenian Brotherhood.[3] Monro did know that Millen had reported to both Sullivan and Tevis 'attributing his failure to the close vigilance of the police'.[4] He did not yet know that Sullivan had sent Moroney and the others.

Six days after the Jubilee celebrations started Millen and his wife left Boulogne for Paris. Inspector Melville got there first, played a hunch and booked a room at the Hotel du Palais, where sure enough, the Millens turned up. They were joined by their two daughters, Kitty, who had been staying in London, and Florence from Dublin. Melville became friendly with the family and helped the girls with French lessons.[5] Kitty Millen had been staying in Thurloe Square, near the Museums in South Kensington, for the last six months, and when she returned to London, her French tutor happened to leave Paris at the same time. He followed her to South Kensington where he quietly handed over responsibility to Patrick Quinn.

Kitty and Florence met an Irish MP at the House of Commons and Kitty passed to him, as instructed by her father, a package of letters recommending one Joseph Melville (Moroney) to three Irish MPs.

Between August and November Monro pursued Moroney and his co-conspirators just as Millen had been pursued in France. His aim was to harass these potential dynamiters into leaving without having done any harm, and in this he succeeded. It was old-school Scotland Yard practice, favouring 'open and constant surveillance': deterrence rather than entrapment.

Of the conspirators in England only Moroney had any money – he had gone to Paris to get it – and he, like Millen, did little except travel around, in his case with a Miss Kennedy, a milliner from Boston. The Clan-na-Gael funds (or more accurately, the Land League funds) he received were spent on hotel rooms in Paris, London and Dublin and the frothiest of fancy lace Miss Kennedy could find in the capitals of Europe.

Littlechild's men – specifically McIntyre, Quinn and Walsh – pursued the two other men who had arrived with Moroney from New York on the day of the Jubilee. These fellows remained in London in impoverished circumstances. (When, later, Clan-na-Gael members insisted on proper accounting for the funds, the plight of the dynamitards and the families left behind emerged as an issue. Some were destitute and abandoned by the movement far from home.) An associate – an associate seen with Moroney and Millen in Paris – died of tuberculosis. Monro used the inquest to expose the Jubilee plot and its association with General Millen before a large number of invited journalists.

In the final months of 1887, dynamite powder was found dumped in a back yard in Islington. Moroney's co-conspirators were arrested. The one who had dumped the dynamite was broke and sick; he had in his possession a Smith and Wesson revolver and a cutting from a newspaper about the future engagements of Arthur Balfour. He could not read, he said, but it was a highly suggestive find, considering the odium with which 'Bloody' Balfour was regarded in Irish nationalist circles. The prosecution's case was that these men were pawns in the Jubilee dynamite plot, and for that they received long jail sentences. (One died in prison and another was released, after petitions to the Home Secretary, after six years.)

On 22 October 1887, General Millen left for America. After abortive attempts to carry on spying in Central America he would die of natural causes in New York in 1889. No doubt Lord Salisbury was relieved. So was Monro; and in justification of the way he had handled the Jubilee plot, he wrote in November of 1887:

To have permitted the plot to ripen, taking measures only to ensure the apprehension and punishment of the criminals, would have involved comparatively little cost of thought or effort or money while the result would doubtless have impressed the public with a belief in the zeal and efficiency of the police. But the policy I have adopted, and steadily pursued, though of course a thankless one so far as the public is concerned, will, I venture to hope, receive the approval of the Government.[6]

In March of 1888 the rewards were doled out. Inspector Melville came second to top of the list after Chief Inspector Littlechild and received the then generous sum of £25.

It seems that at this time Melville was officially posted to Paris.[7] Since no one had yet told Monro that both Patrick Casey and Carroll-Tevis, its most notorious Irish-American residents, were in the pay of the British, the Special Branch could certainly have justified a permanent posting there. Every conspirator who crossed the Atlantic seemed to visit those two and they were worth watching. The Prince of Wales also made frequent trips to Paris and it is quite likely that Lord Salisbury wanted an eye kept on him for diplomatic reasons, quite apart from any threat of attack.[8] Inspector Moser, who had worked for Monro in Paris before, had now left the force and was running an 'Anglo-Continental Enquiry Agency';[9] Melville seems to have taken his place as Monro's man in the capital.

On 17 May Monro told Matthews that a plot was afoot to assassinate 'Bloody' Balfour, the hated Secretary of State, and the would-be assassin was in Paris. Matthews informed the Foreign Office at once, and the following was telegraphed to HM Ambassador:

Private and Most Secret. Home Office have information that plot to assassinate Mr Balfour and others is being prepared by the notorious J.P.Walsh who is living under assumed name in Paris at the Hotel d'Industrie 31 Rue Dunkerque. He should be followed.

Home Office have agent in Paris who will call at Embassy place
himself at Your Excellency's disposal. Further particulars by next
messenger.

According to a key informer, J.P. Walsh had been among the
instigators of the 'Irish Invincibles' who had claimed responsibility for the Phoenix Park murders of 1882. He had been living
in America. The murders – and it is worth remembering this as
a footnote to what follows – had been committed by stabbing
with surgical knives bought in Bond Street by an American 'Dr
Hamilton Williams'. In Monro's view of events in 1888,

> [The dynamitards]… resolved on a new line of tactics. They pro-
> fessed to think that Irish Americans were not good agents for
> outrage, as their accent called attention to them. This sounds pru-
> dent; the real reason was that the Irish American had had enough
> of the danger and judiciously wished to throw the burden on the
> shoulders of other persons. With this object in view they resolved
> to inaugurate a system of assassination… to be carried out by
> Irishmen, not Irish Americans.[10]

Walsh was understandably averse to landing on English soil and
allegedly intended to direct the plot from France. A Scotland
Yard detective, probably Melville, followed Walsh and one day
saw him deep in conversation with another Dubliner called
McKenna under the Arc de Triomphe. Monro wanted Walsh
interviewed, and had to wade through channels, in the usual way,
via the Foreign Office and the Ambassador, to get the French
police to order him to attend the Préfecture to be questioned.

Walsh, informed that he must pay a visit to police HQ, was
sublimely unconcerned. Six years earlier the French Department
of Justice had declined to extradite him from Le Havre, when he
was caught fleeing Dublin after the murders. He had been mind-
ing his own business in Brooklyn ever since, so they couldn't
hurt him now. In he swaggered to the Préfecture, little knowing
that among his French interrogators, speaking to him through

an interpreter, would be one William Melville, whose account continues:

> Walsh arrived at 9.30 a.m. at the Préfecture and was questioned through one of his officers by M. Goron, Chef de la Sûreté. In answer to questions he said his name was John Stephen Walsh, and he was born at Milford, County Cork, and was single and by profession a labourer. He took the name of Walters because he had come to France to receive some money which a man in England owed him. If this man corresponded with him (Walsh) he would bring himself under suspicion there, as he (Walsh) was outlawed in connection with the Phoenix Park murders. He was now staying in Paris for pleasure.
>
> He said he would prefer to be hanged to revealing the name of above man, but said that he met him at Boulogne on 14th inst. when he received £20 from him. That was at the Hotel de l'Union, but neither of them stayed there, each returning home.

Melville, as a Frenchman, put a question. What job did this man do?

> In reply to me, he said the man that gave him the money was a publican. Knowing that Walsh had received two letters yesterday, one from Omaha, United States, the other from Manchester, I questioned him as to his correspondence, when he said he had received a letter also from Preston, but declined to say from whom, but it was clear it was from the publican. On my briefing him re American acquaintances, he said that for the months up to November last, he worked at the Brooklyn Navy Yard, and was well known to a Mr McGee a foreman there. During this time he lodged with John Ross 96 Adam Street, Brooklyn. Last January he went to Omaha to look for work and admitted meeting Thomas Brennan there. Pressed as to his letter of yesterday from Omaha, he said it was from John Groves of that city, but would not give his address. He said latter was a clerk or kept an office.

Thomas Brennan was also wanted for the Phoenix Park murders. Melville was well informed; he knew the names, and where certain Irishmen were hiding out, and he knew who he was looking for. He relentlessly asked questions in French, heard them interpreted, and heard the answers back in English – and made scribbled notes as they were interpreted to him in French. This Groves had sent Walsh some money: £60 in three notes. Melville said he did not believe this story – how could it be in three notes? Walsh asked if he had to produce the notes and –

M. Goron said it was voluntary, but I said quickly that he should show them. On this he drew from a belt worn inside his trousers three £20 Bank of England notes. M. Goron said this was a delicate matter, there being no charge against Walsh. I however snatched the notes hurriedly and found that they were:

1st   Serial No. 59/W No.66929. of 17th February 1887. This one was stamped at some office apparently with the figures 5989 and also 8668.

2nd   4/V No.64906 of 20th March 1886.

3rd   4/V No.85348 – *ditto*

Walsh refused to give any answer as to why Groves sent him the money beyond that he was a friend, and thought, he (Walsh) might want it. He had no acquaintances at Paris but knew a Mr Casey, whom he saw when in custody at Havre in 1883, but did not see him since.[11]

Melville asked him about a 'carroty' fellow in whose company he had been seen (probably McKenna, living in Paris as Sylvester). Walsh told him the carroty man was an American he'd met by accident. And yes, he had met him again yesterday, but said it was by chance.

This pushy French policeman was making him uneasy. He hadn't walked in expecting a grilling. He would answer no more questions. He demanded reassurance from the Préfet, who had been quietly observing, that none of this information about himself, or the banknotes, would reach the English police.

The silence was broken by Melville: 'Walsh, man, I am an inspector from Scotland Yard.'

Walsh's exact response is not recorded but we have it on Monro's authority that it was 'more emphatic than reverent'.[12] He was allowed to go and McKenna was shadowed – so obviously shadowed that he dared not meet Walsh, but had to go back to his hotel. The two detectives sat down at a restaurant across the street and ordered *un verre*. After some time McKenna came out. The detectives got up to follow him. McKenna turned around crossly and came back. This he did several times. He was not a happy man. When finally he came out again they waved him over for a drink. He had been worn down; he could not resist. The glasses were on the table and the rounds were being thoughtfully consumed when around the corner who should come but – Walsh. When he saw McKenna sitting with two detectives he sprang to a certain conclusion about the cause of his own predicament. And he said so to McKenna, roundly abusing him. In the stand-up shouting match that followed, the two detectives crept away.

A couple of days later both men were gently escorted to Le Havre by train, Walsh travelling with Melville and McKenna with Sergeant Flood.

The two conspirators were so irate still with one another that they declined to travel in the same carriage. On the way to Havre Walsh attempted to pump Inspector Melville as to the ports which were watched by the Police. Inspector Melville naturally was not lavish in the information given, but he rather implied that there was not a port in the world where Scotland Yard was not strongly represented. On arrival at Havre, many of the employees at the wharves and shipping who knew Melville well owing to his having been formerly stationed at Havre, came forward effusively and greeted him. To Walsh this sight suggested that all these men must be allies of Melville in the police, and his comment, with an oath was 'There are scores of them.'[13]

Monro gleefully informed the press that Walsh and McKenna were on their way home from France with their tails between their legs. Someone in America issued a denial that Walsh was in Europe at all; he was in Omaha. At this Monro sent a wire to Pinkertons, suggesting that if any American newsmen cared to see Walsh and his former friend Roger McKenna for themselves they could meet SS *Gascogne* when she arrived from Le Havre.

Walsh and McKenna were greeted on the New York waterfront by about forty news hounds. Walsh was in an abusive mood, and no one was left in much doubt that he had been made to look foolish. 'Thus the Walsh assassinations scheme was extinguished by the slaughter and ridicule of both England and America', concluded James Monro, recalling the event with great satisfaction fifteen years later.

Perhaps Sir Charles Warren felt, in the summer of 1888, that his Assistant Commissioner was stealing the limelight. His own standing with the public had never been lower. In November of 1887 he had called out thousands of troops to assist in policing a demonstration in Trafalgar Square; shots were fired and two people killed. The *Pall Mall Gazette* called it Bloody Sunday. Notwithstanding the roar of protest that greeted his rigid and heavy-handed methods, he threw his weight about more than ever. Henry Matthews, the Home Secretary, could not keep him in check; 'indeed he took the attitude that the Commissioner once appointed by the Crown had certain powers by statute in the exercise of which he was responsible to no higher official.'[14]

He was particularly incensed by Monro's direct line of communication to the Home Office. The long working hours and endless ramifications of the Dynamite Plot had pretty much worn Williamson out, and he had to take sick leave. Monro put forward the name of MacNaghten, an old friend of his from Bengal, to the Home Office, suggesting that he should assist with Williamson's work under the title of Assistant Chief Constable. The Home Office agreed but Warren 'blocked the appointment with a mean little whispering campaign.'[15] As for Monro, he was summarily removed from the room that the

Assistant Commissioner had always occupied at Scotland Yard ('one of the best in the collection of dog-holes in which the Metropolitan Police have their headquarters')[16] and sent to work alongside Section D at Whitehall Place. This inevitably marginalised the work of the section, besides causing offence to the man on whom rank had so obviously been pulled. 'The department itself, established in another street, was looked upon somewhat as… a rival rather than a branch of the same business.'[17]

There were mutinous rumblings throughout the Metropolitan Police generally. Since taking over from Henderson, Warren had expected a militaristic style. Not only did he fail to understand that policemen needed to use their own initiative, but he could not grasp that detectives, to an even greater extent, must be relied upon to take decisions without referring upwards. As the *Pall Mall Gazette* pointed out, 'the effect of this was felt throughout the entire force'.

> The essential difference between a soldier and a constable is that the former is seldom or never used out of formation, while the latter is seldom or never in formation. That is to say, the soldier is an integral part of a machine, the efficiency of which presupposes the absolute and mechanical obedience of all its parts. The constable, on the contrary, is called upon at all hours to exercise his own judgment, to solve knotty practical questions of law and of fact, to compose disputes, to dispense rough-and-ready justice, and in short to act as an independent unit. For every policeman is the bishop of his beat, with jurisdiction almost like that of a magistrate. If he winks he can suspend the operation of the law. If he pleases he can convert the law into a weapon of oppression. The soldier is never left alone. He never acts on his own initiative. He is always under the eye of his officer, and his supreme quality is unhesitating and unqualified obedience. The constable is always left alone. He is constantly acting on his own initiative, and his supreme duty is the habitual exercise of self-reliance and common sense. Hence militarism is fatal to the force. But with Sir Charles Warren militarism is supreme.[18]

By mid-August of 1888 Monro had had enough. He resigned, with dignity, in a brief note to Mr Matthews. Sir Charles Warren said nothing to Monro's men and 'sinister rumours', according to Anderson, were circulating about who would take over on 31 August. Robert Anderson was made Assistant Commissioner but 'for some occult reason', as Anderson put it in his memoir, 'the matter was kept secret, and I was enjoined not to make my appointment known. I had been in the habit of frequenting Mr Monro's room as we were working together on political crime matters; but when I did so now, and Sir Charles Warren took advantage of my visit to come over to see me, it was at once inferred that he was spying on me because I was Mr Monro's friend.'[19]

Anderson, laden with added responsibility for the 'ordinary' CID work on the very day in August when the Jack the Ripper murders began in Whitechapel, was floundering. He was not the sort of man who could withstand Warren at the best of times and with Monro gone, no one else was, either.

The Commissioner had introduced a crowd of yes-men, all of them former soldiers, who saw it as their job to issue orders to the Metropolitan Police. These proved both unpopular and ultimately counter-productive. The height requirement for CID entry was arbitrarily raised to five feet nine inches, as though there were some correlation between height and cunning. Uniformed constables could be fined a stupendous £50 (approaching a year's pay) for being caught with a glass of beer when on duty. If they exerted their authority and made a mistake they risked being hauled before superior officers and dropping a 'class'. As it could take eight years to get from one 'class' to another and gain a pay increase of twenty per cent, this did not seem a punishment proportionate to the offence.

Melville, in France, was fortunately spared most of this. He could still work autonomously, reporting directly to Littlechild.

In London police morale was low; police officers were entirely demotivated and assertive action by the force, from murder investigation to crowd control, was disastrously affected. So disastrously, in fact, that with the Jack the Ripper killings of September and October the public began to grow restive and the Queen feared 'that the detective department is not so efficient as it might be'. In October the *Pall Mall Gazette* printed an article that could only have been inspired by Monro, banished to some Home Office backwater but fighting hard. It demonstrated intimate knowledge of Scotland Yard and was entirely unsympathetic to Warren.

Warren at last resigned on 10 November, the day after the final Ripper murder. There had, according to historical consensus, been five Whitechapel murders between 31 August (the date of Monro's official departure) and 9 November. During this time Anderson had been occupied with the Parnell Commission as it looked into the truth of the allegations in *The Times* linking Parnell to the dynamitards. Matthews privately dismissed him as 'a tout for *The Times*'.

Monro emerged from his exile at the Home Office. On 24 November, the Cabinet having discussed his candidacy at length, his name was submitted to Queen Victoria who was graciously pleased to appoint him Commissioner.

Anderson was officially, and openly, Assistant Commissioner in charge of CID. With Monro's guidance in navigating the waters of 'ordinary' crime as well as political crime, he got on top of the job.

The Metropolitan Police breathed a collective sigh of relief and the line of communication between the four-man Special Branch, the Assistant Commissioner and the Home Office once again included the Commissioner.

Had it been generally known that the man strongly suspected of being Jack the Ripper had been in police custody in November, but had been allowed, probably by men working for the CID, to escape, there would have been an outcry. Francis Tumblety's position as chief suspect had been common knowledge in the United States in his lifetime. In England it did not emerge in public for over a hundred years. Even then it came into the light of day only after years of dogged research sparked off by the discovery of a letter from Littlechild.

In 1912, in retirement, the ex-Chief Inspector explained in a private letter to a journalist that Tumblety, a fifty-five-year-old American 'quack' doctor who was in London at the time, was very likely the culprit.[20] He was a homosexual abortionist and a violent misogynist. He practised what he called 'Indian medicine', using herbs and potions and carrying out abortions, all over America. He never stayed in one place for long and always had plenty of money. His appearance was flamboyant and his conversation full of hatred and violence towards women. He used aliases – and decades before at the time of President Lincoln's assassination by John Wilkes Booth had used the name Booth, which, allied with his general eccentricity, had been enough to get him arrested, briefly. While living in Washington DC during the 1860s he owned an anatomical collection which included wombs he kept in specimen jars.

He had spent time in London before, notably in 1882 when he may have been that 'Dr Hamilton Williams' who bought the surgical knives used to kill Lord Frederick Cavendish and Thomas Burke in Phoenix Park. According to a Ripperologist called Nick Warren, 'Dr Williams' was a Fenian who had a practice in Demerara, British Guyana, and 'hung around the capital for several weeks attempting to gain employment with the Irish revolutionaries, only to be refused by them because of his 'violent language'.[21] There are indications that Williams and Tumblety were one and the same.

The pathology departments of two London teaching hospitals had been asked in the months before the Ripper murders for the wombs of women for which the buyer, 'an American doctor' would pay a high price. They declined to discuss this with the press, which may indicate that the police had told them to keep quiet because they were already on the trail of the very same American doctor. Tumblety was of Irish extraction and had relations in Liverpool, where he would have disembarked from America. There were almost certainly members of the transatlantic crew who spied for the British – John Patrick Hayes, for instance, one of Jenkinson's Irish-American informants, was a ship's engineer.[22] There could in other words have been enough of a link to 'Doctor Williams' to make Tumblety of more than passing interest to the Sections B and C – the Special Irish Branch and the Port Police – who by 1888 (though not in 1882) were watching the ports for characters just like him. This seems to be confirmed by the Home Secretary's memo to himself of 22 September: 'Stimulate the police about Whitechapel murders. Monro might be willing to give a hint to the CID people if necessary.'[23]

In October Scotland Yard asked the San Francisco police for a sample of Tumblety's handwriting. In November he was arrested for offences under the 1885 Amendment to the Criminal Law Act, that is, what were then called 'unnatural' offences involving men or boys. The *New York Times* of 19 November wrongly alleged that Tumblety (a well-known character there) had been held on suspicion of complicity in the Whitechapel murders but 'when proved innocent of that charge was held for trial in the Central Criminal Court' on these other, less serious charges.

Tumblety hadn't been found innocent at all and nor had he been held for trial. There was insufficient evidence to charge him with murder and he was granted bail on the Criminal Law Act offences. He promptly skipped the country. As 'Frank Townsend' he boarded *La Bretagne* at Le Havre on 24 November – the very day that Matthews wrote to Her Majesty submitting Monro's name as Commissioner.

On the evidence, it was cock-up rather than conspiracy. There seem few possible reasons other than incompetence why bail was not more strongly opposed. It later emerged that the two men who stood bail in the sum of £1,500 had known Tumblety for only a couple of days. Tumblety seems to have lived in London in shabby rooms in the East End and to have had only casual acquaintances,[24] and if this was the case then the police had no particular reason to think he would be able to put up a large bail or find anyone who could. £1,500 was an enormous sum.

Even so, once bail was offered and granted, Tumblety should have been shadowed constantly.

The senior policemen working on the case were CID detectives, not Williamson's Special Irish Branch men. They were Chief Inspector Swanson at Scotland Yard, who reported to Anderson and, later, Monro; Inspector Moore, the senior man, and Inspectors Abberline and Andrews, in H (Whitechapel) Division; and as many men as could be mustered on the ground. After the trial Tumblety is said to have 'immediately fled south'. Had he fled north, he would probably have left by railway to Liverpool for the transatlantic boat. What is certain, though odd, is that around 20 November, twelve extra constables were deployed at Euston and St Pancras Stations in order to examine the belongings of passengers arriving *from* America.[25]

He had money and at that date needed no passport, so his fastest escape route was to the South Coast and across the Channel. The Port Police in France could have been telegraphed by way of warning but there are no surviving papers to say that they were. Tumblety got out of England. He took a ferry to Boulogne, travelled to Le Havre apparently unregarded, and embarked for America.

The procedure – as in the case of Walsh above – for getting co-operation from the French police was tortuous and by no means immediate. The Commissioner must send a formal note to the Home Secretary. The Home Secretary must request that the Foreign Office contact the Ambassador in Paris. The Ambassador in Paris would be informed of the gravity of the case in writing from the FO. (In the case of Walsh, the Ambassador had been warned to expect Melville to call; he did not warn his staff, who would not at first allow Melville to see him, and Melville had to get in touch with London again, *et cetera, et cetera*. So human error could draw out red tape even further.) The Ambassador would contact somebody in the Ministry of Grace and Justice – and in this case, would have to convince him that the man was a *Jack L'Eventreur* suspect, not just a hounded homosexual. The Minister would speak to the Prefect of Police, the Ambassador would send a wire to Consul Bernal in Le Havre who would speak to M. le Préfet locally, and so it went on. In short, 'Frank Townsend' could cross the channel and be on a boat to America while telegrams flew between London and Paris and a Special Branch man gritted his teeth on the dock at Le Havre.

Melville was the Special Branch man at Le Havre and anecdotal accounts from within the family relate that he was indeed involved in the pursuit of the Ripper.[26] It was not, however, until the discovery of the Littlechild letter in February 1993 that these accounts took on a new perspective and meaning. It seems clear from the actions of the London police in alerting the NYPD and in the immediate despatch of detectives for America, that there was a prompt awareness of Tumblety's exit via Le Havre. It is equally difficult to believe that Melville would have stood by and done nothing to try and prevent 'Townsend's' departure, and yet his past experience of the French authorities demonstrates the extent to which he was bound by cumbersome procedures that could have made action inadvisable or impossible. Crucial police files on the Tumblety case have disappeared; whether the fact that the police had allowed him to slip through their fingers was the reason behind the cover-up and indeed the missing files must therefore remain open to speculation.

And all this happened in the two key weeks of November when the police force was without a Commissioner. Anderson, as the next senior man in charge, could have set the whole arrest-and-extradition case in motion but did not. He was distracted by concerns about the Parnell Commission. Or maybe he was not asked. But that he seems to have failed in his duty is implied by Monro's reticence in later life, broken only by his response whenever the Ripper case came up that it was 'a very hot potato'. [27]

Tumblety was chased back to New York. He passed the week-long voyage in his cabin, arrived on Sunday 2 December, bundled his bags into a cab and set off for lodgings on East 10th Street, closely followed by two American detectives.

Inspector Andrews and two other policemen pursued him to
America, apparently via Toronto, but they did not arrive until
23 December.[28] Before they arrived, in fact within a day of
Tumblety's landing, an English detective whose identity and
purpose were perfectly obvious was seen parading jauntily
about outside his lodgings. A New York newspaper, most likely
getting its slant on the case from the New York police whose
chief had been publicly dismissive of the efforts of British
detectives, ridiculed this deterrent approach. The New York
police, many of whom were of Irish extraction, were strong
supporters of the Fenian cause and would never help English
detectives on principle; and certainly there was no reason to
arrest Tumblety on American soil. However, it seems that in this
case Chief Inspector Byrne of the NYPD was doing his best to
get the Ripper watched while evidence-gathering continued in
London; he told a reporter from *The World*:

> I simply wanted to put a tag on him so that we can tell where
> he is. Of course he cannot be arrested for there is no proof of his
> complicity in the Whitechapel murders, and the crime for which
> he was under bond in London is not extraditable… If they think
> in London that they need him and he turns out to be guilty our
> men will probably have an idea where he can be found.[29]

'Complicity' is interesting; it could imply that the Yard thought
more than one murderer was involved.

In London, the papers – with the sole exception of an article
in February in the *Pall Mall Gazette* – said not a word about the
hunt having moved to America. By now Tumblety had been
lost. It seems he may have gone to Central America, there to
commit a remarkably similar run of murders in January 1889.[30]
The papers of Inspector Andrews, who was involved with the
Ripper hunt from the start and pursued him to America, have
been lost or destroyed. Abberline and Moore were H-Division
men who by 1888 were based at Scotland Yard. In the summer
of 1889 Abberline was taken off the Ripper case to investigate

the Cleveland Street homosexual brothel scandal. Moore stayed until the investigation fizzled out in 1892, and then investigated other murders in London, with notable successes in solving serious crime in the French and Italian communities in Soho; he probably knew Melville well as they had been near contemporaries in Peckham in the 1870s.

The third man, Andrews, who pursued Tumblety to America, retired in August of 1889, at the age of forty-two, with thrombosis in his leg. Nothing further is known of him.

Writing in 1912, Littlechild stated his belief that Tumblety had committed suicide after leaving Boulogne. MacNaghten, in a report produced in 1894, believed that the murderer had fled to America and there died in a lunatic asylum; but MacNaghten did not officially join the Metropolitan force until nineteen months after the last murder. In fact Francis Tumblety died of a heart attack in St Louis in 1903, having booked into a hospital run by an order of nuns founded in Dublin. He died under the name Frank Townsend and he left almost $140,000.[31] One can only speculate about the extent to which his wealth played a part in his escape.

FIVE

War on Terror

The Melvilles returned to England in December of 1888 (just after Tumblety's escape). They went back to Brixton, to 51 Nursery Road, which was just around the corner from Tunstall Road where they had lived in that summer when William was born but Margaret Gertie died. Now Kate Melville, wife and mother, caught pneumonia, and on 19 March 1889 she too died.

It was a terrible homecoming. When the condolences of friends and relations and colleagues were accepted, and the funeral was over, Melville was left with Kate and William, James and Cecilia, respectively aged seven, six, four and two, to bring up alone, and a job that demanded work at all hours. He had only recently started living in England again after a five-year absence. New men had joined his colleagues, much had happened since he left, and he had to readjust in order to fit in; and now he had lost his dear Kate.

The children were new to England. William and little Kate must go to school. All the children had suffered the loss of their mother and must be looked after. There must be a live-in housekeeper, so Melville hired a woman he judged competent and kind, and got on with his job.

From June of 1889 Melville became responsible to a new Commissioner. It had all happened out of the blue.

James Monro had been far-sighted. Understanding the importance of efficient working conditions and high morale, he had commissioned a new building to replace the 'collection of dog-holes' in Scotland Yard, and had worked hard for months over proposals for a Metropolitan Police pension scheme. When the pension scheme was rejected, in June, he resigned. The men were sorely disappointed and at Bow Street there were outraged meetings, after which forty policemen were sacked. Salisbury smoothly explained things away by telling the Queen that Monro had

> posed not as your Majesty's servant… but as if he had been captain of a band of allied troops taken into your service… It was owing to this contrivance that first Mr Jenkinson, afterwards Sir Charles Warren, were induced to resign.

Monro must have suffered from back-stabbing such as this for some time before finally becoming discouraged, for judging by his past record he was not a man to give up without a fight. He was replaced as Commissioner by a one-armed hunting man, formerly of the Indian Police, who had only weeks before returned from escorting the Prince of Wales's eldest son on a tour of the sub-continent. Sir Edward Bradford, as Secretary of the India Office's Secret and Political Department, had like Monro and Jenkinson before him acquired guile in many years of colonial counter-insurgency. Also officially appointed was another old colonial: Melville MacNaghten, Monro's friend from Bengal, came in as Assistant Chief Constable to assist Robert Anderson.

In the first week of July 1889, Inspector Melville was charged with protecting a sexagenarian, middle-eastern potentate on a state visit to London. So far as the Queen and Lord Salisbury were concerned, nothing in the world was too much trouble for the Shah of Persia. He and his retinue of forty were accommodated in Buckingham Palace. He visited the Queen at Windsor, was taken to the play at Covent Garden, to luncheon at the Guildhall and to dinner at Marlborough House; he was invited to the sparkling glass wonderland of the Crystal Palace at Sydenham and cheered in the streets. The newspapers slyly suggested his moustachios were suspiciously black for one of his years, and the Prince of Wales giggled as he told his intimate circle how the Shah had advised the decapitation of some nobleman who was visibly wealthier than the royal family – but in public, all was dignity, majesty and pomp. The Shah's kingdom blocked Russia's route to India. The Shah must be stroked and humoured like a tabby-cat.

The Tsar of Russia would be watching closely, of course, as would the Germans and the French. So the Royal Family played a trump card: they announced an engagement. The Shah simply must stay longer for the Queen's granddaughter's wedding at the end of the month. His two-week visit was prolonged to three and his visit to France postponed. His parting gifts to the staff at Buckingham Palace were lavish and he even stayed with one of the Sassoons at Brighton for a few days before finally tearing himself away from this delightful country. The message was clear. The Shah was a loyal friend of the British.

He had barely departed when Kaiser Wilhelm II arrived at the beginning of August for a state visit. He was still in his twenties and the Prince of Wales could not stand him. They purred at each other, hackles raised, the younger looking down his nose and the elder suppressing hostility.

The Irish Republican Brotherhood was still a concern, though Melville's attempts to recruit informers mostly failed. According to the 'Black Notebook' of Michael Davitt, Melville paid a few Irishmen he met in East End pubs for information, although a number went straight back to Davitt with the tale, pocketing their pieces of silver in glee.[1] No row ensued, for throughout the first half of 1889 all eyes were on the Parnell Commission. At great expense Anderson had persuaded his key spy, Le Caron, to end his clandestine career, cross the Atlantic, and swear to Parnell's support for bombing and mayhem. His evidence was heard and his role in loyally informing for England exposed to the world. Yet English people had very serious reservations about spies; in every class of society, sneaks were unpopular; and suddenly, a few weeks later, the Commission hearing turned into a triumph for the Home Rule-ites. A hack called Pigott admitted that the letters were forgeries and he, not Parnell, had written them. He then fled, and when Inspector Quinn caught up with him in a lonely hotel room in Spain, he shot himself.

Jenkinson rejoiced for Parnell. He had known the truth about the forgeries for some time and, at long last, he had got his revenge on Anderson.

Home Rule looked like becoming reality, the fear of terrorism receded and the Special Irish Branch, Section B, was decidedly under-employed. As Scotland Yard expanded in 1890 and 1891 into the new building on the Embankment designed by Norman Shaw, there was no urgent call to accommodate the SIB. Funding for counter-terrorism depended – as Jenkinson had known only too well, hence the Jubilee 'plot' – upon a *perceived* threat. The section was reduced; hovering between twenty-five and forty officers, in the next couple of years it was at its lowest ebb.

Special Branch, Section D in which Melville worked, was in the fortunate position of having a less exclusive brief. It was supposed to guard against violent anarchists, and if it needed extra men, it had other CID sections to draw on. Accordingly Special Branch's attention turned from 'Irish duty' to England's role as refuge for foreign anarchists. Freedoms of speech and assembly were highly valued, but vigilance was necessary.

Foreign governments favoured scrutiny of socialists as well as anarchists. Special Branch were not particularly interested in socialists, wherever they came from. The existence of international socialist clubs in the East End was known and tolerated. The trickle of refugees from Russia had grown to a flood in the 1880s.[2] Most were poor and worked in the garment trade around Whitechapel. Those were the sort of people who went to these clubs. The majority were politically aware but powerless, and spent their time working towards a more prosperous future and maintaining their identities as Jews, rather than agitating about the persecution they had left behind them.

French, Italian and to some extent German dissidents congregated in Soho and Fitzrovia but might live anywhere in London, and most of them were harmless enough.

When the police were asked by the Austrian Government in 1890
about projected May Day demonstrations in Britain… the best
they could come up with was a newspaper cutting; which does not
suggest any very active surveillance of left-wing groups.[3]

As for home-grown socialists, they were part of the scenery. John
Hyndman and William Morris, Annie Besant and Eleanor Marx
were well-regarded members of the establishment who on balance were markedly less likely to present a physical threat than
Parnell was. Sergei Kravchinskii, the Russian who now used
the alias Sergei Stepniak and who had assassinated the Chief
of the Secret Police inSt Petersburg in 1878, lived in England
and enlisted the assistance of just such a group of respectable
socialists, freethinkers and Fabians in setting up the Society of
Friends of Russian Freedom. He seemed perfectly in accord
with their agenda.[4] They would do all they could to publicise
the Russian cause in England and if their accounts of oppres-
sion and pogroms were smuggled into Russia, in Russian, so
much the better; but both he and they were opposed to violent
action in the Russian cause outside that country's boundaries.
English socialists were persuaders and demonstrators rather
than violent activists and Stepniak referred disdainfully to anarchism as 'middle-class individualism pushed to the ultimate'.[5]
Whatever Melville thought of Stepniak, and as we shall see his
view diverged from the official line, as a 'socialist' the Russian
was generally disregarded.

Anarchist clubs and pamphlets were altogether more threatening. Many of the anarchist refugees from the continent were
wanted men abroad. Foreign governments had an awkward habit
of asking for information about fugitives, and a blank response
increased suspicion that the English were actively encouraging
refugees to use London as a base from which to mastermind
revolt at home. The Foreign Office was anxious to promote the
impression abroad that the English police were in command of
the situation. They constantly defended the English *laissez-faire*
attitude but a major plank of their defence was a keen and

knowledgeable secret police – which as far as the English public were concerned, was alien to the national spirit of tolerance. Special Branch was not in an easy position.

Traditionally there had been no secret force, just inoffensive Inspector Tornow on surveillance duty unknown to the public, and the French in particular had employed their own agents to watch anarchists in London. In fact, as the following recollection by a Special Branch detective shows, from at least 1887 English policemen were watching

> …prominent propagandists, and [men] being suspected of complicity in various explosions… One could never be sure of what these fellows would be up to at any moment, so that Scotland Yard had an anxious time keeping every movement of theirs under surveillance. We knew the addresses of most of them, and the places where they worked, when they did any honest work, and we kept watch on those places; that should anyone be absent, even for a few hours only, we should have no difficulty in cornering him and making him account, if he could, for his absence.[6]

Foreign governments were somewhat mollified by the efficiency of the police in Irish affairs, but Special Branch would never really gain their confidence until they were able to respond swiftly and knowledgeably to their queries and collaborate productively with foreign police spies in England. Reformed character or not, Stepniak's freedom to live unpunished in England remained a source of annoyance to the Russian Government and they had not given up trying to get their hands on him.

At Scotland Yard Anderson was disappointingly unconcerned. He was otherwise occupied collaborating in the destruction of his old adversary, Parnell, as the unfortunate politician was dragged through the divorce courts. Having lost a battle, Anderson was determined to win the war. Captain O'Shea, the cuckolded husband of Parnell's lover Kitty, had been one of the Black Propagandists behind the forged letters. He and Anderson were still fighting to destroy Parnell's good character. At the beginning of 1890 Gosselin was retailing gossip to Anderson about the marital scandal in which Parnell was about to become embroiled –

> …when young O'Shea returned from Germany in December last, he went with his father to Brighton… he went to his mother's house. She not having dressed could not see him immediately and to pass the time he entered a room next his mother's and there found enough to show Parnell was in the habit of using it – pill boxes, medicine bottles addressed to 'Charles Stewart' and his clothes were all about the place. On this the lad attacked her… he retaliated and made admissions which he told his father… [7]

This was Anderson's day-to-day obsession. Back and forth flew allegations about whether or not Pigott's orphaned sons had been given money by the Government, or whether attempts had been made to bribe this or that informer during *the Times* case of 1888-89, or who had seen Parnell going into Kitty's house. The world had moved on, yet agitators from the continent, whose surveillance was so key to the Foreign Office's relationships overseas, barely registered with Anderson.

The Special Branch was small and had not yet proved its worth. It could save itself from plunging into the doldrums by getting a grip on what was happening in non-English-speaking communities. For one who had so recently returned from abroad, Melville seems to have made his mark forcefully, and quickly, on the Special Branch, so he is likely to have been voluble in support of this strategy; it would have been nothing new to him. Violent anarchism was of particular concern at this time on the continent, where there had been attempted political assassinations in France, Russia and Spain.

There was no shortage of requests for information from abroad. But to what extent did the original members of Special Branch understand the ideologies they were opposed to? Had they merely followed orders, as soldiers do, they would have been inefficient. As detectives, Special Branch men were required to grasp, although not to concur in, the ideas that distinguished one group of immigrant dissidents from the next. Since their overriding aim was maintenance of the Queen's peace, they would not seek to antagonise their targets. They would approach them softly while keeping an eye on them and if they needed to make an arrest prior to extradition, the Home Office preferred the excuse of 'ordinary' crime abroad.[8] This was necessary not just to protect the Government from charges of illiberalism, but because of legal difficulty in obtaining an order to extradite from England. In 1890 an extradition order had been quashed on appeal on grounds that the murder which had taken place abroad had been political in origin. This set a precedent: anyone who could prove a political motive for a murder committed abroad was probably safe.

Special Branch often found that foreign governments asked them to investigate threats that proved exaggerated. To at least one historian

> This suggests that the Special Branch discriminated. It was less
> impressed by hearsay than its continental informants, and less apt
> to confuse sedition with dissent.[9]

In this the Branch officers were not alone. Opinions expressed in the English press, in magistrates' courts and by respected members of society generally, indicate that a clear distinction was made between a sane, legal desire for radical change and a determination to commit propaganda by the deed.[10] Melville was a sophisticated observer but no liberal. In his own mind there was a clear distinction between self-deluding 'anarchists', who might be dropouts but were probably harmless, and violent anarchists whom he preferred, by every means at his disposal, to exclude from society.

Enrico Malatesta, a follower of the deceased Russian anarchist Bakunin, had been expelled by the largely communist interna-tional in the 1870s as a potentially violent extremist. The Italian

Government was interested in Malatesta, and in the late summer of 1890 they received a report from London announcing his arrival in England. He was much admired by the London anarchists and did not leave until the spring of 1891, when Inspector Melville wrote on 27 April:

> I beg to report that the Italian anarchist E. Malatesta has recently been residing at 112 High Street, Islington. Information has been received that about a week or ten days ago Malatesta and a most intimate friend of his named Consorti (another desperado) left this country *en route* for Italy, and supposed[ly] for Rome, for the purposes of fomenting disturbances on 1st May.
>
> The few Italians in London who are aware of Malatesta's departure are very silent respecting it, and with a view to deceiving any person who would give information to the Italian Government about it, hand-bills are being printed announcing that Malatesta will speak in London on 1st May. From this circumstance it is believed that Malatesta has gone to Italy on very important business.[11]

This is the amended version. Littlechild, to whom this was passed, adjusted two phrases such as 'my informant is of opinion that' to the diplomatically passive 'it is believed that' and passed it on to the Home Office for transmission to Italy.

With Malatesta out of the way for a while, Melville continued his clandestine investigation of other continental 'desperados' in London. His domestic life had taken a turn for the better. Amelia Foy, aged thirty-nine, had become a more or less permanent visitor at 51 Nursery Road. How could Melville have shared his life with anyone who did not understand his job? Her first husband, another Irishman called William, had died early in 1888. Melville knew him – he too had been among the first officers of the Special Irish Branch, and had been posted to Southampton when Melville went to Le Havre. Amelia had been born in Guernsey and is believed to have moved to London at some time in the 1870s.[12]

Not long after he submitted the report on Malatesta there was another tragedy at home. The littlest of Melville's four children, all of them under ten, fell ill. The little girl had an ear infection, as so many children do. There were two ladies in the house to help with her care; besides Amelia, Alice Darcy, a widow in her early thirties, lived in with her little boy and supervised laundry, cooking and cleaning. But no amount of attentive nursing could cure meningitis, and in the middle of April little Cecilia Victorine, who was just four years old, passed away as her father sat with her.

In Cowes Week of 1891 Amelia and William Melville married in a Roman Catholic church at West Cowes.[13] (He had probably been on royal duty.) Some time afterwards, the family moved from Brixton to the heights of genteel Clapham. Lydon Road is in the quietest part of the Old Town, the village near the Common, and the new house was larger and convenient for the station at Wandsworth Town. Melville went back to work.

He relied heavily on informants. Not only was Melville among the original members of the first Victorian Secret Police section but he was among the first of Queen Victoria's secret policemen to command a foreign language and culture. He could have returned after almost five years abroad to find himself a back number, but instead he was in the vanguard of a new police initiative and had the great advantage of being able to talk to foreign agents already engaged on surveillance work.

By now, thanks to his contacts in the Préfecture, he would have learned that the French Secret Service had run full-time undercover agents in London for years.[14] It is likely that his first contacts in the anarchist community were among these men and that he approached them as a result of introductions from friends in the French police. Following universal police practice, he would not in the normal course of events have revealed their identities to fellow officers in the Special Branch. They in turn would have introduced him to potential informants among the French community. One such man, known to

him from early 1890 onwards, was Auguste Coulon, a member
of the Autonomie group of anarchists which met at a club in
Fitzrovia.[15]

Collaboration with foreign policemen was welcome, and
on the whole they shared an ideology.[16] It was also mutually
beneficial; and none of them could work without informants.
Special Branch laboured under a number of disadvantages. It
was tiny, and royal duty depleted its numbers all the time as
did other protective functions. In 1890, for instance, at least
two of its members, Sweeney and McIntyre (lifted from royal
duty at Osborne) were engaged for months in protecting Henri
Le Caron after the Parnell Commission.[17] Yet shadowing a
suspect meant employing enough detectives to work three
shifts in every twenty-four hours. While there were insufficient
men for round-the-clock surveillance, men borrowed from the
SIB would have had to be paid for, since the SIB had a different source of funds, and men from private detective agencies
were not only expensive but might be considered a security
risk. Besides, attendance at clubs and political meetings meant
passing oneself off as a continental anarchist and McIntyre
and Sweeney, Melville and Quinn – had they been available,
which they often were not – would have found it almost impossible to remain undiscovered at meetings. The others were
not fluent linguists and not even Melville – who was fond of
using disguise and spoke the language – could pass as a native
Frenchman.

So information must come from following up queries by foreign governments, from foreign informants, from the anarchist
press, and from the suspects themselves, usually on entry into
Britain. When fugitives disembarked they were grilled by the
Port Police about where they intended to live. The Port Police
telegraphed ahead, and on arrival at a London railway station the
suspect would be followed to his lodging. Anarchists were not
inconspicuous. Like members of any sub-cultural group, they
cultivated a certain look. At this time it tended to involve very
dark, shabby clothes, preferably long overcoats and soft hats with

the brim shading the face: fashion to skulk in, worn as described
by Conrad in *The Secret Agent* by men who looked

> ...generally as if they were not in funds. Some... had the collars
> of their overcoats turned right up to their moustaches, and traces
> of mud on the bottom of their nether garments, which had the
> appearance of being much worn... With their hands plunged deep
> into the side pockets of their coats they dodged in sideways, one
> shoulder first, as if afraid to start the [shop] bell going.[18]

For Melville, informers and informants were the most important source by far. The Special Branch's 'special account' from
1888 onwards shows that while most were occasional informants (such as a landlady in the Jubilee plot case who received a
reward) a handful were, like Le Caron, on the payroll for over a
decade. The rest were employed for anything from a few months
to several years.[19]

Many who lived among the London refugee community were
not mere informers to Scotland Yard, but long-term agents of a foreign power under deep cover. Of those who knew or collaborated
with Melville, the most extensive record is found in the *Archives de
la Préfecture de Police* in Paris. Their letters survive, written in long-
hand and signed with *noms de guerre* such as Zéro, Zéro numéro 2 or
Monte Carlo. They often enjoyed the confidence of key anarchists
and were not in the least suspect; whether or not they were always
aware of one another's true identities is uncertain.

The first mention of Melville is in 1892, when a French correspondent reports that an anarchist bomb plot involving, of all
things, English protagonists plotting in the English provinces, has
been foiled. Perhaps it occurred to them from the outset that
the Walsall Plot was a sham designed to increase that *perceived*
threat which was so important in obtaining Treasury funds for
Special Branch without a murmur of objection. After all, justice
must not only be done, but be seen to be done; yet undercover
work among London's fringe political groups did not – must
not – hit the headlines.

A dynamite plot in Walsall was alarming enough to make the news, but sufficiently far geographically from most foreign anarchists to deter them from snooping around what they might suspect was a fit-up. And Melville was at the bottom of it.

Late in the summer of 1891 a socialist working men's group in Walsall, Staffordshire, was approached to find work and accommodation for a couple of Frenchmen of similar outlook and background. This they did, although with some difficulty as one of the men – a colourist and painter called Laplace, alias Clément – spoke no English at all and the other, Victor Cails, did not settle easily to the jobs that were provided for him. Laplace returned to London.

The original approach had been by letter from Auguste Coulon. He was half French and half Irish and worked with Louise Michel, the well-known anarchist, running a school for children of expatriate anarchists in Fitzrovia, that part of London just west of the Tottenham Court Road and north of Oxford Street. Coulon had met a young man called Joe Deakin from the Walsall club at an international conference some time before and it was Deakin who had received the letter seeking assistance for Cails and his friend.

Some time in November of 1891 Cails, now in Walsall, also received a letter. This came from London and requested assistance in fabricating the casting of a 'device'. It seemed obvious enough that émigré workers in London should seek help of this kind in Staffordshire, as this was where the most engineering expertise was located. The comrades decided it would be quite in order to help in some small way since they understood that the 'device' would be used against the cruel régime in Russia.

An egg-shaped bomb casting – harmless, of course, on its own – was made and when with some difficulty it was at last paid for, Joe Deakin was sent to London with it. There he was to meet an Italian he already knew by sight, for the man, Jean Battolla, had visited Walsall.

No sooner had Deakin been greeted by Battolla on Euston Station than Melville, McIntyre and two other officers leapt forward and arrested both of them. They were escorted back to Walsall, where along with Cails and several others they were thrown into cold bare prison cells and half-starved. The Chief Constable of Walsall, a Superintendent Taylor, was only too pleased to assist Scotland Yard.

Deakin protested from the start that this was the work of agents provocateurs. He lay awake in his icy cell trying to work out who had set him up. Cails was suspect; on the other hand so was Charles, another accused; and so was Battolla. In London the anarchists could see the Walsall men had fallen into a trap; Russia, indeed! – Coulon wouldn't know the first thing about Russia. They knew it was a sham designed to spread fear in the English population. The members of the Autonomie Club demanded to know where Coulon got his money. It wasn't as if a part-time schoolteacher earned any to speak of. Coulon protested that he was a true anarchist, and lived by plunder.

The Walsall case came to trial in the spring, and an agent sent a cutting from the *Birmingham News* to Paris about Melville's earlier, rather over-zealous arrest of a pillar of the community (presumably on a tip-off from Chief Constable Taylor) in the course of the investigation. He had a quiet Handsworth street blocked off and having barged uninvited into the man's home with a couple of Staffordshire policemen, he found him recovering from the 'flu on a sofa in his living room.

Mr Cavargna is by birth a Swiss, and is 55 years of age. He is the local representative of the Provident Association of London… In the locality he is very well known indeed, and has always been considered a quiet, unassuming and inoffensive gentleman. The company with which he is connected have the highest esteem for him, and by his clientèle he is justly respected. The house he resides in with his wife and daughter… is plainly but comfortably furnished, and our representative noticed a number of books and magazines about, showing that Mr Cavargna reads not a little. The portrait of the Bishop of Salford in his robes was pointed out by Mrs Cavargna – 'When in Manchester we knew him very well', said she, 'he used to call upon us.'[20]

Phew. This was not going to be one of Melville's finest hours. He and his subordinate officers, having talked to the invalid and 'enjoyed his whisky and cigars', were shown his patent bomb-making equipment. The patent had been taken out because Mr Cavargna was not just an insurance agent; he was an inventor. In response to a competition run by the Government of New South Wales which offered the huge bounty of £10,000 for a method of destroying rabbits, which were a pest, he had invented and patented small egg-shaped bomblets, to be tied around the necks of those unfortunate rabbits that had been caught; upon release they would scamper happily back to their warrens and explode within, suicidally destroying their entire family.

Melville unaccountably took Mr Cavargna into custody. Despite sympathetic treatment by magistrates, doctor's notes, dozens of letters of support and protest and ultimately, a squirming explanatory letter from the Chief Constable to the Home Office,[21] the poor gentleman spent several weeks in the dismal confines of Winson Green prison before being released.

For the genuine 'Walsall plotters', bail was set extremely high, and Deakin and the other main actors in the drama spent a couple of months on remand awaiting trial. At Stafford Assizes in April before Judge 'Hanging' Hawkins, Auguste Coulon was not called to the witness stand. Nor was he even arrested, although counsel for the defence mentioned the part he had played more than once. Inspector Melville was cross-examined.

> [He] stated that he had known for two years previous to that time Auguste Coulon, who was a member with the prisoner Battola of the Autonomie Club group of anarchists. Asked by Counsel whether he had paid Coulon any money as a police spy, Inspector Melville declined to answer and the judge over-ruled the question on grounds of public policy. Counsel for the defence remarked that his object was to show that all which was suspicious in the case was the work of Coulon; in fact that it was Coulon who had got up the supposed plot.

It was further submitted by Counsel for the prisoners that it had not been shown by the Crown that any of the prisoners had possession or control of any explosive substance or material for the manufacture of an explosive bomb, and that all that was produced against them was a rough sketch of a bomb sent from London, a leaden pattern, a brass screw, some lead and plaster castings, and a small bit of time fuse commonly used by minders in the locality for blasting.[22]

The Walsall 'plotters' got ten years' hard labour, except for Deakin who got five.

The panic about anarchism had been exacerbated by another bomb from Ravachol in Paris in March. When Ravachol was caught at the Café Véry after a tip-off from a waiter, his capture was quickly avenged by a bomb at the café which killed its proprietor and a couple of customers. Two men, Meunier and François, were wanted for questioning after the revenge attack.

Majendie began circulating a note recommending international preventative laws.[23]

All this was going on during the Walsall trial, but English anarchism had barely existed until it was identified as such during that very trial, and now the sentencing of Deakin and the others met with indignation in a small-circulation journal called *Commonweal*. In May the publisher, C.J. Mowbray, and the editor, David Nicoll, were charged at the Old Bailey with 'maliciously soliciting and encouraging certain persons unknown to murder the Right Hon. Henry Matthews, Secretary of State for the Home Department, Sir Henry Hawkins of the Judges of the High Court of Justice, and William Melville, an inspector of the Metropolitan Police'. Nicoll had written that these people were 'not fit to live' and Sweeney and another policeman claimed, not very convincingly, to have heard him inciting murder in a speech in Hyde Park. In his defence Nicoll

...denied that this article was intended by him as an incitement to anyone to commit murder; it was written in hot blood, when the news of the issue of the infamous Walsall police plot reached him, and with a similar provocation he should probably write as hotly again. His opinion of the conduct of the persons he had denounced was in no way changed, and he suspected that this charge against him was brought to get him out of the way, because the police knew that he was collecting evidence of the vile means they had used in concocting their Walsall plot in conjunction with the provoking-agent Coulon.[24]

Observers agreed that Chief Justice Coleridge was fair, but Nicoll got sent down anyway.

Eighteen months later, Zéro numéro 6 wrote a full report on the whole affair. It is not accurate in every respect; he seems to think that Mowbray, the publisher of *Commonweal*, was somehow involved; but he does say that the plot

...is universally admitted to have been set up by Melville and by Coulon who in my view was his unwitting accomplice. Coulon is a knowing fellow who speaks English and French but he is a bit off his head. He enjoyed the confidence of all.

On the pretext of having *fourneaux* [casings for combustible substances] to make, he sent several anarchists to Walsall... They [including Battolla, a shoemaker and 'a very nice man'] were condemned on simple presumptions. A mock-up of a bomb was found at the home of one of them and drawings at the home of another and at the home of another, the issue of *Internationale* in which Molasse describes the easiest way of blowing up the Opéra.

...On the advice of Delbecque, Thompson who was Battola's lawyer asked why letters from Coulon had been found at the homes of all those accused, and why he was not being searched. Melville replied that he didn't have to reveal the names of anarchists who worked for him. This reply gave Coulon's enemies more reason to accuse him. Coulon defended himself, accusing Nicoll, Capt and others of being narks, but up to now this hasn't done him any good.[25]

According to this report, Coulon had no friends left; his former friends wouldn't speak to him, and two of them wanted to sack him from the general store they had set up in Balham.

Patrick McIntyre worked on the case for Melville and three years later had cause to resent him after Melville took disciplinary action that led to his resignation. McIntyre published a sensational memoir over successive weeks of 1895 in *Reynolds' Newspaper* which included the following:

> Some time previous to what was known as the Walsall bomb conspiracy, Coulon wrote a letter to Scotland Yard offering his services to the police. Now, the police generally take advantage of any offer of this kind, in view of the necessity of keeping secret political agitations under surveillance....

> It is not my desire to round on my former colleagues and it would be especially unbecoming of me to say anything to the disparagement of Inspector Melville, with whom I have been acquainted since I joined the force. Certainly it was he who carried out the inquiries that resulted in my own reduction, but I found no fault with him on that account, for he had to perform his duties. I am obliged, however, to allude to his connection with the Walsall business. At the time that Coulon wrote to the Yard, Melville was senior officer, and the letter was handed over to him, and it fell to him consequently to go and see Coulon. And Coulon afterwards became his 'property' – that is to say, all information that Coulon supplied was taken possession of by Melville, who submitted it to Mr Anderson, the Assistant Commissioner of Police. Anderson would direct what action was to be taken in the matter. A police officer of any grade, from superintendent to constable, has to act under the orders of his superiors. In serious cases every iota of information has to be reported to the Assistant Commissioner...

> It is noteworthy that Coulon was constantly in London in the days and weeks following the trial. The last time I heard of him he was living in the neighbourhood of Brixton in a style that favourably

contrasted with his humble circumstances when I first knew him
as a resident of the Italian quarter, near Hatton Garden. Anyhow,
the Walsall business appears to have enabled him to migrate to a
semi-fashionable neighbourhood.[26]

Melville did not lie in court. He simply 'took refuge' in McIntyre's
words

> behind the usual excuse that on public grounds he was not
> called upon to answer the questions. In this he was upheld by
> the Judge.

Coulon never admitted to being a *provocateur* although he conceded, in a letter published in *Reynolds' Newspaper* on 21 April
1895, that he had been paid. The extent of his role is only now
apparent. Special Branch 'special accounts' show that he received
his first payment from Melville as early as 18 July 1890. From
1891 onwards he was on the payroll (under the alias Pyatt). He
got extra money in the spring of 1892 during the Walsall case,
and briefly in April 1894; after that he received a regular income
until his final £10 pay-off in 1904.[27]

The archives show how excited the French were by all this. The
arrests of Cails and Charles were reported back and cuttings from
English and American newspapers were sent to Paris. Dynamite
terror continued in the French capital and Kropotkin, the elderly
theoretician exiled in England, predicted that the workers were
about to arise. As far away as San Francisco, newspaper reports
thrillingly described the arrest in Paris of a friend of the dynamitard Ravachol 'suspected author of the Boulevard St Germain
dynamite outrage'.

The full-time spies returned a stream of incidental intelligence to
the Préfecture which has great immediacy. It must have been sent
by diplomatic bag. On 11 February 1892, for instance, one wrote
that he hoped to be admitted as a member of the International
Club next Sunday and in consequence, to 'facilitate research'.

He was more and more certain that Meunier and François lived nearby, which could not be better for them, as the *quartier* was crowded and there were a lot of 'French Jews' and 'everything that was most *crapule* in London'. It would have been this agent's business to track them down; Meunier (this is before the Café Véry outrage) was wanted for the bombing of a barracks.

The International Socialist Club was at 40 Berners Street off the Commercial Road in the East End, and was of interest to foreign police, although generally disregarded by the English. The anarchist network was largely based in the West End, specifically in Fitzrovia. This was a seedy, lively, Bohemian place, notorious at the time for the Cleveland Street affair of the previous summer.[28] It was a straggling grid of ill-maintained, third-rate Georgian terraced houses fronting the street and a few picturesque squares, with a bookshop or a pub, a tobacconist's or a restaurant, on every corner and cramped rented rooms occupying the three or four bug-ridden floors above. A fugitive new to London could find friends in the back room of Victor Richard's grocer's shop in Charlotte Street, or at the Autonomie Club and library which occupied three storeys at 6 Windmill Street, or at Lapie's bookshop at 30 Goodge Street.

Typical reports describe, in cursive handwriting, who has been seen and what is being said.

> Last night, for instance (10 February) there was a meeting at the Autonomie Club, in German, about whether or not meetings should generally be multi-lingual; no conclusion was reached. On 18 February the socialists will hold a demonstration, but none of the anarchists will bother to turn up. The attempt to raise money for Meunier and François hasn't raised much, and some of the comrades (Delbecque being one) think that François should look after himself, but Meunier should be helped to get away as soon as possible.[29]

In July, agent Black reported from London that the gang with Schouppe in it had gone to Paris to steal and blow things up; some of the booty would be distributed among out-of-work comrades and some would be kept by Schouppe and a few others with the aim of getting Pini out of jail…

> Here, [i.e. in London] the anarchists are very pleased with themselves. When you mention the arrests to them, they say so what – we're organised now, and everything's working out.

> The police here know François' wife's address.

> François and Meunier are here and François will soon be tracked down – there's a new lead. Meunier was in hiding with a M. Magret when he lived at 30 Fitzroy St. The Melnotte woman, who lived almost opposite, came often with her lover to see the Teron woman who lived in the same house as Magret. Last Saturday Melnotte and Magret moved away…[30]

Agent Black had airily suggested about a month before that Meunier and François, once they were found, might well be kidnapped with paid assistance from the English police. The cost and tactics of this coup had obviously been the subject of animated conspiracy over a bottle of wine.

> According to a conversation with an informer here, the police will co-operate if the price is right and you could have the two of them in the bag within a week. Would the Government be inclined to donate a certain sum to be divided among those who took part? Because it would mean special surveillance and there'd be a certain number of men to organise.[31]

Nothing more of this master plan remains in the files, although both Meunier and François were eventually nabbed – by Melville.

In August of 1892 agent Zéro numéro 2 reports that he has spoken to comrades Delbecque and Gardrat, who are fed up with having to keep François & Meunier, who would never have had any trouble if they'd kept their mouths shut and not boasted to all comers; the explosion at the Café Véry would have been just as effective. Jourdan, 'of whom much has been said of late', corresponds with someone called '*l'éveillé*' ('wide-awake') who's written to him. He has shown the letter around and the agent encloses a copy he has managed to make.[32] In September, the same agent sends a useful recipe (recently passed to him by a named visitor) for a bomb made of nitro-glycerine and coal which can be detonated from a distance, and asks for a password 'so that if Monsieur F comes to London we can arrange a meeting without risk'.[33] Meanwhile agent Zéro is keeping abreast of plans to publish. It seems Gardrat (who prints *L'Autonomie)* will print a new paper with the financial backing of Malatesta, Delbecque, Bordes and others. And so it goes on; accumulated in the archives is the small change, the va-et-vient of intrigue, every passing argument and infidelity, dream and boast, itemised, year after year, until the agent has formed opinions about who is dangerous, who is treacherous, and who is merely huddling together with his compatriots for warmth.

One of the agents contributes a cutting from an unnamed French journal of 20 September headed La Bande à Melvil – '*Melvi*lle's gang'. It complains that Delbecque was hounded 'as far as the homes of his clients' and nearly lost his livelihood because of it. His wife, with the five-month-old baby, was interrupted by the police bringing false information about her husband, worrying her, trying to drag a confession out of her – and as a result her milk went bad and the little girl died. She emerged from the house of mourning to the hearse outside, and there stood police on the corner of Charlotte Street. They were responsible for the death of her child.

> The leader is called Melville, and within his trade he has the rank of Inspector. He is a nice-looking, kindly-spoken gentleman. As for his henchmen, anybody in London's French quarter could point them out: a big devil, like a squaddie, with a rough red moustache and boxer's fists, and a portly fellow with brown side-whiskers and greying hair who looks like a retired shopkeeper. These two are always together [The first is believed to be McIntyre and the

second Sweeney]…Then there is the attendant rabble of pimps and boot-lickers who swell their coffers with the small change that narks always get. We all know who they are.

One Monday, 1st August in the afternoon, while Delbecque was in his workshop, the Inspector did get in to see his wife and told her, with all the slyness of his trade, 'Look here, you're not well, your little one is very sick. For heaven's sake be reasonable! Aren't you tired of this endless struggle? I can get you out of the hole you're in. Listen to me. You need rest and a quiet life. You can have it. Just tell me that Meunier lived here, tell me where he is now and I'll leave you alone. You, and your six children and your husband. Can I say fairer than that? And don't worry. No one will know. It's between you and me.

'…You don't want to know? Too bad. Your husband won't stay in work, you can be sure of that. We are very well informed… and then the kids… Look, understand this. It's in your own interest. You're a good woman and a good mother. It'll be no joke when your children are howling from hunger. Look, I tell you what: five hundred pounds. And that's just for starters. Five hundred pounds right away.

'…You won't listen? All right. I'm off. But think about it. There'll still be time tomorrow…Think of it: your husband out of work and your children with nothing to eat…'[34]

By mid-November the anarchists' cheerful mood of the summer had plummeted. François, one of the alleged Café Véry bombers, had been arrested, in a blaze of publicity, by Melville – and against all expectations had been extradited to France. People were not sad for him (though they were sorry they'd lent him money) but worried about his children, who were still in London. As Zéro numéro 2 reported, Bordes couldn't keep them for ever. Schouppe and Mathieu had a month's work house painting, but that was about the only bright news for the community which was otherwise, by universal agreement, entirely infiltrated by cops.[35]

The arrest and extradition of François was considered a personal triumph for Melville. The prosecution had cleverly argued that, since the Café Véry bomb had gone off as an act of revenge for the arrest and trial of a single person (Ravachol, executed in July), it was not a political crime. Its success had repercussions far and wide. At least one Russian diplomat (or possibly a policeman) proposed to leave for England in hopes of seeing Stepniak, too, extradited at last. The Okhrana's (the Russian Secret Police's) Paris archive contains a document in Russian, unsigned and undated which reads in translation:

Before you leave for London I consider it my duty to warn you against being too enthusiastic about English 'loyalty' and to express my misgivings based on bitter experience of Russo-English relations.

According to the 1886 Convention, we have the right to demand that S. Kravchinskii [Stepniak] be extradited as the murderer of General Mezentsev. But one of the Articles stipulates that political criminals may not be extradited, nor may those who 'can prove' that their extradition is being demanded from a desire to punish them for a political crime.

Previously, when we have demanded the extradition of various petty rogues, the English judges have displayed an extremely nit-picking attitude towards our evidence: the exceptional personality of such a villain and murderer as Kravchinskii, therefore, will present them with an even greater temptation to exhibit their customary pedantry and arrogance and flaunt their ancient traditions of asylum even though the latter are totally inapplicable in the present case.

As you know, through his lying and deception Kravchinskii has got himself patrons not only in English society and the press but also among Members of Parliament. Their understandable sense of self-esteem will not allow them to admit that a vile criminal has pulled the wool over their eyes; they will be ashamed of the extraordinary 'Society of Friends of Russian Freedom' which was founded on his initiative, and falsehood will be upheld *quand même* throughout the extradition proceedings. The wide scope for inter-preting the above-cited article of the Convention in different ways will undoubtedly lead to well-publicised hostile propaganda against Russia and compel the judge to forgo a just assessment of the crime and truckle to this propaganda. Already, following the extradition of François, concerns are being voiced in the English press that Russia might demand the extradition of nihilists (even though these are murderers) and it is openly being announced *in advance* that nine tenths of the population will condemn such an extradition. The latter, of course, will happen precisely when your English friends are reassuring you that extradition is beyond doubt.[36]

Nobody trusted the English. The Russian Government didn't, and neither did the French socialists. At the height of the Paris bombing campaign in April a French paper, *l'Autorité,* had com-plained bitterly that:

…John Bull, inventor of the Trade Unions, is very much responsi-ble for all the crises we've been through, and will continue to go through unless we hurry up and stem the rising tide of anti-social theories with which – in a reversal of the truth – the anarchists besmear the great name of socialism.[37]

According to this article, Ravachol and his friends learned bomb-making from the Anglo-Saxon dynamitards of 1882–85. And:

Que dire des policiers londonniens? C'est l'incapacité multipliée par la vénalité et la sottise.

(What can one say of London policemen? They represent incom-petence made worse by corruptibility and dimness.)

The Walsall case led to new interest from the French police, as well as the press, in the political scene in England, and they had rather more respect than *L'Autorité* did for the Met. One of their agents wrote a long report from London just after the trial, tracing links between English socialists and foreign anarchists. It was conceded that they didn't mix much, although they knew each other. In England, the report pointed out, it was not the bourgeois who were afraid of the anarchists (as in Paris) but the anarchists who were afraid of the bourgeois. The anarchists, very much harassed by the police, want to get rid of Matthews, Hawkins and above all, that enemy of Stepniak, Inspector Melville

> …who perhaps does not possess the admirable perspicacity of the late Williamson,[38] but is an agent with great experience and much in favour with the Queen; and who – particularly in the matter of Russian refugees – would (had he not been prevented by his superiors) have rendered the greatest service to the Russian Government – whose cause, in this matter, is linked to that of any modern society.

> Melville is perfectly well aware of the links between English and foreign anarchists, of the complaisant attitude of the Fabians, and the indulgence of even moderate English socialists towards nihilists, communists, Fenians, Irish 'invincibles', Italian irredentists, and German and Austrian demagogues. There isn't a London embassy that hasn't had recourse to his services, no diplomat, no matter how unconcerned by all this, who hasn't sought to get to know him, and in his opinion English anarchism – once suffocated in its cradle as it just has been – is of no danger to England. He reserves his opinion regarding foreign countries.[39]

As far as these foreign intelligence agencies were concerned, it was Melville who mattered, not Anderson. In the course of his obsessive pursuance of Parnell, Anderson had lost his grip, and in May of 1892 he was already floundering:

> May I here take the opportunity of explaining that it is only in the case of refugees officially expelled from foreign countries that I can rely upon obtaining definite particulars… [where other refugees are concerned] it is a matter of difficulty even to obtain their names…[40]

The late Superintendent Williamson had been fond of telling Melville 'The four essentials for a policeman are truthfulness, sobriety, punctuality and tremendous care as to what you tell superiors.'[41] Melville was tight with information, and as a result, for the first time a senior policeman knew more than the Assistant Chief Constable. He also knew more than his Chief, Littlechild.

SIX

A MAN TO BE TRUSTED

1892 ended in triumph for Melville. His public image was exactly what he wanted it to be: he wanted trouble-makers to know that he would play dirty.

On the other hand, English and foreign anarchist groups felt a new bitterness towards London's police, and they attracted sympathy among radicals generally. The publisher of *Commonweal* had lost his wife just four hours before his arrest, and it was said that Melville's men had dragged him into custody leaving the children alone with the body of their dead mother. Melville himself is supposed to have manipulated the feelings of Madame Delbecque as her baby lay dying. And this from a man who knew what it was to lose a wife and a child. How could he live with himself?

Presumably he managed just fine, because he believed that the end justified the means; and also, that everyone has choices. Mowbray had chosen to publish an incendiary article and Madame Delbecque had chosen to cast in her lot with an enemy of society. They must take the consequences. He drew a sharp line between his sentiments as husband and father and the immediate needs of his job.

Certain Paris newspapers at the end of 1892 read like public relations for the Met.

The word on the street in London is that the anarchists are resolved to revenge themselves for François' extradition – both on Melville, and on English justice in general. Everyone blames the English and the number of French anarchists in London has doubled... But the anarchists are trailed by police close as sheepdogs. The police miss nothing. English police are also at ports including French ports,

and at Anvers in Belgium – always in plain clothes… Melville, who
captured François, has seen correspondence between London and
Paris anarchists in an as yet impenetrable code.[1]

What is being set up is a thrilling battle: the sleuth against the
forces of evil – and it is no coincidence that this period sees the
first success of the detective novel.

The French agents are equally impressed, although momen-
tarily alarmed by a report that Anarchist Central now seems to
be London with its driving force in America.[2] Agent R in Paris
sees an end to London as a haven: he has been told by an informant who is 'in a high position in anarchist circles in London' that
since the extradition of François, the foreign anarchists no longer
feel safe in London and have decided to move to Barcelona.[3]
This confirms other reports and there is also talk of moving to
Geneva, where it might be easier to print anarchist papers. From
January of 1893 agent Z describes how the French and other
anarchists are extremely nervous – mainly of each other. Barely
a week passes but a meeting is held and one of them is accused
of being a grass.

To Melville's satisfaction, the London anarchist community
was imploding from within.

Behind the scenes the Russians were trying to sort out extradition treaties. In April of 1893 they were able to announce
success in reaching agreements with France and the United
States; but the advice to Russia's envoy to England proved correct. The English stuck to their 'liberties' and the Foreign Office
and Home Office were unwilling to collaborate. Melville could
not assist.

Chief Inspector Littlechild, according to a not-altogether-reli-
able informant, told his officers to act openly, that is, never to
pretend to political sympathies they did not have in order to get
information since 'it was degrading to the service for an official
to play the part of a spy'.[4] Either overwhelmed by the growing
hegemony of Melville's less honourable tactics, or because he

saw a more lucrative future as a private enquiry agent, he retired 'for reasons of ill health' on 9 April at the age of forty-five. He took three weeks' holiday before his official retirement date.

So from Monday 20 March 1893 – ten years to the day since he began work for 'Dolly' Williamson in the old office in Whitehall Place – Melville took over as head of Special Branch.

He could look back on his progress to date with some satisfaction. He had begun as a sergeant in a new, under-resourced department. By 1893 Special Branch, for the past two years located in the New Scotland Yard offices, was answerable only to Anderson who reported directly to Home Secretary Asquith. In some ways Melville's job gave him more power to defend the realm than any English policeman including the Commissioner, and he knew it.

One man who had been with Sergeant Melville as a constable in Williamson's outfit in 1883 was Patrick McIntyre, who would later get his revenge over the Walsall plot. Now, in the spring of 1893, McIntyre was recovering from his involvement in a curious affair that had arisen last year out of his ramshackle private life and questionable contacts.

An American doctor, a real one this time but again an abortionist, had come to London in the autumn of 1891 and had taken lodgings at Waterloo. And again this was no ordinary doctor, but a murderer; and in the course of the winter and spring of 1892 he led several unsuspecting young prostitutes to a horrid and painful death by the administration of strychnine. At the same time he wrote anonymous letters accusing unlikely strangers and prominent people of having murdered them. The poisoner was being sought, and Dr Neill Cream's behaviour was suspicious, but there was no proof and he was not arrested; there were many suspects.

In April of 1892 Cream made the acquaintance of a former private detective called John Patrick Haynes, who lived in the Westminster Bridge Road above a photographer's studio. Haynes was from Philadelphia and now, like Neill Cream himself, appeared to be rather down on his luck. He grew quite friendly with Neill Cream, seeing him most days and going to music halls with him, although he listened with dawning suspicion to his wild talk about the poisoned women and the men who (according to Cream's alleged inside knowledge) had murdered them.

Haynes confided his doubts to a drinking partner of his, Sergeant Patrick McIntyre. McIntyre encouraged Cream to talk and he too became friendly with him. McIntyre and Haynes drew Cream into a trap. In fact it was thanks to their subtle approach, and to subsequent research in America which showed that Cream had already served time there for murder but had been released insane, that he was arrested. He was hanged in London in November of 1892.[5]

Despite this bit of resourceful detection Haynes was still out of work and Sergeant McIntyre was still a sergeant when Melville took over. Somehow in the summer of 1893 McIntyre so offended Melville that in September he lost his position in Special Branch. There were plenty of opportunities for detectives to defraud their employers; they could put in false expenses claims or pay non-existent informants, for instance; in McIntyre's case the stated reason for dismissal was a fraudulent claim for a day not actually worked. But these things never arise out of the blue and there does seem to have been some mistrust between them already. Melville had disciplined McIntyre for insolence before. Also McIntyre allegedly fell out with Le Caron, whom he had been set to guard. McIntyre may have been a fiery and undisciplined, troubled man; he was certainly resentful enough of his sacking to want to cause trouble, two years later, with the articles about Walsall in *Reynolds' Newspaper*. But he blamed his dismissal from the Branch on a suspicion among his superiors that he was growing too fond of an anarchist's daughter. It is a fine romantic tale but perhaps there were other, more mundane reasons.

'Haynes', the out of work detective who had befriended Cream in the first place, was none other than John Patrick Hayes, the Irish American who had spied on Fenians for Jenkinson in America and Paris in the mid-1880s and had later been paid to seek support for *The Times* against Parnell. Hayes certainly knew, and may recently have sought work in London from, Inspector Maurice Moser who was stationed in Paris for Monro from 1884 to 1887. Moser, like Hayes, knew Patrick Casey the British agent; Moser, like Hayes, had worked for *The Times* on the Parnell case.[6] He was now, in 1893, running his private detective agency out of 2 Southampton Street, Covent Garden, and doing a bit of work among the anarchists for the French Sûreté.[7] Moser reported directly, not through Scotland Yard: for instance in this letter to M. Goron, Chef de la Sûreté, Paris, dated 26 April 1893:

Cher Monsieur,

I am sorry that as a result of enquiries made by the London police, Corti has been sacked from his job. He came to see me yesterday and was furious, believing that I had something to do with it.

He didn't want to reveal any secrets of the Rinard affair, where there was still more to know (*encore d'autres marchandises*). I offered him money but he vehemently refused.

He tells me that Pavesi has just done something in Belgium and is expected in London on Sunday. He promised to tell me as soon as he arrives.

So far as the anarchists are concerned my informant has just got me a circular (appended) and tells me that at the meeting of Autonomie, 6 Windmill Street, yesterday, it was decided not to send delegates in view of the May 1st demonstration in France; Dr Merlino was in the chair…[8]

One or two anglicisms indicate that Moser wrote this himself. (Melville, the French agents, grasses, private detectives – no wonder the anarchists were paranoid.) But it does indicate that Moser might need workers, sometimes, in surveillance. At Cream's trial Hayes (as Haynes) claimed that he had been working against anarchists in 1892. He was not on the payroll of Scotland Yard (who did not trust him)[9] although Jenkinson had given him a testimonial. Inspector Moser was one of the few people in London who knew his history and would give him work.

McIntyre knew Hayes but how did they meet? He would surely not have met him in the course of his Irish duty, since McIntyre was in England in the 1880s while Hayes was in America or France. But they had apparently known each other for some years and they both knew Le Caron. It is possible that they both worked for Moser in his snooping duties for Monsieur Goron. Moser was in a position to offer occasional work to detectives. This of course is highly irregular. Even today, policemen have been known to moonlight for private detective agencies. But moonlighting – and we cannot prove it – is a more convincing reason than romance for Melville to have sacked McIntyre, whose police career came to a final and ignominious end as a beat policeman in October 1894. Having sold his story to the papers, he took over a pub in Southwark, and faded from history.

The first half of 1893 passed in truly dreadful confusion among the foreign anarchist community. The archives make nervous reading…Weil got a letter saying that Gardrat is a grass. Gardrat stormed out telling them all to go to hell; a man who defends him is accused of being a nark; Schouppe isn't going to get any money out of this writer, because if it's lent he'll wonder where it comes from; Mathieu has gone to ground – Meunier has probably gone to Argentina – Marocco moves so often that nobody knows where he lives – Jourdin's come to London probably to shop somebody to the police – Schouppe has been arrested in Brussels but according to the anarchists themselves, the only thing he understands about anarchy is expropriation – he's just a robber. Parmeggiani and his wife have been in a dreadful brawl outside a pub… A couple of anarchist papers have been burned out; there's a gang believed to be in the pay of the German police, people think they did it …Nobody will say *anything*.[10]

In July agent Y3 reports that the German police chief is said to be snooping in London. He might well have been, for in May, three misguided members of the Autonomie Club, in court in Berlin, had sworn that it was a social club, not a political one, and the prosecution in Berlin asked for confirmation of this from the English Government in order to 'assist the defence'. As a result the Home Office commissioned a report from Melville. Then they wished they hadn't.

Its members are composed chiefly of advanced and prominent anarchists and are of all European nationalities, but Germans are in a large majority... the club has been used as a centre for forwarding anarchistic literature to the continent, but more particularly to Germany, and for generally propagating anarchistic doctrines... Funds have frequently been sent from the Autonomie Club to various continental countries for propagating anarchism, and as occasions arise subscriptions are made for fugitives from justice from the continent if their offences are of a socialistic or anarchistic nature. I am informed that the club is affiliated with similar clubs in Germany, Belgium, France, and Italy... from the number of foreign refugees who arrive there, I have no doubt but it is so affiliated. The club may be described as the foyer of foreign anarchism in this country.[11]

Melville added a postscript saying that the building had recently burned down, while empty. And standing alone, his parting shot: *It was heavily insured.* Sir Edward Bradford wrote a two-page covering letter to the Home Office before submitting this. Anyone could see that the whole thing was so politically embarrassing that it simply could not be forwarded to the German Government. After a few panicky notes between civil servants a silkily bland reply was decided upon: HM Government regretted that no response could be given, as to do so, in such a way as to bear witness for either side, was not in accordance with HM Government's practice, and would set a dangerous precedent...[12]

François, having been found innocent by a French court, was back in London, sitting in pubs drinking absinthe with his friends but keeping a lookout for the comrades who got him busted. There was a meeting at the Autonomie, at which Louise Michel spoke for an hour. Plenty turned up and talked revolt 'but in private, everyone wanted to go their separate ways; enough of organisation'. People don't seem to be quite so hard up; Parmeggiani and Cova are selling wine and sausage to Italian suppliers; Coulon is setting up a printing press.

In September, Y3 was in Paris, and writing a report that summed up his feelings quite frankly.

> The English press especially the *Daily Telegraph* and the *Morning Post* are totally fazed by recent anarchist attacks in Barcelona & Vienna, agitation in London, violent manifesto &c – and have no remedy; they are totally bowled over by it. The *Daily Telegraph* thinks the police of Europe and the United States should work together against the 'human wolf'. But the English won't have it. Have just been discussing this with Mr Ricksmann from the German Embassy here – who controls information coming from London – he says the *Daily Telegraph* solution is impractical – they do co-operate… but not formally – which would not work. The German anarchists already find life on the continent intolerable. Now that the Marshal Campos affair [assassination attempt] has happened Spanish will chuck anarchists out – America has at last signed a treaty with Russia and will do with France – only the English are outside the pale legally. So it will remain, a free town for such types – because it suits everybody that way. We know them. On the continent we know them. We need a safety valve or it would all be much worse.[13]

In November there was a stupendous anarchist bomb outrage in Barcelona, with thirty dead and eighty injured; the heat was on. Agent Monte Carlo was in constant touch with Melville, and tipping him off.

> Three anarchists have come in from Brussels and one of them, Charles Decord, is dangerous. He's short, about 1m 52; wears an overcoat trimmed with imitation astrakhan, big collar, round at the

back; little bowler, pink tie with blue knot …hitches his trousers up all the time. Used to make bombs with Carriola – has been off the scene – will let you know the train he'll be on back to Paris. Melville is going to have them all watched.

And three days later:

Melville, chief of Special Branch at Scotland Yard, has been made aware of the robberies at LeVallois and St Ouen. He will take measures to ensure that these people are watched until the moment extradition is granted…

Four days pass and Z6 writes:

The whole Melville squad has been watching the *quartier* for two days – too late to nab Edouard or Le Breton, but they'll have to come back when the police presence has died down, they can't afford to stay away, and then they'll be picked up. You see police every night at the Club and the pub.

Monte Carlo was writing again at the end of the month about various anarchists spotted in the neighbourhood, none of them Spanish:

Some of them are about to rob gold and jewellery &c and some of the proceeds will go to 'propaganda'… Anarchists will make no headway in London. People are too well off and peaceful. All the same Melville's men are all over the *quartier* and the anarchists are very leery, they think there's something up.[14]

On 28 November Z6 sent to Paris an (unidentified) issue of *The People* in which there appeared an interview with Melville and counterbalancing view from a radical MP (probably John Burns). This must have attracted the attention of French editors as well as French policemen, because within days a journalist from *Gil Blas* was in Goodge Street. Everyone knew which comrade had been talking to this man at the club, who'd been seen with other French journalists – and then in the middle of it all, on the first Sunday of December, the *Commonweal* people had a meeting in Trafalgar Square, in the course of which the Barcelona bombers were congratulated for their enterprise.[15] The police broke it up; another French newspaper reported in awed tones that 'none of the cops was less than six feet tall'. [16] *Truth*, the paper run by well-off liberal Henry Labouchère, had employed a private detective to look into the Walsall affair and now it printed allegations about how Deakin was fitted up and Coulon escaped. John Burns, the radical member of Parliament, was to ask questions in the House of Commons about this. The agents wrote all about it to Paris: anything about Melville was of interest, it seemed.

What Burns wanted, and never got, was an enquiry. What other MPs wanted was a ban on anarchist publications; they never got that, either – Asquith told them on 7 December that he thought it best to leave things as they were. On 14 December and 19 December there were more questions in the House. What are we doing about 200 anarchists expelled from France, who are coming over here? What are we doing about these people preaching sedition and wreckage? Asquith for the Home Office, and Sir Edward Grey for the Foreign Office, gave bland replies. Some of the French agents were now sending reports twice a day, and were keeping in close touch with Melville, and sometimes reined him in…

London, Zéro 6, 4 December

Grandidier is a wanted man, hiding out in Camden up the Hampstead Road with Latour (Lutz), a Swiss mandolin maker – very tall with a glass eye and a light maroon overcoat. Malatesta lives at 112 Camden High Street. Grandidier sometimes goes to see Corti at 18 Little Goodge Street, 3rd floor; or Marceau, who is 19 and has a hoarse voice (cross reference to a report by another cop.)

London, Monte Carlo, 8 December

A Frenchman is in town who speaks good German and has a big dog – Melville's men are watching him. In future I will be Jarvis, not Monte Carlo. One of my letters from you was opened, and I had to show it round saying it was an attempt to hire me as a nark. It worked well.

London, Jarvis, 8 December
Melville's men are watching Latour; he and Grandidier and the others are trying to leave for Buenos Aires.

London, Jarvis, 12 December
At the Trafalgar Square meeting last Sunday Malatesta got two black eyes, and Agresti had his left cheek smashed up, by Melville's men.

London, Jarvis, 12 December
Squabbles at the Autonomie meeting over funds – how to defend anarchy against new anti-anarchy laws. Escaré suggested subsidising a kind of cheap canteen with theatrical performances like the one on Sunday. Melville wanted to close down the Lapie bookshop, but was dissuaded.

Melville's personal profile was high. The people he was dealing with were not all, by any means, hopeless idealists or useless windbags; some of them were dangerous, not merely with a bomb in their fists but with a knife. He was running a considerable personal risk by being so constantly in public view. And in February of the new year, just in case anyone doubted that there was a risk from bomb-makers in England, one Martial Bourdin blew himself up in Greenwich Park.

This was the event which resounded over a decade later in Conrad's classic *The Secret Agent*. In Conrad's version, which is heavily influenced by the later case of Rubini as well as by the Greenwich Park tragedy, an anarchist in the pay of a foreign embassy is ordered to create an explosion in order to frighten the public into an awareness of the anarchist threat. He employs his simple-minded brother-in-law who unwittingly goes to his death.

The real-life explosion took place at dusk on a winter's day and probably was an accident. On Thursday 15 February Bourdin, an inarticulate, unremarkable young man, took a late-afternoon train from Charing Cross to Greenwich, a distance of about four miles. Emerging from the station, he turned in the direction of the empty park. He walked through the winding High Road away from the river, turned up the lane alongside the Royal Naval College and passed through the imposing gates set into a brick wall. The park would soon close for the night. Before him rose the steep green hillside, dotted with ancient trees and surmounted by the Observatory. (Why he was going to the Observatory, no one ever did make out, unless it was the only unguarded public building he knew.) Up he climbed, up and up in his heavy overcoat, gasping from the exertion; from on high he could have turned back to see the river twinkling under a red winter sunset, the Pool of London crowded with lighters and barges and high-masted, ocean-going clippers, the docks, the City lamps twinkling into life and the blackened dome of St Paul's. But he probably didn't look. Bourdin tripped on a tree root; and that was the end.

According to the ticket inspector at Greenwich, only one other man had alighted from that train. There were reports that Bourdin was followed by 'a French spy'. There was something unconvincing about the whole event. Nothing was clear-cut, neither the motive, nor the chain of events. The flash and bang on that cold Tuesday afternoon shook the neighbour-hood, and a park-keeper panted up the hill to find a young man with most of an arm and both hands blown off, his face and overcoat covered in blood and his entrails gleaming in the dusk. A finger and bits of scarlet flesh were found in the trees days later.

Bourdin pleaded to go home. What was left of him was piled onto a stretcher and carried down to the Naval Hospital, where he died within half an hour of the explosion.

All anyone knew was that he was a tailor who worked with his brother at a shop in Great Titchfield Street in Fitzrovia; he had something to do with an anarchist rag, and had once lived in Montréal. His brother and sister-in-law, who lived in Kilburn, didn't want anarchists at the funeral.

It was more sad and disturbing than frightening. But it was the excuse for a major raid on the Autonomie Club the following night, and as was usual with Melville, journalists were present. The *Daily Graphic* reported

Inspector Melville and a large force of men quietly took over the club at nine o'clock. There were not yet many present, but the anarchists who were there were immediately conducted to the basement, where detectives searched them for documents while other detectives, armed with bulls' eye lanterns, made a minute inspection throughout the club.

As other members arrived, the door was opened for them and they walked into the arms of the police.

'This way', said Inspector Melville with his best smile, showing them to the bar where he immediately began to interrogate them in French and English, their answers being noted down by secretaries...

'Are you armed?' our reporter asked one of the detectives.

'We didn't come here with rosewater sprays, I can tell you that much. We've a fine haul downstairs, about seventy altogether.'...

There were very few Englishmen. Most were French or German. The Inspector met them at the entrance in the most friendly fashion.

'Just the man I wanted!' he would say as newcomers arrived. 'Come this way a moment.'

'I don't speak English', one would sometimes respond.

'*Qu'à cela ne tienne*', Inspector Melville would reply, in excellent French. '*Vous êtes tel et tel?*'

'*Oui.*'

'*Où demeurez-vous?*'

And so on.[17]

Melville was a public figure; the hero of the hour, for the popular papers. Among the crowd at the Autonomie Club was at least one German journalist. A week later a Frenchman turned up to interview him in his office.

> M. Melville immediately told us not to reveal his name, as the Government wouldn't at all approve. We therefore accept entire responsibility for breaking a promise which was, besides, made in the most ambiguous way possible.

> The office of the Chief Inspector [He was not officially a Chief Inspector until July] into which we were shown is remarkable for that sparkling cleanliness so typical of an English office. It is furnished with numerous complicated speaking tubes, and one might (so different is it from our own administrative offices with their grubby green carpets and worn chairs) believe one was in a bank, were it not for certain symbolic insignia above the immaculate walnut mantelpiece: namely two service revolvers and two truncheons – so innocuous in appearance, and such skull-crushers in reality…

> M. Melville does not look at all fierce or at all like a typical policeman. Full-faced, welcoming, yet sometimes you catch that sharpness that you see in our own Chief of Security, M. Goron – towards whom Melville professes the greatest goodwill, as towards M. Jeaume and M. Fédée.[18]

He could do no wrong. He spoke French; he had lived in France; most of the London anarchists, he said, were Germans. Only the Germans were less *active* than the French; more prone to theorising. As for English anarchists, there was no such thing, he insisted, telling the journalist that

'When Bourdin's cortège went past, people hissed and whistled it all the way. The red flags that had been brought were torn up before they were even used. Nobody showed any respect to the coffin, as you would in France no matter who it was. People here think that if they showed respect to a murderer it would be an insult to decent people.'

'But if anarchists are so despised, how can they continue to live here?'

'It depends how they behave. In the last few days we've had to protect their club from being torn to the ground…'

The French were almost envious. The previous week there had been another café bomb in Paris. Yet here – the police were so efficient, and M. Melville so stern. He showed them. That was the way. Could Melville's reputation rise higher?

Mais oui. At the beginning of April he arrested Meunier, who like François was wanted for the Café Véry bomb, at Victoria Station. George Dilnot, in *Great Detectives and their Methods* published in 1928, has him spotting the furtive Meunier in a railway carriage, disguised as a hunchback and carrying a gun.[19]

Melville was entirely unarmed. He did not even have a walking stick. To enter the small compartment in an endeavour to make the arrest would give Meunier such an advantage as to make the attempt almost suicidal. He would have to be lured into the open. Quietly Melville summoned a railway official. 'There is a hunchback in the fifth carriage from the engine. I want to get him out of the train without arousing his suspicions. Will you inspect his ticket and tell him that he is on the wrong train?' The official agreed and, with Melville keeping in the background carried out his instructions. Meunier, a little concerned at the mistake he had made, sprang hurriedly for the platform. As he emerged the detective leapt at him. Together they toppled to the ground, the anarchist underneath, fighting like a mad dog. Amazed passengers gathered round while the two men writhed and twisted for mastery. Strong man though Melville was he had all that he could do to retain his grip. Meunier strove with all that was left of his strength to drag his captor under the wheels of the train, which was on the point of starting. They were on the verge of the platform when some railwaymen came to the aid of the detective. Even then the fight went on for minutes, but the odds against the fugitive were too great. He was overpowered, and uttering oaths and threats, he was taken away.

Contemporary reports were less highly coloured. Journalists must have been primed to be on the scene; there was a sketch of the arrest, a full action shot with Melville, black of moustache and stern of mien, dominating the cowed criminal, appropriately in the *Daily Graphic*. Another man, Ricken, had been arrested at the same time and appeared before the magistrates first, as he spoke English.

Chief Inspector Melville stated that at 8.20 on Wednesday evening he was on the London and Chatham platform of Victoria Station just as a train was leaving for Queenborough. He saw the prisoner speak to Meunier as they passed each other on the platform. The witness spoke to the railway officials, telling them who he was, and then laid his hand on Meunier's shoulder and seized him by the arm. He said to him in French 'Meunier, I arrest you.' Meunier began at once to struggle violently, but the witness was assisted by the railway officials. While the struggle was going on the prisoner Ricken rushed up and said in French 'What are you doing with that man?' At the same time Ricken tried to drag the witness and the railway officials away, the other prisoner struggling furiously in the meantime. Eventually Meunier and the prisoner got separated, and the former was detained by the railway officials, and witness kept hold of the latter, and told him he would be charged with attempting to rescue a prisoner. He still struggled violently, and had to be thrown to the ground. He was afterwards taken to Bow Street and charged. He made no reply. The witness added that during the struggle he told Ricken that he was an inspector of police. He also shouted out 'This man (meaning Meunier) is wanted for murder!' He recognised Meunier by his photograph.

Melville was now forty-four, and as ready to jump into a brawl with a dynamitard as he had been twenty years before, arresting shop-lifters in Lambeth. Meunier (who was unusually handsome, according to the astonished *Standard* reporter) would, much to the consternation of the Autonomie crowd, be extradited a few months later and would spend the rest of his life in jail.

Later in April Melville was involved in another sensational case. Like Bourdin's, it was poignant with wasted life. An Italian boy called Polti, whose teenage wife had just miscarried with twins, had been determined to blow something or someone up and himself as well, and had fallen in with an anarchist called Farnara (known as Carnot). Farnara had directed Polti to an ironworks in the Blackfriars Road where he could get a casting made. Of course, the manager of the ironworks – knowing perfectly well that this order could only be intended to contain a bomb – alerted the police, who watched.

Melville sent Inspector Quinn and a couple of others all the way out to Stratford to arrest Farnara in the middle of the night. The place was a doss-house. Farnara slept in a room with six other men, sharing a bed with a stranger; he owned nothing but the clothes he stood up in and a change of shirt. The police trooped through the house in their big boots at 2.00 a.m. and shone their lanterns onto the cots until they found him.

As for Polti, his situation aroused universal sympathy but he seemed determined to make a martyr of himself and when arrested had already written a suicide note to his parents. An account of everything he said appeared within twenty-four hours in the *Standard:*

Polti declares that Carnot was chosen to direct operations in
England... the money was always brought to Carnot in coins
by a companion. How for such a long period Carnot has succeeded in changing the foreign coins into English money without
being discovered has yet to be explained, and active enquiries
are in progress... Polti asserts that Carnot was responsible for the
manufacture of the bomb which exploded in Greenwich Park,
and handed Bourdin the money found on him after he was found
fatally injured.[20]

'It is curious', a Home Office hand has written on the cutting
provided 'that so much information should get out – not from
examination in open court – but from what would appear to
have been communicated by the police.' Melville, it seems, had
no sooner questioned a prisoner than he related the whole conversation to some journalist.

It had been Farnara's intention to make a bomb for use in
France or Italy, but he could not afford the ferry fare; so he
decided to destroy the Royal Exchange because, he said, it was
the seat of capitalism. Everyone looked pityingly at him and supposed that he must mean the Stock Exchange. He talked wildly.
If he had had a gun, he could have shot Melville, he said. The
court could not hurt him – he would soon be dead anyway.[21]

The tragedy of poverty and endless disappointment stood
like a spectre in the dock beside a highly dangerous, unhinged
individual like this. Maybe Melville saw it. He occasionally had
sympathy for someone he investigated. Later in the year, after
rewards for the Farnara case had been distributed and he had fin-
ished guarding the Tsar during a state visit, he sat down to write
a report on the Countess Clémentine Hugo of 55 Guildford
Street, widow of a brother of Victor Hugo.

At present this lady is reduced in circumstances and is endeavouring to obtain a livelihood by writing books &c. She frequents
the British Museum daily. It is said that when in France she was
exceedingly generous to any person requiring assistance... I have

spoken to the Countess a few times, principally on anarchism, when she was eloquent in denouncing outrages &c. She is however to my knowledge intimately acquainted with Louise Michel, Malato and other leading anarchists but I believe this is due in great measure, if not entirely, to the fact that those persons are generally in a chronic state of want, and the Countess invariably assists them, even when her means are very slender. [She]… loses no opportunity of denouncing what she calls the mad ideas of Louise Michel and those acting with her. At the same time she says she has much sympathy with the poor classes who she says have been badly treated, but I do not think she would go beyond this.[22]

His view of this lady is unusually calm and reasonable, and might just have been influenced by her social position. Was Melville a snob? He was conscious of rank, as respectable Victorians were required to be, but had he been obviously subservient he is unlikely to have got on as well as he did with the Tsar, the Shah, and the Prince of Wales. Being a royal protection officer is rather like being a royal doctor: you have to maintain the appearance of deference while making your charge do as you wish – and you must be prepared to issue peremptory orders in order to save the life that is in your care. Unlike a doctor, however, you are also expected to put yourself between the King and the assassin's bullet.

Melville was keen to defend the people at the top of the social heap. He lived at a time when royalty were more than figureheads: they occupied an important political position. It could be argued in defence of his attitude that had there been self-sacrificing protection for Archduke Ferdinand in 1914, the First World War might not have happened. But it would never have occurred to most English people that Melville's position as defender of kings needed to be justified. Yet this loyalty to the monarchy, loyalty which could have meant sacrificing his life, does highlight one of several contradictions in the character of one who always thought of himself as Irish and brought up his children to remember their Irish heritage.

SEVEN

THE LODGING HOUSE

As Chief Inspector of the Special Branch, Melville cleverly exploited his contacts with the press. One cannot write 'contacts with the media'. There was one news medium only – print – and no mass communication other than the newspapers, which were only just beginning to use photographs.[1] Since the arrest of Meunier, Melville had developed a public profile. His bravery was a model for the public's acceptance of, and indeed their growing fascination with, covert detective work. But given that the enemy were so often young hot-heads determined to kill heads of state or chiefs of police, his cheerful self-advertisement was an act of defiance. It was a way of standing up to bullies: 'Here I am; what are you going to do about it?' Also, more importantly, the press stayed well clear of his investigations when it was necessary that they do so, and that was part of the deal.

In 1895 Patrick McIntyre got his own back and he too exploited the power of the press. From February onwards he told the story of the Walsall anarchists in *Reynolds' Newspaper* in such a way as to cast doubt on Melville's good character. By that time Melville was unassailable, and despite murmurs of protest and a criminal libel suit by Coulon (which failed) the Government refused to revisit the events of 1892. Too much would have been revealed.

Yet Melville was kept in check. In May Sir Edward Bradford, the Commissioner, refused to allow him to accept the *Légion d'Honneur*.[2] And Melville was certainly not expected to assist foreign governments on his own account. Sometimes the Foreign Office made enquiries of Special Branch, out of courtesy on request from ambassadors in London;[3] diplomatic channels, of course, were perfectly in order.

Had the public known that Special Branch occasionally helped the Russian regime to prosecute, some might say persecute, their political refugees, Melville would have been dropped into very hot water indeed, if only to save face.

The Imperial Russian secret police was the Okhrana; he knew its chief officer for Western Europe, Piotr Rachkovskii, who was based in Paris, and they renewed the acquaintance during 1896 when Melville was guarding the Tsar at Balmoral.[4] Rachkovskii was a self-dramatising character and Melville once told a friend that the most difficult aspect of royal protection, when it came to the Russians, was

> ...looking after the foreign police who accompanied their Majesties. The Russian police had to be taught that they could not shoot at sight and that suspects could not be carried off into the unknown without certain formalities.[5]

Melville remained interested in Stepniak and his Society of Friends of Russian Freedom, presumably because Stepniak had stabbed to death a previous head of the Okhrana. Against the Society were ranged Olga Novikov and her influential liberal friend from the *Pall Mall Gazette,* W.T. Stead. From the early nineties, Novikov had 'embarked on a crusade against the Society with the purpose of whitewashing the Tsarist Government'.[6] Liberal opinion was unconvinced, and support for the Society's cause widened thanks to its eloquent speakers and trustworthy news reports from Russia. As for Melville's own attitude to the Tsar's repellent regime, we can if we are feeling charitable assume that he was not necessarily a supporter of all it stood for but rather a hater of anarchic violence under any circumstances, and of police assassins in particular. He was also on friendly terms with the French police, who collaborated quite happily with the Russian police while sharing their mistrust of the Germans.

Stepniak was killed in a railway level-crossing accident at Bedford Park, Chiswick, in December 1895. There were witnesses – the unfortunate man had simply ambled across the track deeply engrossed in a letter, and failed to hear warning cries. A number of Russian and English 'Friends' took over publishing and distribution after Stepniak's death, and the Society continued to smuggle anti-Government literature into Russia. Melville was particularly interested in a prominent member called Wilfred Voynich, a Russian Pole who ran a bookshop in Soho Square and specialised in rare medieval manuscripts. A young friend of Voynich in the Society, and newcomer from Russia via Germany and France, was one Sigmund Rosenblum.[7]

Then aged twenty-two, he is believed to have left Paris in the last week of December 1895 with a large amount of money gained by the robbery and knife murder of an anarchist. The victim, an Italian, was making his way out of Paris by train, probably heading towards Switzerland with funds collected for the comrades.

Early in 1896 Rosenblum set himself up in a spacious new flat in Albert Mansions, Vauxhall, London, and began trading as Rosenblum & Co. of 9 Bury Court in the City of London. His business was the patent medicine racket, marketing miracle cures to the desperate and gullible.

In the summer of 1896 he obtained a fellowship of the Chemical Society, and in the spring of 1897 he became a Fellow of the Institute of Chemistry. He was good company and a wonderful storyteller, but also a man who would say, and promise, anything.

In the spring of 1896, in the course of his application to the Chemical Society, his Russian birth certificate was scrutinised by Special Branch. A report to Melville by Special Branch Sergeant O'Brien showed that the young man had been born Salomon Rosenblum in the *gubernia* of Kherson, north-east of Odessa near the Black Sea, in March 1873. Later he claimed that he had had an affair with Ethel Boole, a writer nine years older than himself who later married Wilfred Voynich. He certainly knew her, and all the other leading lights of the Society of Friends of Russian Freedom in which he is known to have played an active part.[8]

These contacts eased Rosenblum's absorption into émigré circles in London. Informers were the most significant intelligence sources Special Branch had in terms of the Russian and Polish émigré communities. Some were recruited through the course of everyday enquiries while others offered their services. As Chief Commissioner Sir Edward Bradford reflected a decade later, this area of intelligence gathering was a most difficult one for officers due to the language and cultural barriers of the community they were seeking to infiltrate. Whether they were approached or had volunteered, their motive was usually the same – monetary reward. Although Rosenblum was reasonably well heeled, he was somewhat of a spendthrift and a gambler. Money was one of the prime motivators in his life and was, without doubt, the reason he became a Special Branch informer.

In 1897 he met through his patent remedies the Reverend Hugh Thomas, a very comfortably-off invalid aged sixty-two. He attended this gentleman both at the Manor House at Kingsbury, North London and at Thomas's town house at 6 Upper Westbourne Terrace, Paddington. To Sigmund Rosenblum, the immediate fascination of this new client was his twenty-three-year-old wife Margaret.

At around the same time the Russian police in St Petersburg received the first (April) issue of a new émigré paper called *Narodovoletz*, printed in London, and edited by one Vladimir Burtsev. The Deputy Director of the Police Department, alarmed because an article appeared to incite the murder of the Tsar, passed the first issue to Rachkovskii in Paris, who wrote to Melville asking his opinion. For Melville to respond without referring the matter to his superiors was highly irregular. He was not supposed to be co-operating with the Russian secret police, which now had an 'almost universal reputation in Britain as an agency of tsarist tyranny'.[9] That he was able to manipulate events indicates the extent to which Special Branch operated beyond political control.

Early in July Melville responded to Rachkovskii as follows:

A copy of the newspaper… was passed on to me by someone
who provided me with a summary of that issue's contents, and
I did not discern anything serious in it. However, since you are
writing to me about it, I shall naturally not rely on the impression
I have formed of it since, as you yourself well know, one cannot
trust translators.

Where the question that you put to me is concerned, our laws are
very strange. I do not think that our laws could punish the editor or
managing director of a newspaper in which terroristic ideas, murder
&c are advocated in a vague form, so to speak. It is a different matter
if an article propagating such ideas *identifies* particular people; then
we are dealing with a crime that is covered by English laws.

He cites as examples the Most case and the *Commonweal* case, both
of which resulted in successful prosecutions, and continues:

If you found it possible to bring a case against Burtsev & Co., you
could only go about it in the following way. Send the aforemen-
tioned newspaper to the Russian Ambassador in London, having
marked in it the most relevant passages, and accompany it with a
letter in which you insist on the need to prosecute the editor. Ask
the Ambassador to bring this letter to the notice of our Foreign
Secretary, who, in his turn, will send it to our Home Secretary. The
latter will surely pass it on to me. As you see, one will have to act
through the diplomatic channel.

For myself, I need hardly mention that I shall be happy to be of
service to you and to get at these scoundrels, who essentially are
neither more nor less than common murderers. In a word, you may
be sure that I shall neglect nothing that may facilitate the successful
completion of this matter. I should very much like you to make
the above-mentioned approach, because even if nothing comes of
it I, at least, will gain the opportunity to worry these fellows and
drive them from one end of London to the other. Furthermore,
information about the methods Burtsev & Co propagandize for

their struggle will make our Government turn its attention to them and, whether it comes to a court case or not, the matter will pass through my hands, so I shall avail myself of the opportunity to inform the Government what these fellows are.

Around the 1st of August I am going away for about three weeks to take the waters in the south of England. I hope the file will arrive on my desk either before or after my holiday. At the moment, Burtsev is working on the second issue of his newspaper. The nihilist Feliks Perl has just arrived in London and is staying in Beaumont Square with Dembskii, who will shortly move to a different flat.

Finally, I hope you will be able to construe my long letter and I assure you that I retain the most pleasant memory of the time we spent together.[10]

Burtsev was not a member of the Society, but he had been living in London since 1891, had known Stepniak, and knew its leading members well. Some of them warned him that the English police would not put up with provocation to regicide, and they were right.[11] Melville seems to have an efficient informant among the Russian community and it is likely to have been Sigmund Rosenblum, who in his private life at this time was wooing the besotted Mrs Thomas.

In August 1897 Melville may well have spent some time 'taking the waters' but his letter left the Russians with plenty to do. The Chargé d'Affaires in London made his feelings known to the Foreign Office, which in September presented its report on *Narodovoletz* and that paper's opinion that throughout the last seventeen years under Tsars Alexander III and Nicolas II

...reaction ought... to have given rise to the strongest resistance on the part of the revolutionists, and to have caused their plan of campaign to be summed up in one point, *regicide*, and if it appeared necessary *a whole series of regicides, and a systematic political terrorism.*[12]

Wheels turned exactly as Melville had said they would. By
December Mr Burtsev of 16 Westcroft Square, Ravenscourt
Park, London W. was legitimately in his sights. Melville himself
made the arrest, which took place on 16 December when the
astonished young man was leaving the British Museum Reading
Room. Later that day he took Burtsev's keys and, with some
fellow officers, travelled to Ravenscourt Park and turned over
the flat. A van-load of documents was removed; Burtsev was
the unofficial archivist of the Russian revolutionaries abroad.
When, before the trial, Rachkovskii and other Okhrana agents
required sight of these they were prohibited from seeing them.
The Society of Friends of Russian Freedom breathed a sigh of
relief and kept on raising money for Burtsev's defence fund. A
question was asked in parliament and

> ...assurance was given that the papers were under seal. They had
> been seen by no one except the prosecution and would not fall
> into the hands of any foreign Government.[13]

Melville's action in confiscating these documents may have saved
lives. We still do not know what happened to the incriminating
material.

In February of 1898 the unfortunate editor of *Narodovoletz*
was sentenced to eighteen months' hard labour. Melville received
an effusive thank-you note from Rachkovskii in French (the
language in which they usually communicated). The Okhrana
supreme in Europe congratulated him on the 'outstanding outcome' and the fair-mindedness of British juries who were not
swayed by political considerations and continued

> I don't need to add that the success of this case has saved us from
> any inconvenience at a personal level: I would have been sorry to
> see you so badly rewarded for so much goodwill.[14]

One wonders what 'inconvenience at a personal level' Inspector
Melville avoided with success in the British case. One implication

could be that he sometimes worked for two masters – Russian as well as English; and somebody, perhaps in St Petersburg, had demanded results, or a cessation of funding. However, there is nothing in the Okhrana files to confirm this.

At the shop in Soho Voynich, meanwhile, was also attracting unwelcome interest from the security services. He was not only distributing what the Okhrana saw as seditious material, but his business was believed to be a conduit for revolutionary funds. Special Branch knew this, and it seems likely that they knew because Sigmund Rosenblum kept Melville informed. Melville was of course interested in this unprincipled young man, and not just because native Russian-speaking informers were almost impossible to find; Rosenblum was also clever, daring and could talk the birds out of the trees.

In March of 1898 the invalid Reverend Thomas died suddenly in a Newhaven hotel. For the past year he had been in the care of a nurse who, unknown to him, was a murder suspect who had evaded the law abroad.[15] The death certificate was signed by a young Dr T.W.Andrew, MRCS, who, according to the researches of this author over a century later, did not exist under that name; he was seen by hotel staff, but quickly left; the burial took place within two days. Thomas had made a new will just twelve days before he died, and left his great wealth to his widow Margaret (who just five years before had been employed as his maid).

By the summer of 1898 Melville knew that Rosenblum wished to marry Mrs Margaret Thomas, and he knew also that Rosenblum was keen to change his identity. He wished to return to Russia, but could not do so under his current identity, as he was eligible for army service, which he had effectively evaded when he left in 1893. Melville was aware of Sigmund Rosenblum's value as an informant and would go out of his way to assist. Circumstantial evidence for his role in what followed is strong, particularly since Rosenblum now prepared to adopt the surname of Melville's first wife Kate.

The oldest known way of satisfying officialdom about one's identity is to produce evidence of place of birth. It was not until

1971 that Frederick Forsyth's best-seller *Day of the Jackal* revealed
to the world the ease with which a deceased infant's identity can
be assumed. Melville would have known about it in the 1890s
as Special Branch sometimes needed to create new identities for
people. It so happened that a Sidney Reilly had been born to
Michael and Mary Reilly in Belmullet, County Mayo, in 1878
and had died soon afterwards. Quite what relationship Michael
was to Kate Melville is unclear. (Civil registration of births in
Ireland did not begin until 1864.) But since Michael Reilly bore
Kate's name and came from the same small place, it is on balance
probable that Melville knew of the baby Sidney Reilly's birth
and almost immediate death.[16]

The birth of a single Sidney Reilly in Ireland, in the 1870s,
was traceable; that would be enough. At the time Irish-born men
and women were subjects of the Queen.

When, in August of 1898, Sigmund and Margaret married, both
the witnesses were future sons-in-law of a man called Pannett,
who worked for the Royal Mail and knew Melville in a professional capacity. In the register Margaret, whose maiden name was
Callaghan and who had been born and brought up in Ireland, gave
her father's middle name as Reilly (which it was not).

Shortly after the wedding Sigmund Rosenblum departed, well
supplied with money, for Spain, leaving Margaret to move out
of the Manor House in Kingsbury and dispose of the contents.
They would henceforth reside at Upper Westbourne Terrace,
Hyde Park. Rosenblum, with his fine-eye awareness of appearances, never called it 'Paddington'.

Quite what his business in Spain was is unclear. He could have
been doing something for Melville, who had been approached
through diplomatic channels by the Spanish Government in the
past. They had recently deported a number of anarchists, inevitably to England, and there were moves afoot to co-ordinate
international reaction to violent anarchists who now appeared to
favour assassination by knife or gun, rather than bombs in public
places. In 1897 the Spanish Prime Minister Canovas de Castillo

had been murdered by an Italian and, in September 1898, the Empress Elizabeth of Austria-Hungary was killed.

Late in 1898 an anti-anarchist congress was held in Rome. The participants were, on the hard-line side Russia, Austria-Hungary and Germany; on the other, Britain, France and the rest.[17] Before the conference, Robert Anderson wrote of the congress's intention that certain laws should be co-ordinated:

> The chief effect upon my mind produced by reading these documents is to deepen the misgivings I entertain that the Congress will result in increasing our difficulties – serious enough at all times – in dealing with the alien revolutionists who congregate in London. I am clear that the level of peace and order which we have been able to maintain in recent years has been due to action taken by this department which was (if I may coin a word) extra-legal; I hesitate to use the ordinary word which seems applicable to it. But if the proposed legislation is obtained at the cost of a public statement of what are the actual powers of the police in this country, then the methods which successive Secretaries of State have sanctioned, and which have been resorted to with such excellent results, will be shown to be without legal sanction, and must be abandoned. Sir E. Lushington's memo brackets 'surveillance' with expulsion as 'practices unknown to English law.' But is it not strange that foreign anarchists should be unaware of this, having regard to the statement in Sir P. C[illeg.]'s declaration 'I do not need to add that any individual suspected of intending to commit one of the criminal acts already referred to in contravention of English law is subject to scrutiny by the police.'[18] Such indeed has been our practice in dealing with anarchists. So recently as a few weeks ago it enabled us to break up a conspiracy for the assassination of the King of Italy.

Someone has scrawled in the margin beside this last sentence – *This appears to me very far-fetched* – PRIB.

After the conference, Robert Anderson wrote an even clearer confidential memo pointing out that the law should be left as it was and the Expulsion of Aliens act tightened, since the police seemed quite effective at driving anarchists away rather than prosecuting them; and regarding anarchy in general

> ...I would say emphatically that in recent years the police have succeeded only by straining the law – or in plain English, by doing utterly unlawful things – at intervals, to check this conspiracy; and my serious fear is that if new legislation affecting it is passed, police powers may be thus defined, and our practical powers seriously impaired. Within the last few weeks I have by means such as I allude to driven away two of the most dangerous anarchists in Europe, who were plotting to murder one of the crowned heads of Empire. A power to expel such men would prevent such plots altogether.'[19]

Within weeks the Foreign Office concurred that in return for an agreement on the part of the other countries not to deport all their anarchists 'wholesale' to British shores, the British should consider tightening their own laws.[20]

In the winter of 1898–99 the Rosenblums were living at Upper Westbourne Terrace. Nearly seventy years later, Robin Bruce Lockhart asserted that shortly after their marriage, Margaret sold the Hyde Park house and the couple moved into St Ermin's Chambers, Caxton Street, Westminster.[21] In fact they held onto the Church Commissioners' lease of the Paddington house until June 1899 when they left the country.

Rosenblum was still friendly with Voynich, who is said to have made money for the Society by selling fake medieval manuscripts, having obtained a supply of fifteenth-century paper from continental Europe. Now he needed to make the inks as authentic as possible. Early in 1899 it was Sigmund Rosenblum who, as Sigmund Rosenblum FCS FIC '&c', applied for and was granted permission to use the British Museum Reading Room. Here he had access to a range of medieval books and manuscripts that contained the formula for a range of ancient inks, pigmentations and colours.

It seems that having gained expertise in the field, he may have turned his attention to still more lucrative opportunities.

On 17 April 1899, Rachkovskii wrote to Melville alerting him
to the presence of a massive rouble-counterfeiting ring operating in London. His friend Fiodor Gredinger, the Deputy State
Prosecutor of St Petersburg, was on his way to London to take
charge of the case and would much appreciate Melville's assistance
(and any costs incurred would naturally be reimbursed.) To quote
my own account in *Ace of Spies – the True Story of Sidney Reilly:*

> The counterfeiters had a contact inside the currency-printing firm
> of Bradbury and Wilkinson, and the contact obtained a plate that
> was copied by an engraver. The counterfeiters then carried out the
> printing themselves using their own ink and paper. Rosenblum's
> name was not initially connected with the investigation. It
> emerged when attention turned to how the forged money was
> being shipped out of the country.
>
> According to Okhrana records, Rosenblum had an interest in
> the Polysulphin Company in Keynsham, Somerset. The factory
> produced a host of chemical products including soap, which it
> exported abroad. This was an ideal vehicle for smuggling money
> and indeed other commodities… [Also] in order to perpetrate
> such a scheme an expert knowledge of printing inks would have
> been required. As a chemist with some experience in this line,
> Rosenblum would therefore have played a wider role outside
> that of mere distribution. Once Rosenblum's role was uncovered,
> Melville would have had good grounds to fear that his connection
> with Scotland Yard might prove a severe embarrassment…[22]

Melville's cleverest agent must vanish from the scene at once. In
the first week of June 1899, Mr and Mrs Sigmund Rosenblum
gave up their lease; Mr and Mrs Sidney Reilly sailed away from
England. Sidney, at least, would be back.

A year later, another unknown adventurer from overseas was
to find himself in Melville's orbit. Eric Weiss, who ironically
shared the same birth date as Sidney Reilly, arrived in London
with his wife Beatrice in May 1900 and moved into theatrical
lodgings at 10 Keppel Street in Bloomsbury. Weiss, better known

to posterity by his stage name, Harry Houdini the handcuff king, had so far made little impact in the United States, his adopted home. He had therefore resolved instead to conquer America by first making a name for himself in Europe. Knowing that a good number of successful acts whose reputations had been made in London, Paris and Berlin had an exalted value in New York, he set about securing London bookings. According to Beatrice Houdini, after some days of unsuccessful interviews, C. Dundas Slater, the Manager of the Alhambra, gave him an audition on 13 June.[23] Apparently not wholly convinced of the young man's abilities, he offered him a contract on the condition that he must first, 'escape from handcuffs at Scotland Yard'. Slater was apparently acquainted with Melville and arranged for himself and Houdini to visit the Yard the following day.

At the appointed hour they were welcomed by Melville who immediately ridiculed the notion that anyone could escape from Scotland Yard handcuffs. Stage handcuffs were one thing, he told them, but Scotland Yard cuffs were the last word in scientific manacles. Houdini, unabashed, insisted on rising to the challenge. Later that day he told Beatrice that within seconds Melville suddenly grabbed his arms, encircled them around a nearby pillar, produced a pair of cuffs from his coat and snapped them tightly around his wrists. 'I'm going to leave you here and come back for you in a couple of hours' Melville told him as he and Slater headed towards the doorway. To Melville's astonishment, Houdini replied, 'I'll go with you' as the opened cuffs fell to the floor. For over a century no corroboration of Beatrice Houdini's recollections was thought to exist. However, in December 2003 a record of the meeting was found in New Scotland Yard records.

Melville, although somewhat taken aback, held out his hand to Houdini in genuine astonishment, offering him his unreserved congratulations. Two weeks later, on 27 June 1900, Melville was Houdini's guest at a special performance of his stage act at the Alhambra Theatre in Leicester Square. There the London press were treated to his full routine of escapes from a variety of trunks, cabinets, chains, padlocks and shackles, many brought along by the audience themselves.

It has often been maintained that Houdini could compress his knuckles so that they became smaller than his wrists, thus enabling him to slip out of manacles. In fact, he was unable to perform such a feat, relying instead on giving them a single sharp rap in a certain spot. For more complex manacles he used a unique picklock he had devised while working for a locksmith in Appleton, Wisconsin. He could also improvise a picklock from a piece of wire, a pin or a watch spring, all of which were easily concealable. Over and above this, he had an encyclopaedic knowledge of every type of lock and locking system imaginable and a unique collection of locks and mechanisms. Melville was to remain an acquaintance of Houdini's long after their first encounter at Scotland Yard and, like a number of other police officers around the world, gave Houdini a glowing written testimonial. When, a decade later, Melville began his Spy School lectures to new Secret Service recruits, he often gave advice on the art of entering locked premises, and could well have drawn on the knowledge that Houdini was rumoured to have imparted to him.

Around the turn of the century Special Branch had done such a good job that the general public were no longer threatened by terrorism. Fenian bombs were a thing of the past, the wilder English elements were mutinous but had never succeeded in doing any harm, and foreign anarchists could hardly make a move without its being reported, and knew it.

Covert detection was no longer regarded as sly or underhand, but rather as an intellectual challenge worthy of the finest minds. There was a perceptible change in attitude. There could be many reasons for this, all of them plausible; the fact is that while Conan Doyle's first Sherlock Holmes story, *A Study in Scarlet*, failed to make a stir in 1887, ten years later Sherlock Holmes was wildly popular.[24]

Conan Doyle could not have plucked his hero from the ranks of the police because such a hero would not be believable. Everyone knew that 'the finest minds' were those of sophisticated, international, and classically educated men. Class prejudice was endemic. Policemen could be brave, as the newspaper-reading public knew since the arrest of Meunier, but everything was somehow *obvious* about a policeman. The progress of his career was there on paper for all to see. Policemen, with their nondescript backgrounds, suburban families and thumping boots,[25] lacked the urbanity, the mystery, of the upper-middle-class detective, free of domestic encumbrances in his book-lined room. However:

> Values were changing, no doubt under the pressure of material circumstances. Old taboos were lifting, and among them the Briton's old maidenly blushes at the thought of a plain-clothes police. Whether this would spread to embrace *political* police was yet to be seen. Plain-clothes detection and disguises were only a step away from espionage, but it was still a very long step… The spy story as a genre had not yet been born.

In naval and military circles, the old preoccupation with honour-able conduct − not sneaking or spying − was beginning to lose ground, faced with the need to prevent the Boers from obtaining guns from Europe and to keep up with German technical progress. Now that the Europeans had carved out their Empires and there was no easily conquerable land left in Africa or elsewhere, the threat faced by British governments was more likely to come from other states than from isolated terrorists. But the Army and Navy would not turn to Scotland Yard for expertise, for they had cobbled together their own intelligence services over the years.

So Special Branch had been too efficient for its own good. Like any department of Government, it could only increase in importance by developing a larger workload. At least one Special Branch policeman therefore turned his attention to a phenom-enon he considered equally capable of destroying the social fabric. The Naughty Nineties had seen coverage in the newspapers of the Oscar Wilde trial, and Inspector John Sweeney was among those horrified by its revelations. Littlechild, now a private detective, had had a walk-on part as discoverer of a nest of rent-boys in Alfred

Taylor's flat at 13 Little College Street. Three years later in 1898, when Sweeney turned his beady eye upon it, the 'Legitimation League' hardly represented what Bernard Porter calls 'sexual anarchy'.[26] It was founded on nothing more than a well-meaning desire to remove the taint of bastardy from illegitimate children. But Inspector Sweeney single-mindedly pursued these people in the belief that they posed a threat to the foundations of society. He persuaded the League's secretary, who made a living from the sale of progressive literature, to sell him Havelock Ellis's *Psychology of Sex*, a book intended as a serious scientific study of homosexuality. No sooner was it handed over than he arrested the fellow on an obscenity charge. Sweeney persuaded his terrified prey that if he pleaded guilty, he would get off with a fine and no publicity; but he must shut down the League and its publication, *The Adult*.[27]

Quite what Melville, who presumably sanctioned this pursuit of the Legitimation League, was thinking is unclear. It has been suggested that the prosecution would have appealed rather to Anderson, 'who was just the kind of person to perceive a threat to the national fibre in the encouragement of free love'.[28] This was the one occasion on record when the Special Branch seems to have acted in a frankly paranoid way toward liberal progressives who did not claim to be anarchists, and it calls the personality of Melville into question. Was he obsessively straitlaced? Surely he could not have done his job if he was. Nothing he wrote implies any kind of moral disapproval: despair at the foolishness of mankind perhaps, strong dislike of violent anarchy certainly, but perhaps something more akin to Conrad's dismissal of the average anarchist as hopelessly lazy and cowardly rather than 'evil'. There is no apparent obsession with other people's sex lives. His easy familiarity with people in all walks of life implies a certain tolerance, his writings indicate a sense of humour, and his Will shows that he was kind and considerate. The Legitimation League affair was in Sweeney's own opinion one of his finest achievements,[29] but Melville did not take any credit for it.

He and Amelia had, as it happened, had a little girl together in 1896. She was a child of their middle years; Amelia was forty-four when she gave birth. Unbelievably, he lost this third little daughter to meningitis. Amelia Norah Melville died, aged three, in the Throat Hospital in Golden Square, Soho, in August of 1899.

In October David Nicoll's play about the Walsall affair, its villain *le vile Melville*, was performed at the Athenaeum Rooms in the Tottenham Court Road to raise money for Deakin and the others who had just been released.[30] Special Branch was hardly bothered. English anarchists represented about three per cent of those they knew about.[31] What was more worrying was the continuing shift among violent anarchists on the continent from bombing campaigns to political assassination, and the diplomatic awkwardness that resulted from attempts to get the formal co-operation of Special Branch. This came to a head after 1900, the year in which the Prince and Princess of Wales were shot at by a teenage boy in Brussels and King Humbert of Italy really was assassinated, by a Mafioso from New York; perhaps Anderson's story had not been so 'far-fetched' after all.[32]

Count Hartsfeldt, the German Ambassador, approached the Foreign Office in the summer of 1900 with a request that Prussian police commissioner Ossip should bring six of his constables to London 'for the purpose of improving their knowledge of police duty in attendance on the Royal Family and in the Criminal Branch'.[33] The Commissioner, on the basis of advice filtering up from Melville who had now been created Superintendent, would not countenance the idea; and it fell to Sir Thomas Sanderson at the Foreign Office to compose a suitably diplomatic response based on what Sir Edward Bradford had told him.

> As regards attendance on the Royal Family he says that efficiency does not depend on any rules of practice, but on the possession of a large amount of common sense, judgement and presence of mind, and the power of dealing with difficulties and emergencies irrespective of rules and without reference to a superior officer.
>
> With regard to the general work of the Criminal Branch, the laws which govern the work of the Metropolitan police are so

different from those in Germany that Sir E. Bradford believes that
any attempt to derive instruction from our practice would rather
confuse than assist your police officers.[34]

In case that was not enough to see off the Prussians, the letter
concluded with the Government's view that collaboration with
foreign police would prove unpopular with the public.

The Italians enquired next. This was all very complimentary;
Special Branch were obviously doing a better job than any other
royal protection squad, but as Anderson had pointed out to the
Germans, this was not merely a matter of training but of police
culture and public expectation. In January of 1901 Signor Sessi,
the Commissioner of Police for Rome, approached the Italian
Consul General in London asking for information about how
the English did things – there having been a 'great misfortune'
in July 1900 (the assassination of the King at Monza), in response
to which the Italian police had set up a criminal investigation department within the Royal household. Sessi wanted the
answers to ten questions, among them 'are any of the officers
ever sent abroad among the anarchists for the purpose of obtaining information?' and 'are there any agents on cycles?' and 'what
measures are taken to ensure the safety of foreign princes, guests
of the state?'

Anderson resigned a few months later, apparently after
many difficulties with Sir Edward Bradford. As similar queries
landed on the desk of Sir Edward Henry, his successor, the
groans from that office must have been audible right down the
corridor.

If one of the Kaiser's own police officers is to be believed,
Melville appears to have been perfectly happy to work with the
German police so long as they collaborated without professional
formalities. In January 1901 Queen Victoria lay on her death-
bed, and Gustav Steinhauer, as the royal bodyguard, was sent
to England with Kaiser Wilhelm II who wished to pay his last
respects.[35] Melville had heard that assassination attempts were
planned for the funeral. Both the Kaiser and King Leopold of

the Belgians were allegedly in danger. He discussed the matter with Steinhauer within hours of the German party's arrival.

This Melville was a silent, reserved man, never given to talking wildly.

'I have spoken to the Prince of Wales', he informed me, 'and he has requested that neither the Kaiser nor any of the members of his suite shall be told what is in the air. The Prince thinks it more than likely, if the Kaiser has any reason at all to fear assassination, that he will not attend the funeral. That would be disastrous from a political point of view.'

The Queen died and as the funeral approached Steinhauer consulted Melville again.

'Tonight', said Melville slowly, 'I hope to arrest three of the most dangerous nihilists in Europe. It may be that I shall want your assistance. In the meantime, not a word to any one.'

By now they were both at Osborne, and that afternoon Melville took Steinhauer with him to London by train. On their way to Waterloo –

'Steinhauer', he began, 'I hope you have made your will.'
'So', I said, 'it is as bad as that!'

It was. It was worse.

At Scotland Yard, Melville issued Steinhauer with a revolver, ammunition and a black silk scarf with which he must, later that night, cover his face, bandit-style, and his white shirt-front. He then took him to Simpson's Grand Cigar Divan in the Strand, where one could dine in discreet opulence off such rib-sticking British fare as steak-and-kidney pudding or roast beef followed by syrup roly-poly. After dinner and 'one or two bottles of wine' they sat over their coffee and cigars until 11.00 p.m. when Melville judged the time right to leave.

1 South Square, Sneem. The Melvilles' pub and bakery is third from the top right-hand corner.

2 Fenian bomb explosion at Scotland Yard, Whitehall, 1883.

Clockwise from above left:

3 Jack the Ripper suspect Francis Tumblety managed to evade Melville in Le Havre and flee to New York under the name of Frank Townsend.

4 The Walsall bomb was only too real, but had the plotters been unknowingly set up by Melville?

5 Following his dismissal from Special Branch in 1893, Sergeant Patrick McIntyre revealed the truth about the Walsall Plot in the national press.

6 *Above:* The original Metropolitan Police Headquarters in Great Scotland Yard, Whitehall, where Melville's Special Branch career began.

7 *Right:* Melville shortly before his appointment as Head of Special Branch in 1893.

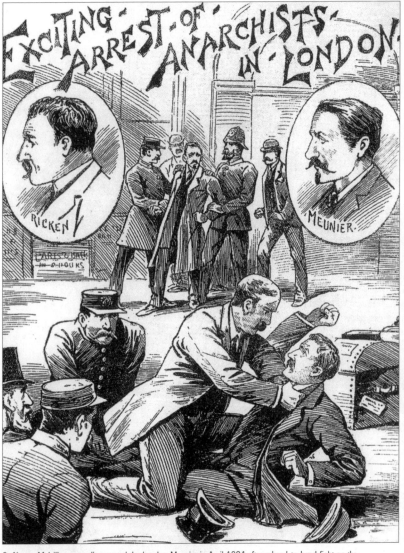

8 *Above:* Melville personally arrested the bomber Meunier in April 1894 after a hand-to-hand fight on the platform at Victoria Station.

9 *Opposite above:* At the Bow Street trial of Meunier and Ricken, defence barristers were unable to get many straight answers from the wily Inspector Melville.

10 *Opposite below:* Melville at his Scotland Yard desk, a drawing by a colleague *c.*1894.

MEUNIER
IN THE DOCK.

MR. INSPECTOR
MELVILLE
IN THE
BOX.

RICKEN
EXPLAINING
HIS CASE.

THE HEARING OF THE CHARGE AGAINST THE ANARCHISTS MEUNIER AND RICKEN AT BOW STREET POLICE-COURT.

THE ANARCHISTS IN LONDON: SKETCHES AT THE POLICE RAID ON THE AUTONOMIE CLUB. (See page L)

11 *Opposite above:* Armed with two revolvers, Melville led a posse of Special Branch officers on a raid of the anarchist Autonomie Club in February 1894.

12 *Opposite below:* Known as the 'King's Detective', Melville was frequently rewarded by foreign monarchs for protecting them on visits to England. In 1902 Tsar Nicholas of Russia presented him with a Fabergé cigarette case and two gold fob watches.

13 *Above right:* A personally signed photograph sent by Melville to his cousin in March 1903, shortly after the dramatic mission to Cannes.

14 *Right:* In 1903 Colonel James Trotter of the War Office wrote to Melville offering him the job of Spymaster.

15 *Above left*: Here, at Winchester House, St James Square, Headquarters of Military Intelligence, Melville was interviewed by Colonel James Trotter.

16 *Left*: Sir Francis Davies oversaw intelligence work at MO3 during Melville's first three years at the War Office.

17 *Above:* Le Grand Hôtel, Cannes, where Melville sought to prevent William Knox D'Arcy selling his oil concession to the French.

18 *Below left:* William Knox D'Arcy's 1908 Persian oil strike led to the creation of BP, today the world's fifth largest company.

19 *Below right:* Sigmund Rosenblum was given a new identity by Melville: as agent Sidney Reilly he later provided the inspiration for Ian Fleming's literary creation James Bond.

To Katie
with affection from
Father
April 1906

J. F. Langhans

20 Melville in 1906, a signed photgraph for his daughter Kate. In early 1906 M succeeded in obtaining plans for the mobilisation of the German Army.

Clockwise from right:

21 25 Victoria Street, Westminster, where Melville set up a two-roomed office under the name of 'W. Morgan, General Agent'.

22 64 Victoria Street became the first Headquarters of the Secret Service Bureau in October 1909.

23 Captain Mansfield Cumming, head of the Secret Service Bureau's Foreign Department, the forerunner of MI6.

Clockwise from top left:

24 Major James Edmonds, on whose initiative the Secret Service Bureau was created in 1909.

25 Colonel Vernon Kell became head of the counter-intelligence arm of the Secret Service Bureau in October 1909.

26 Melville moved his headquarters to Temple Chambers, Temple in June 1909.

27 *Top:* The Secret Service Bureau moved from 64 Victoria Street to 3 Paper Buildings in February 1911, just around the corner from Melville's office in Temple Avenue.

28 *Above:* After a mere eighteen months, the Bureau moved from Paper Buildings to Watergate House, York Buildings in September 1912.

29 *Above:* To commemorate the 1918 Armistice, MI5's G Branch posed for this unique group photograph.

30 *Below left:* German Spymaster Gustav Steinhauer, Melville's chief adversary throughout the First World War.

31 *Below right:* Karl Muller. After Muller's execution in early 1915, it was decided to impersonate his handwriting and continue to send back 'double cross' reports to his German controller.

Clockwise from right:

32 Along with Haicke Janssen, Willem Roos sent reports to his German controllers in the guise of cigar orders. He was executed for spying on the same day as Janssen.

33 Posing as an American journalist, George Vaux Bacon was arrested in his Dublin hotel room, where maps of Royal Flying Corps bases were found concealed within a novel.

34 German spy Haicke Janssen posed as a cigar salesman. Melville's search of his room revealed codes and secret inks that secured his conviction and execution for spying on 30 July 1915.

35 *Above left:* Sir James Melville, William's second son, became a successful barrister and Labour politician, serving as Solicitor General under Ramsey McDonald.

36 *Above right:* A friend of Melville's son James, fellow barrister Henry Curtis-Bennett was recruited by MI5 in 1916 to assist in the questioning of spy suspects.

37 *Below:* Melville's final resting place at St Mary's Cemetery, Kensal Green, London.

Outside, in the brilliantly-lit Strand crowded with people, we got into a hansom cab. Melville gave the driver an address somewhere in the neighbourhood of London Bridge. With my nerves tingling with excitement, we drove up Fleet Street, through the deserted thoroughfares of the City, and thence over London Bridge to some squalid street close by the station. Telling me he would not be more than a minute or two, Melville, surprisingly active for a middle-aged man,[36] jumped out of the cab, and without knocking went inside a house that was in pitch darkness.

When Melville emerged from the house (in Vine Lane, off Tooley Street leading down to the river) he was followed by a woman in a dark mackintosh who got into another cab, which theirs followed. They were conveyed over the bridge towards the East End. In an alleyway somewhere in Whitechapel the first cab stopped, followed by the second.

'Now', whispered Melville, 'mind you obey instructions and keep your pistol handy. We are getting near the spot.'

They followed the woman on foot as she made her way through a neighbourhood that 'fairly reeked with smells foreign to London'. When she entered another darkened house, Melville and Steinhauer lurked unnoticed in the black and silent street. She emerged and took Melville into the house. Then she came back and Steinhauer followed her. He felt her be-ringed fingers through her glove as she took his hand. Inside the house was 'blacker than ink... one of those terrifying darknesses you can almost feel'. He and Melville stood motionless and waited.

Then, so rapidly that we were taken unawares, there was tragedy on the floor above. We saw a flash of light from an open door, heard the crash of a pistol shot and an agonizing cry of pain in a woman's voice. In almost the same moment there came a hail of bullets from above.

Bang! Bang! Bang! One, as we discovered subsequently, went through Melville's hat, another struck me on the arm. But it did no great damage beyond a temporary numbness; it must have ricocheted from the wall and spent its force – luckily for me.

Our own pistols were out almost as soon. Like madmen we blazed away into the light above and were rewarded by a cry and a fall which proved someone had been hit.

Upstairs, the woman and a man lay dying. Two men had leapt from the window into the street; they dashed off in a cab and succeeded in giving Melville and Steinhauer, who pursued them in another cab, the slip. Back to the house went the two policemen, only to find the upstairs room empty.

The girl had disappeared, and so had the man who had been lying wounded on the floor beside her. The handcuffs Melville had put on him… had been broken off and lay on the floor. We lit the gas and saw a scene of terrible disorder. The room itself looked as though it belonged to a woman of the streets. There was a bed in it, a table, two or three chairs, a couple of mirrors and a small oven. On the walls were photographs of actresses. Over the bed were a number of pictures in the nude and a large paper fan which Melville took away with him. There was blood all over the floor.

It seemed that the runaways had returned for their friends. Why Melville wanted the fan is unclear. The idea that a crime scene should remain undisturbed for forensic examination *in situ* had not yet emerged. However forensic science was on the horizon and fingerprinting was probably in his mind. A Home Office committee had recently reported upon methods of 'Identification of criminals by measurement and fingerprints'. The new Assistant Commissioner in charge of CID, Sir Edward Henry, had a passion for the subject and was publishing a book, *The Classification and Use of Fingerprints*. The subject was not entirely new, but Henry's appointment in the spring of 1901 represented commitment to a fingerprinting system and rejection of the old unscientific Bertillon system, which had proved useless since it relied largely on cranial measurements, definition of the 'stunted' criminal physique, chaps whose eyes were too close together, and so on.

Three Russian nihilists had got away, but the body of the woman informer was dragged from the Thames some weeks later.[37] Melville told Steinhauer she was an Italian, who had volunteered information about a Russian plot to kill the Kaiser and King Leopold after being rejected by one of the men. When her lover's two companions arrived from the continent one dark night, she travelled to Melville's private address to alert him. She was able to show him their plan to escape from the funeral procession: this had been torn up and thrown into the fire, but she retrieved enough of the charred map to satisfy Melville that she told the truth. The anarchists were not found in London, although long after the funeral

A clue to their fate came in Berlin one day when an official of the Russian Secret Police informed me that two anarchists who had come from England had been hanged. One of them had had an arm amputated on account of a shot in the left shoulder. The description of this man strikingly resembled that in the possession of Melville.[38]

Never very communicative at the best of times, Melville no doubt continued the chase long after my return to Germany. What astounded me more than anything else was the cleverness he displayed in keeping the details of this dramatic affair out of the Press. Such a thing would not have been possible in Germany.

In America, President McKinley was assassinated in September. The German and Russian Governments once again hinted that British practice should fall into line with theirs in dealing with anarchists. A certain sense of *déjà vu* develops. Edward Henry presented two reports in 1902 which, though couched more tactfully, and even disingenuously, than Anderson's, followed the usual line:[39]

...the police have always been compelled to keep a number of suspects under more or less sustained observation, an observation not sanctioned by express provision of the law but by usage only and by the general acquiescence in it of the community who realise that it is worked under direct departmental control and under the indirect but effective control of the Courts to whom any person aggrieved by police action can apply for redress. It is to this form of observation exercised not only through plain-clothes officers, but also through other agents that anarchists are subjected, and it is quite certain that the working efficiency of the police would not be much increased if an Act of the legislature conferred upon them special powers in this direction.

And precious little help they were getting, either:

Their work... has been carried on under difficulties, the Special Branch receiving but little assistance from the Continental Police. It is true that periodically they receive from France, Belgium, Italy, Austria, Hungary, Greece, Switzerland and Holland reports from either the Police or the Minister of Justice regarding the anarchist movement in these countries and when expulsions are made the fact is occasionally noticed but such expulsions are often made weeks before the reports arrive. The last list of expulsions received from France is dated December 1901, the preceding list having come in the January of that year. No such list has at any time been sent by Germany, Russia, Spain or Italy...

Having rehearsed once again the concessions the British were and were not prepared to make, Henry went on to say that no interference with the freedom of the press was required either. The newspapers of Most, Burtsev and Nicoll had been put out of action by existing laws and English juries. Some flexibility was desirable; all sorts of newspapers were currently telling their readers that Mr Chamberlain:

…because he is recognised to be a masterful exponent of a policy of colonial expansion of which their readers disapprove, has been pilloried in their publications as responsible for the blood that is now being shed in South Africa and for all the deaths among the women and children of the refugee camps. Without any express intention of so doing these writers have enlisted to their side the active partnership of anarchist association by whom Mr Chamberlain… is denounced as the common enemy of the human race and there is little doubt that the more violent and desperate spirits among them would view his removal as a laudable and meritorious act. Thus indirectly these newspapers are inciting irresponsible and unreflecting persons to commit crime, but no legislation that could be devised would meet the danger…

Behind all the objections and excuses lay mistrust of the competence of certain foreign police. The need for secrecy in dealing with informers and informants was as important to Melville as it had been to Jenkinson and Anderson, and the issue was brought into the foreground by the Rubini case in 1902, the year of Edward VII's coronation.[40]

The man known as Rubini was an Italian anarchist who arrived in England in May 1897 and did not come to the attention of Melville's surveillance team until September, when he wrote to *Reynolds' Newspaper* praising Agiolilli, the assassin of the Spanish Prime Minister. Rubini married an Englishwoman in Soho in the December after his arrival, and thereafter worked as a newsagent for various employers in Soho. The couple had a baby. There was a pattern of petty theft, frequent changes of address and failed attempts to set up in business alone or with a partner.[41] In June of 1900, having been denounced in a widely-circulated leaflet as a spy for the Italian police, Rubini was no longer able to obtain work in the expatriate community and could not pay rent or buy food. Special Branch's observations confirmed that he was peddling worthless information to an Italian policeman at the embassy. As he was, so to speak, on their side and out of favour with the comrades anyway, they watched him less keenly from then on.

In May of 1902 with the Coronation looming, the Italian Ambassador wrote a memorandum to the Foreign Office suggesting collaboration between an Italian police officer, living in London since last year, and Scotland Yard. In view of the Rubini case, this got a dusty response from Sir Edward Bradford.[42] Special Branch had known of Inspector Prini's arrival, and 'have been in a position to appraise the value of the information he received and transmitted to his Government.' He had deliberately exposed his informer to danger by circulating a leaflet.

> This leaflet printed in Italian, headed WARNING and addressed to 'Companions and the public' calls attention to one Rubini who has been proved to be a spy in the service of the Italian Agent, gives the address of the Agent and also of Rubini, and mentions the assumed name as well as the real name of the Agent.[43]

Rubini had been called to account by the anarchists but instead sent a letter, admitting that he had been an informer but had fed Prini only lies. The bearer of the letter admitted that he too had been approached, and had indeed been told 'that there was money in the business as it would be easy to concoct plots with a view to their being discovered'. In Sir Edward's opinion, the Italian Government was making matters worse. Not only were they inciting violence and making fools of themselves by paying for dud information, but their treachery impelled the anarchists to greater secrecy. The door to collaboration between English and Italian police was slammed and bolted, and at the Foreign Office Lord Lansdowne smoothly issued the usual response about different practices being incompatible.

Later in the year Rubini resurfaced. He was arrested in Belgium, having made an attempt on the life of Leopold, King of Belgians. He was also apparently plotting against Edward VII. 'I marked down the English Prince of Wales for death! It has been tried once! You have got me, but somebody else will take on the job!'[44] Melville and the Special Branch were asked for information. They intercepted mail and immediately traced and interviewed Rubini's wife. She had left him after the financial disaster of his betrayal to the comrades, and had gone to live with her sister. By now the sister had agreed to adopt the child and the young mother had found employment as a cook. They were given to understand that Rubini had indeed been receiving a handsome retainer from Prini, amounting to three pounds ten shillings a week (more than double a working man's wage). He had bought a revolver too; detectives interviewed the shopkeeper who sold it to him.

This time Sir Edward Bradford was able to point out that both Rubini and Agiolilli had been incited to murder because, having been betrayed, they must restore their own credibility, Agiolilli also having been drummed out of London as a police spy.[45] His fear that the Italian police's leaden-footed activities made violence more, rather than less, likely had been proved well founded. Secret informants must not be compromised.

Melville was shifting his position on other police forces. At one time, having worked closely with the French police, he had been disposed to treat the police of all other nations as an international brotherhood transcending cultural barriers. It was in this spirit that he had gone out of his way to help the Okhrana over Burtsev. But times had changed. As early as 1896, when he was talking to one of the Tsar's bodyguards at Balmoral, he found doubts creeping in. In 1904 he would write about Rachkovskii's colleagues in the Okhrana in Western Europe:

I also know Harting well. He occupies the next position to Rataev. For about the past five years he has been stationed in Berlin, in charge of the Russian officers apparently engaged respecting nihilists in London and the protection of the Tsar and Tsarevitch. For immediately either of the latter left Russia they followed on or preceded them for protection. I feel convinced however that they were also engaged as a matter of course on espionage. In 1896 they were with the Tsar at Balmoral and on that occasion Harting in conversation remarked that he had been several months in Ireland, but did not further refer to it. I thought at the time, what could he be doing there? Certainly not after nihilists.[46]

Late in 1899 Special Branch undertook to investigate a Russian called Mitzakis, who was believed to be reporting to a Russian agent in Paris called Hansen. At this time Mitzakis lived with his wife and child in a flat in Earls Court while also appearing to maintain a smart house in Drayton Gardens, South Kensington, which was kept empty, locked and in the charge of a servant. From time to time it was used for overnight stays by Mitzakis's colleagues. Inspector Sweeney reported that Mitzakis and two other men, all three either Russian or Greek, occupied offices in a City building where they appeared to do little but accept mail; they were associated with a military fellow, living at the Cecil Hotel, whom Sweeney suspected of having shown them 'plans of fortifications'.[47] The military man proved to be associated with a respectable English railway syndicate. Mitzakis, Rachkovskii the head of the Okhrana in Western Europe, and an Okhrana man called Golschmann[48] were 'endeavouring to form a syndicate which would have the monopoly of sending English coals to Russia'. The three of them were also

> ...engaged in Paris with a poor Italian inventor who brought out an electric accumulator which was patented on the continent, but Mitzakis brought it to London and exploited it on his own account making thereby an immense amount of money... Mitzakis was correspondent of some newspaper using some such initials as E.J.B...[49]

The newspaper accepted mail as 'Paris Tid-Bits', 87 Bd de Courcelles.[50] Mitzakis 'followed Rachkovskii everywhere, even to Copenhagen,' yet when Melville made discreet enquiries of Okhrana agents he knew they 'always characterised him as a *filou*' (a crook). Melville must have been rather puzzled and disappointed by this dubious connection between the Okhrana and the Establishment. In his memoir he wrote:

> When in London Rachkovskii always called on me at New Scotland Yard. He was a very hospitable man and of genial char-

acter, but still he was mysterious. On calling upon me he would always say 'I only arrived this morning. I could not rest until I called upon you.' (This of course I put down at its proper value) – 'I brought no person with me from Paris.'

Without knowing exactly why, I got somewhat suspicious of Rachkovskii. One day he called to see me at New Scotland Yard, told me the same story – I suddenly called the same afternoon at the Hotel Cecil. I learned he had been there for a week and had several gentlemen with him. I went upstairs to his suite of rooms and found Rachkovskii at a table with six or seven others, all apparently writing. He certainly looked very silly over it... What was his object in thus deceiving me? Of course I did not refer to the matter but it left an unpleasant impression on my mind. This was somewhat relieved when on one occasion I was at Copenhagen. Rachkovskii was there at the same time. The Chief of Police, Hensen, was a fine frank sort of man. One day he said to me 'Yes, Rachkovskii is a fine character, but I would like him better if there was not so much silly mystery about him. Why does he tell me he only arrived in Copenhagen last night when I know he has been here a fortnight? Why does he say he is all alone when I know he is accompanied by six of his officers?'

The Russians had a great antipathy to the Germans. They said the latter were all-powerful at the Russian Court, and generally, so to speak, were the lions of society, all through it being known they had the Court behind them.

The Mitzakis plot did not satisfactorily thicken, but remained a confusing minestrone of disparate and irreconcilable elements. When the well-connected Princess who lived with Mitzakis arrived to have a word with Sir Edward Bradford, the investigation was peremptorily halted.[51] ('She moves in good society.'[52]) But Melville's appetite for intrigue was whetted, and his new awareness broadened: enemies of the state were not limited to self-proclaimed revolutionaries.

EIGHT

W. MORGAN, GENERAL AGENT

The new century saw Melville at the prime of life and the peak of his career. At 16 Lydon Road, Clapham, the two eldest children, Kate and William, then aged eighteen and seventeen respectively, were clerks in an insurance office.[1] James, at fifteen, was a pupil at Westminster City School, only half a mile from Scotland Yard. A young woman born in London but bearing the reassuringly Irish name of Bridget Joyce lived in and helped Amelia.[2] There was also a live-in maidservant called Beatrice. Melville's youngest brother George was living in the Ladbroke Grove area of London, married to an Irish girl. They had two children and George was a constable in the CID.

Melville was well known and respected as the royal body-guard: 'the King's detective'. In the autumn of 1903, he had run Special Branch for a decade and had spent the few weeks preceding his annual leave escorting King Edward to Lisbon, Rome, Paris and Vienna.

So the announcement in November that he would retire at the end of the month came as a great surprise.

Ill-informed but knowing types probably allowed suspicion to cross their minds. In the spring, Melville had been put in sole charge of considerable Special Branch funds for secret out-of-pocket payments. Was it possible that some irregularity had come to light?[3] This retirement was so entirely unexpected. Patrick Quinn, hastily appointed Melville's successor, was not yet qualified by examination for the rank of Superintendent. Surely something was going on.

What had been going on, and was now over, was the Boer War. The British Government's struggle to retain control of the Transvaal and the Orange Free State had succeeded, but it had revealed an army intelligence service flawed in both war and peace. Like senior policemen years earlier, many military men were inappropriately fastidious when it came to spying. As late as 1895, Colonel G.A. Furse found it necessary to point out, in *Intelligence in War:*

> In war, spies are indispensable auxiliaries and we must discard all question of morality. We must overcome such feelings of repugnance for such an unchivalrous measure because it is imposed on us by sheer necessity.[4]

This had been understood at the highest level during the Boer War, and a large amount of money and up to 132 specialist officers put at the disposal of military intelligence, *pro tem*. But money and men were not enough: the military culture was all wrong. Very few of these new appointees knew Afrikaans or any African language and they tended to be inappropriately complacent about their own cleverness.[5] And the old amateurism persisted in men like the young Robert Baden-Powell who 'treated spying rather like cricket, as a game for the gentleman amateur'.[6]

Another major problem was lack of co-ordination. Threats to British interests all over the world were perceived and dealt with by a variety of agencies who might employ anyone, from envoys in the palaces of Constantinople to officers braving bullets on the *veldt* and plain-clothes men lurking at British ports.

> Despite the belief that vast imperial interests were at stake there was no attempt to form a unitary intelligence service nor, more importantly, to establish a permanent relationship between intelligence and operations, or intelligence and policy. The Foreign Office, the army on the ground, the War Office in London, the Indian Government, the India Office and various Empire political services all operated more or less independently...[7]

Military intelligence in London around the turn of the century was focussed to an old-fashioned degree on a perceived threat from the Franco-Russian alliance. Sir John Ardagh of the Military Intelligence Department believed the French were grooming Irish elements to support an uprising which would take place should the French confront the British in war. In fact a complex web of treaties and alliances had been forming, breaking apart and re-forming for years, and only the British remained in 'splendid isolation'. Every country ostensibly at peace was busy developing industrial strength and tactical resources in case of war. The Russians (who had concluded a treaty with the Austrians that preserved them from trouble in the Balkans) looked more covetously than ever on Persia and India and were stringing the Trans-Siberian railway right across Asia. The Germans were building a railway from Mesopotamia to Turkey. The American, Japanese and German navies were getting bigger and better, the Germans had implemented the Schlieffen Plan which would preserve them from attack in the west if they decided to make a move on Russia, and most of these newly industrialised nations were jostling for power and territory. The others were catching up. Britain's position at the top of the heap was not half so impregnable as it had been fifty years before.

When great wads of War Office money were sunk into a scheme to set up a coal supply network as the means of gaining intelligence about the French navy, somebody on high decided to pull the plug and there ensued a reorganisation.[8]

It was one of many reshuffles and renamings which took place in the twelve years between the end of the Boer War and the start of the Great War. The Committee for Imperial Defence, led by A.J. Balfour, sat from 1903 with the aim of co-ordinating policy and practice between the Admiralty, the War Office and the Foreign Office. At the War Office, the first changes were dictated by a committee led by Lord Esher.

A new Directorate of Military Operations was instituted, and two of its divisions, MO2 (operations abroad) and MO3 (counter-insurgency) were specifically entrusted with intelligence gathering. During the South African conflict Colonel James Trotter had run Section 13, which included a three-man team devoted entirely to 'watching shipments of ammunition and messages from the continent [to the Boers] and for carrying out enquiries referred from South Africa'. [9] Trotter strongly believed in maintaining a peacetime intelligence system (which insofar as it existed had traditionally been paid for by the Foreign Office). [10] So now that MO2 and MO3 were in place, Trotter and his brother officers would do the analysis – but they needed at least one excellent field operative; somebody who could respond to the demands of counter-espionage in England while acting as case officer for agents abroad. He must have a solid background in this kind of work and be prepared to commit himself for a long time, for in Trotter's recent experience

> Before the war money had been wasted on persons who made sham offers of information, and in other ways, owing to want of… a record of [their] previous history; if the section was made permanent such occurrences would be avoided in future. [11]

Should spies be discovered at home, they might have to be arrested and tried. As only the police could make arrests, the man concerned must also carry the authority and credibility to get swift action from the very top at Scotland Yard. 'I think Superintendent Melville would be a good man, and that I had better write to Henry about him', noted Sir Thomas Sanderson after a meeting with Trotter in September. Lord Lansdowne asked him first to consult Sir Edward Bradford, the former Commissioner, 'whose opinion was favourable'. [12] Sanderson's letter to Sir Edward Henry was duly sent, and Henry (who had received a memo about a man for this new post from Trotter as early as 19 May) wrote back

> I hope to be back on 12th October and will then arrange about Melville. He is shrewd and resourceful and altho' he has a tendency towards adventuring he can keep this in check when it suits his interests to do so.

> For the purpose for which he is needed, to be an intermediary, no
> better person could be secured – probably no one nearly so good
> for the money. The Intelligence Department will make it clear to
> him that he must work to orders and must abstain from taking a
> line of his own.

> We must arrange that he sever his connection with Scotland Yard as
> quickly as possible. His utility to the WO would be much lessened
> if it became known that he had taken service with them.[13]

In the course of his holiday in October, Melville received a
mysterious communication from Colonel Trotter, whom he
visited at once upon his return to London; and Colonel Trotter
offered him the job.

Melville was in no rush to leave the Metropolitan force, but
he had nothing left to prove and already qualified for the full
retirement pension. More importantly, in the course of his work
he had outgrown the view that a few anarchists were the greatest
present threat to British imperial power. He had spent time with
people at court and in the higher echelons of Government and
understood that matters of international business and politics
were subject to forces far more subtle and opaque than, as a
policeman, he was used to handling. Here was a new challenge
that would allow him to investigate complex and far-reaching
events.

His cautious response was that 'if I got a suitable offer, I would
consider it'.[14] Reading between the lines, he could hardly wait
to get started. Terms were quickly settled: he would receive
£400, which with the £280 police pension would add up to
a good living. But nobody must know that his retirement was
prompted by anything other than a desire to spend more time
in his Clapham garden.

At this time bright officers were returning from active service
in the Empire and sharpening the focus of War Office intelligence. Vernon Kell, a young man recently back from China
after serving as ADC to a Chinese General during the Boxer

Rebellion, was among those making his mark. He had been brought up speaking Polish and English. He spoke German, French, Russian and colloquial Chinese to interpreter standard and could read Italian.[15] He would concentrate on information from Germany about war preparations there.

Staff Captain Francis Davies had been a Commissioner of Police in South Africa during the Boer War and was now at MO3. Ex-Superintendent Melville would report directly to him. Among his first tasks would be the hiring of a reliable man to work in Europe. The *modus operandi* of this person, Henry Dale Long, is revealed in a letter from Melville to Captain Davies of 8 April 1904:

> I beg to inform you that Long left for Hamburg on 30th ult. But he had first to proceed to Brussels re obtaining some introductions if possible.

> I gave him full instructions how to act and of course many suggestions. Everything is to be done in a commercial way. To this end he will present attached card which explains itself. I received a telegram from him yesterday from Hamburg stating that his address is Hotel Glaesner, Neuer Jungfernstieg.

> He will do all possible to get in with some *employés* in the firms of Busch & Co and Gottlieb Goerner, both mentioned in précis of reports.

This was accompanied by the business card of W. Morgan, General Agent, of Victoria Street London SW, inscribed 'presented by H.D. Long'.

Melville's next preoccupation would be with events which were already unfolding in France, in which he foresaw a role for an old friend.

Mr and Mrs Reilly had spent an interesting few years abroad. In the summer of 1900 Sidney left Margaret behind in St Petersburg and travelled to the Caspian, where he pursued business opportunities between Baku and Petrovsk in Kazakhstan.[16] At this time the British Consul in Baku employed a useful agent who is likely to have been Reilly. Petrovsk, linked by railway to Baku, was also an important entrepôt along the trans-continental route now opening up between Moscow and Vladivostok. Reilly became aware of possibilities in the Far East.

In September 1900, the couple crossed the Mediterranean from Constantinople, sailed down the Suez Canal and on via Colombo, Penang, Singapore and Hong Kong to Shanghai. Shanghai, at the time an exotic forcing-house of rumour, commercial opportunity and international crime, must have been the sort of place where Sidney Reilly felt at home; but after a few months he and Margaret moved on. There was money to be made in Port Arthur (today Lüshun). The city commands the entrance to the Gulf of Zhili, from which Beijing lies only a hundred miles inland. Port Arthur can be approached across the Yellow Sea. Korea lies roughly east of the Yellow Sea, the Chinese mainland to the west.

The Chinese had leased Port Arthur to the Russians, but the Japanese, lying in wait beyond Korea, were determined to take it for themselves. Port Arthur, and the peninsula on which it stands, would give them access to Beijing and Manchuria. By 1901 the Foreign Office recognised that 'unless Japan could find an ally against Russia, she might be driven to make a bargain with her instead'.[17] The British were negotiating with the Germans but there were strong reservations on both sides. Talks collapsed and immediately afterwards, in January 1902, the Anglo-Japanese treaty came into force. They agreed strict neutrality should either go to war with another country, and assistance if the other party went to war with more than one.[18]

The Japanese needed intelligence about Russian defences and Sidney Reilly needed money. It seems that a deal was struck that satisfied both parties. Reilly also made a good living working for, and with, a wealthy and astute entrepreneur by the name of Moisei Ginsburg, who had been based in Japan for many years and was now represented in all the important ports of the Far East.

Sidney Reilly saw the Russo-Japanese War coming before most people, and in September 1903, Margaret was sent away, no doubt persuaded that this was for her own protection. Off she sailed towards America; and she did not reappear in Reilly's life until the winter of 1904.

Left alone in Port Arthur as the Japanese prepared plans to attack, Sidney Reilly devoted himself to an affair with the Russian wife of an Englishman, Horace Collins, who happened to be Russia's chief intelligence agent in the town. Intelligence was being supplied to all the major powers, particularly the Japanese, who had no difficulty in getting their own citizens into construction gangs working on the harbour defences. The Russians couldn't tell the difference and the Chinese weren't telling, and one result was that the standard of workmanship was not of the highest.

One person who knew about these Japanese masquerading as Chinese was a German spy calling himself Dr Franz von Cannitz, who resurfaced over a decade later as an acquaintance of Melville's and a future British intelligence agent. He was Dr Armgaard Karl Graves.[19] His account of life in Port Arthur at the time is worth quoting.

> Never in any place – and I know all the gayest and fastest places on earth – have I seen, comparatively speaking, such an enormous amount of wine in stock, or such a number of demi-mondaines assembled. Most of the officers had private harems. I often sat in the Casino and watched the officers of the First Tomsk Regiment, the 25th and 26th Siberian Rifles, practising with their newly supplied Mauser pistols on tables loaded with bottles containing the most costly vintage wines and cognacs. At such times the place literally [sic] ran ankle-deep in wine. There were over sixty gambling houses and dancing halls supporting more than a thousand filles de joie.

This colourful account, exaggerated or even untrue as it certainly is, nonetheless indicates the mood of a wild east in which few secrets were retained. Von Cannitz, or Graves, was recalled to Berlin 'exactly seven days before Togo's first night attack'.[20]

It is significant that in the Intelligence Department at Berlin they knew an attack was imminent, although they did not know it at Port Arthur. Furthermore, Russian securities dropped 18 points on the New York Stock Exchange before the official knowledge of the attack came through. This information leaked out through the German Embassy in Washington.[21]

It all *sounds* convincing but we have only Graves's word for it that he was ever in Port Arthur at all. Graves was a great self-mythologiser and the notion that the Germans were best-informed was flattering to him. British intelligence was thoroughly certain, on the other hand, that Sidney Reilly was spying for the Japanese.[22] In February 1904, with the Japanese beginning a long siege of Port Arthur, Sidney Reilly too would leave – for Europe, and an opportunity to assist Mr Melville.

On 1 December 1903, Melville began undercover work as W. Morgan, General Agent, of 25 Victoria Street. His two-roomed office was located just across Parliament Square from Scotland Yard, in a building whose public entrance was bedecked with business names while the second entrance was hidden around the corner. With amazement he found that although

few men at this time were better known in London than I was… during the five years I was there I never met any person going in or coming out who knew me. This could only obtain in London.

Detective work, actually being there and asking the questions, meeting the people and seeing the places where things happened and using the intuition born of long experience, was what he did best, and MO3 would exploit his skills to the full.

My duties were rather vague, but were generally to enquire into suspicious cases which might be given to me; to report all cases of suspicious Germans which might come to my notice; the same as to Frenchmen and foreigners generally; to obtain suitable men to go abroad to obtain information; to be in touch with competent operators [and] to keep observation on suspected persons when necessary.

Melville's role included not only defensive counter-espionage but espionage itself, should he be able to 'obtain suitable men to go abroad to obtain information'.

The 'vague' duties resolved themselves at the start into a mission on which would depend the future of British naval defences and (had anyone suspected it at the time) the foundation of one of the world's biggest companies. The background to the affair is succinctly set out in a letter of reminiscence dated 30 April 1919 from E.G. Pretyman MP to Sir Charles Greenway, the chairman of the Anglo-Persian Oil Company, in which he recounts his own involvement some fifteen years earlier, as Civil Lord of the Admiralty, in securing the Persian oil concession for Britain; 'In 1904 it became obvious to the Board of the Admiralty that petroleum would largely supersede coal as the source of fuel supply to the Navy. It was also clear to us that that this would place the British Navy at a great disadvantage, because, whereas we possessed, within the British Isles, the best supply of coal in the world, a very small fraction of the known oil fields of the world lay within the British Dominions'.

The Americans, Germans, Japanese and Russians had already acquired access to guaranteed supplies of oil. If Britain was to develop oil-powered ships she must have a large and guaranteed supply of her own.

In the months preceding Melville's appointment a wealthy Englishman, William Knox D'Arcy, had approached the Admiralty. Knox D'Arcy, having made his first fortune developing a gold mine in Australia, had bought the rights to exploit Persia's oil reserves and was negotiating with the Turkish Government for similar rights in Mesopotamia (now Iraq). He was convinced that reserves existed, although so far no oil had been found. Petroleum already powered engines in the most advanced factories, agricultural equipment, ships and motor vehicles, and even fuelled the aircraft which the Wright Brothers had just – in this very year of 1903 – flown for the first time in America. Control of oil supplies would surely be important in time of war. But with every month that passed Knox D'Arcy was pouring more money into a hole in the ground. He required massive backing to finance further exploration and told the Admiralty that he would be prepared to sell an interest in the Persian concession.

It all made sense but the Admiralty was unconvinced by Knox D'Arcy's claim that oil would be found in Persia. They did not close the door on negotiations, but waited and did nothing. Quite how they discovered, in December of 1903, that Knox D'Arcy had turned to Lord Rothschild is uncertain, but it may have been learned through 'shadowing', surveillance and secret (illicit) interception of mail or telephone calls, and Melville was their only specialist in this regard.

Knox D'Arcy's proposition impressed Lord Rothschild, whose affairs were much too entangled with those of the British Government to allow him to assist. He therefore decided at the end of the month to write to his cousin in Paris. So it came about that, in February, Baron Alphonse de Rothschild and his team met Knox D'Arcy and a colleague of his, John Fletcher Moulton, in Cannes. Other guests at the Grand Hotel included a London couple, Mr and Mrs William Melville.

It is astonishing that anyone with confidential matters to discuss should pick an hotel to do it in. Unlike personal domestic servants, hotel staff are notoriously willing to trade information for money – indeed excusably so; theirs is a service culture reliant on gratuities. Waste-paper bins, overheard conversations, phone calls intercepted at the hotel exchange, private letters consigned to the post and opened – an hotel is to security as a colander to water, and every leak would have been accessible to a man like Melville. How he obtained this particular intelligence is

unknown, but Melville's reports of the progress of these negotiations between Knox D'Arcy and an incipient French syndicate
were sufficiently alarming to make Mr E.G. Pretyman, an MP
and Civil Lord of the Admiralty, take up his pen:

> I… wrote to Mr D'Arcy explaining to him the Admiralty's interest
> in petroleum development and asking him, before parting with
> the concession to any foreign interests, to give the Admiralty an
> opportunity of endeavouring to arrange for its acquisition by a
> British syndicate.[23]

On receipt of this letter Mr Knox D'Arcy returned to London to
hear what the Admiralty had to say. They promised to approach
Burmah Oil with a view to setting up a syndicate. He was perfectly in accord with this but in a hurry; Lloyds Bank, already
committed to the tune of about £150,000, was demanding
that he put up his Persian concession as security against further
funding. He maintained an adamant refusal, but could not wait
indefinitely for commitment from the Admiralty.

Melville kept an eye on developments.

In the middle of May 1904, at City Hall Westminster, he was
presented with an illuminated address thanking him for his
thirty-one years of police service, and a cheque for well over
£2,000. Subscribers to the cheque included the embassies of
America, France, Germany, Austria-Hungary, Portugal, Belgium,
Italy, Japan, China, Mexico, Rumania and Peru. In his speech of
thanks he said he was 'terribly embarrassed at having to reply to
this outburst of recognition for his services. During his career he
had been in many tight places, but this was the tightest, especially
as he had to thank not only the English subscribers but those of
other nations. The honour had been bestowed on him, but it was
due to the brave and gallant set of officers under his control.'

Shortly after that happy day he learned that Knox D'Arcy
could wait no longer. In late June there would be a meeting
between Knox D'Arcy's agent, John Fletcher Moulton, and
Baron de Rothschild.

Melville could hardly turn up by chance in the south of France a second time. Fletcher Moulton probably knew him at the very least by sight, or possibly as the bearer of the letter from Mr Pretyman summoning Knox D'Arcy to London. And Baron de Rothschild's negotiations were a concern of the French Government, whose agents also knew Melville well from his visits to the Riviera with the King.

Fortunately he had run into an old friend. He arranged a meeting with Sidney Reilly in Paris on 6 June. Here was the very person to take his place. Between them they came up with a somewhat dishonourable idea that Melville was quite happy to pay for.

One of the most effective ways of scuttling the negotiations would have been to sow doubts in de Rothschild's mind concerning the odds of oil being found in the area D'Arcy was drilling. Reilly was a creative fellow. If he saw a desired outcome he would manipulate events in order to achieve it.[24] This particular little scheme could have drawn on his skills as a forger, although it is more likely that he exploited his network of contacts. Because by the time the de Rothschild–Moulton meeting took place later in the month, information from an 'unfavourable outside interest' had cast doubt on Knox D'Arcy's ability to find oil. Fletcher Moulton was offered terms less generous than before and believed that Baron de Rothschild had cooled off the idea following sight of some unknown 'report'.

Thirty kilometres away at the Continental Hotel, St Raphael, Sidney Reilly was writing with satisfaction about a 'most useful report' that had helped him 'turn the tide'. Melville would have been startled, though, had he seen that the Mrs Reilly twirling her parasol in the sunshine of St Raphael was no longer Margaret, but a quite different young woman. This Mrs Reilly is more than likely his first bigamous wife Anna, with whom he fled Port Arthur in early 1904, having sent Margaret packing back to England.

Fletcher Moulton returned to England downcast, but in London he found Knox D'Arcy unexpectedly cheerful. It seemed Burmah Oil and the Admiralty were definitely setting up a syndicate that would continue exploration in Persia. In May of 1905, the deal was signed; Knox-D'Arcy got his backing and Burmah managed the exploration. The first field in the Middle East was discovered at Majid-i-Suleiman in 1908, and the following year the Anglo-Persian Oil Company was founded as a consequence. The British Navy was assured of oil during the First World War, and Anglo-Persian went on to become BP, today the world's fifth-largest company.

Despite their defeat, Boer groups were still plotting under the leadership of a Dr Leyds, who was based in Holland, and it was Melville's business to find out the plans of 'an incessant stream of South African suspects arriving at that time in this country'. Boers were hard to watch as they expected to have Scotland Yard men keeping an eye on them, but his memoir relates how he was once able to obtain a complete run-down of the intended movements of a party led by one Ledebour, 'a very suspicious character', as discussed while they had their boots polished outside Liverpool Street on arrival. Evidently they had spoken English to one another, for the shoeblack was able to oblige Melville with an account of everything they said.

Thus ended one of the exciting episodes Melville saw fit to recall. In fact, he was also intermittently engaged in 1904 and 1905 in assessing the strength of Russian exile movements; but to go into detail, even in a confidential memoir intended for War Office eyes only, at the end of 1917 with the new Bolshevik Government in Russia, would perhaps have been incautious. As Melville dictated his memoir in 1917 some of the people he had pursued over the years were already in positions of power. Burtsev was, of all things, Chief of Police in Petrograd (formerly St Petersburg). As for Lenin, Melville was keeping quiet, but Herbert Fitch, then a detective constable attached to Special Branch, later related a tale concerning the Bolshevik's visit to London in April/May 1905 to attend the 3rd Congress of the Russian Social Democratic Labour Party.

Fitch, who had joined Special Branch when Melville was at
its head, worked on numerous cases where Special Branch and
the Secret Service had a joint involvement. He seems to have
been particularly useful in situations where his multilingualism
enabled him to observe and report on the activities of foreign
nationals. Although prone to embellishment, Fitch's account of
this episode is actually corroborated in its essential details by a
number of other sources.[25] According to Fitch, he was detailed
to shadow Lenin and other delegates, who held covert meetings
in a number of public houses in Islington and Great Portland
Street.[26] Although Fitch does not refer to Melville by name, he
makes it clear that the man he was writing about had left the
Yard, yet is still in a position to call on Special Branch men when
he needs them. The public houses he refers to are not specifically named, although the description of one in particular fits
that of what was, at the time, the Duke of Sussex in Islington.
In fact, a typed list of addresses compiled by Melville in April
1905 includes, 'The Duke of Sussex, 106 Islington High Street;
The Cock Tavern, 27 Great Portland Street and The White Lion,
25 Islington High Street'.[27]

In his own memoir, Melville's lips remained sealed – except
for a brief reference to how the Russo-Japanese War had caused
'severe political tension' between Britain and Russia, resulting in
a decision, 'to get in touch with Poles, nihilist and other discon-
tented Russian elements' in Britain. As a consequence, Melville
had written to an anarchist leader, a Pole called Karskii, claiming
to be 'an American of Polish sympathies', requesting a meeting
at the Charing Cross Hotel. To his dismay, Karskii insisted on
the Nihilist Club, where everyone knew Melville by sight and
knew who he was. He turned up anyway, deeply suspicious and
full of trepidation. Melville found Karskii, 'awaiting me at the
entrance… when he opened the door off the entrance hall, the
odour of garlic and pickled herrings smothered everything'.[28]
Karskii, who was 'a born conspirator, taciturn and mysterious even to his immediate colleagues' spoke to him alone for
some time before ushering him out, unseen, by the back door.

The interview was rather too successful, for it was followed up by others in less compromising surroundings and quite soon Melville found himself discussing plans to land men on the Polish coast and start a revolution. At this point, unsurprisingly

> Our people were getting cold on the subject, and finally I was told to drop the matter… [I] sent him a letter from the SS *St Louis* at Southampton, enclosing £10 for his propaganda fund, and informing him I was sailing for New York the following morning… I duly received the newspaper of the Party, showing a subscription of £10 from an American sympathiser. Thus the door was left open to recommence *pourparlers* for starting an insurrection in Poland, should it become necessary.

Why Karskii? Why would Melville pretend to be an American? Given that a century has passed, this is not easy to do. It is possible that he had heard about Karskii's gun-running ambitions from Sidney Reilly who had heard it from Japanese intelligence or from his old friend Nikolai Chaikovskii; it is equally possible that he had picked it up from an Okhrana contact such as D.S. Thorpe. Nikolai Chaikovskii was a veteran Socialist Revolutionary and leading light of the Society of Friends of Russian Freedom in London in the latter part of the 1890s.[29] Through the Society he knew Rosenblum/Sidney Reilly who spied for the Japanese in Port Arthur prior to the outbreak of the Russo-Japanese War in 1904. The following year Chaikovskii was close to, and a conduit of funds from, the Japanese Colonel Akashi, who, from his base in Stockholm, tried to undermine the Tsarist Government during that conflict. Socialist Revolutionaries were among many dissident groups, including the Polish Socialists and some of the Letts, who accepted Japanese gold from Akashi to promote a Russian revolution. (On the other hand, Chaikovskii [according to the report by Okhrana agent Rataev, which places Chaikovskii and Rosenblum/Reilly together in London] was believed by London's Polish émigrés to be an Okhrana agent. He had been seen meeting Mitzakis.)

In the summer of 1905 Akashi financed the purchase of '16,000 rifles and three million bullets to be sent to the Baltic regions and 8,500 rifles and 1.2 million bullets to be sent to the Black Sea'.

> …It was decided that if the Socialist Revolutionaries took a lead- ing role, the other parties would follow… They therefore set about buying arms… I decided to give the Poles money in advance and a free hand, but the other parties received money only after they had found arms for sale… Parties composed mainly of workers, such as the Socialist Revolutionaries and the Polish Socialists, did not like rifles. In contrast the Finns and Caucasians, who were mainly peasants, preferred rifles.[30]

Akashi also bought, through an English wine merchant called Dickenson, a 700-ton cargo vessel called the *John Grafton*. The arms were transported by train from Switzerland and loaded into it. The ship's nominal owner was an American, Morton, who was believed by Akashi to be an anarchist and somehow connected to Mrs Vernon Hull, an American woman who owned two gun- running steamers, the *Cysne* and the *Cecil*.[31]

The *John Grafton* had offloaded only some of the arms at Baltic ports when everything went horribly quiet. The only person who could tell Akashi anything about what had happened was Konni Zilliacus, the multilingual Finn who was his go-between all over Europe.

> Probably on 25th or 26th August Zilliacus came to Stockholm with a passport in the name of Long from England and said 'I am really puzzled by the *John Grafton* business. She unloaded arms for the Lettish party to the north of Windau on 18th August. But no boat was waiting for her at the arrival point to the south of Viborg on the 19th. The crew were so apprehensive that they sailed her back to Denmark and begged me to give her new orders…'

He did so. The ship then ran aground amid uncharted sandbanks, and within days its cargo became international news, with photographs of the wreckage in the newspapers. As an afterthought Akashi adds

> Prior to this, three machine guns and 15,000 bullets which the *Cysne* had on board were discovered by the English authorities, just before the ship left London. Morton from the United States, the nominal owner of these arms, was arrested and fined.

The identity of Morton raises many interesting questions. It has been speculated, by Dr Nicholas Hiley, that in light of Melville's account of his encounter with Karskii at the time of the Russo-Japanese War (in the guise of an American anarchist), Morton could well be a Japanese transliteration of Morgan, Melville's chief alias at this time.

No record as to whether Morton was in fact fined, and if so where, has so far been located. In light of Melville's own testimony, the theory that Morton and Morgan were one and the same is therefore a plausible one.

As early as 1901, Melville had begun to suspect that spies were interested in English coastal defences. A commercial traveller with the French name of Allain, who sold wines along the South Coast, 'frequented soldiers a great deal', presumably on the pretext that they would purchase wines for the mess. He asked questions about the armaments of the forts around Portsmouth and then turned up in Dover doing much the same kind of thing. Some papers of his were found on a cross-Channel ferry and proved to contain, among other incriminating material, a questionnaire about Dover Castle: 'calibre of guns, strength of garrison, the best approaches thereto, &c.'[32] It was believed that at least three NCOs had taken money in exchange for information. Although they had not been able to supply much of value, it was a worrying case.

At the time, this kind of thing fell into a gap between military security and Special Branch. Later Allain, who was an American citizen, turned up in Cherbourg asking much the same questions, and from this

> …it was evident he was in the pay of Germany. But no person thought of such a thing at the time. In fact Allain came in for little attention from the police although he was under notice from November 1901 to November 1903.[33]

The German *Nachrichten* Intelligence Service, had been run from Berlin by a Major Dame until 1900 and Major Dame had been perfectly happy to co-operate with Colonel Edmonds of the War Office in figuring out what the Russians and French were up to. But there was change shortly before Queen Victoria's death. Dame was out, and a Major Brose was in, and he

> …was known for his anti-English views. Shortly after this Colonel Edmonds learned from several sources that a third branch of the German Secret Service had been formed to deal with England.

In 1904, despite the 'special duties' MO3 being set up, possible spies still received no 'attention from the police' in England and Melville, who was now on the *qui vive* at all times, was frustrated by the sheer innocence of the policemen he met up and down the country. He was working for a War Office conscious that Russia would very much like to invade India, that Germany would take on the British Navy if it thought it could, and that the French were quietly preparing for conflict against the Germans. All these nations needed information about British naval and military strength and must get it by spying. But the average policeman had no idea of this. Germans in particular were accepted without question wherever they went.

> I had to travel to all parts of the country to make enquiries re suspected persons. In these duties I found the police, whether in London or the provinces, absolutely useless. Their invariable estimate of a suspect was his apparent respectability and position.

Just as though only blackguards would be chosen for espionage. But the fact was the police could not understand these matters. The idea was foreign to them.[34]

He was aware that railway lines into London were a prime target for destruction by Germany in the event of war. At Merstham in Surrey there is a particularly long tunnel, and information reached him that a German photographer had taken up residence in the village. Off went Melville to find out more; the German had vanished. The house where he lived was directly opposite one occupied by a police constable. The constable was naturally surprised and impressed when called upon by ex-Superintendent Melville. He knew the photographer of course – very nice chap, took landscapes, not portraits, and splendid they were, too. Melville (one imagines him hunched over the teacups in the front parlour) now approached a delicate topic with a meaningful air.

It must be remembered that in those days I was absolutely forbidden to mention the word 'spy.' All sorts of pretexts had therefore to be resorted to, even with the police… I then spoke to the officer for some time on the fact that the times were strange, and that we all should take stock of those foreigners and have our suspicions of them, &c., &c. 'Yes, Sir', he said, 'I am sure you are right; I believe these fellows are the authors of nearly all the burglaries we have around the country.'

Thus my eloquence was absolutely thrown away.[35]

The German had made a comprehensive photographic survey of the entire district. His landlord, at the house where he lodged, worked at Merstham Railway Station. Among his duties he had to inspect the tunnel at least twice a week, and Melville would soon learn that the photographer had accompanied him quite frequently 'out of mere curiosity'.

Public awareness of the need for vigilance had not yet trickled down from readers of Erskine Childers' *Riddle of the Sands,* which had appeared the previous year and was the first sensational spy novel. The War Office had no permission at this time to intercept private mail. Melville had built up relationships with people in the GPO over the years but outside central London it was a different matter. While up and down the country foreign waiters and farmers, salesmen and language teachers, shopkeepers and 'persons of independent means' explored the countryside and sent and received letters from abroad, among the locals 'not to one in a thousand did the idea occur that Germans might be here on espionage'.

And it takes one to know one. Melville had no difficulty in turning his attention to Germans who might be spies. He was firmly on King Edward's side in this. He was all for an Entente and, by association, civilised tolerance of the Russians, but again like King Edward, was rather lukewarm about Germans and ready to believe they were up to no good. It was a prejudice he had.

His failure to encounter much suspicion in the populace at large was probably partly because the German of popular imagination, the stiff-necked, pompous, conceited, humourless Prussian, was not yet the butt of popular dislike that he later became. The caricature of a Frenchman, on the other hand, the duplicitous garlic-munching ladies' man, had been despised since the Napoleonic Wars. National and racial stereotypes prevailed in contemporary discourse at all levels of society and generally went unchallenged. Melville knew France, and the French, so he would not fall for that one; but the Germans were an unknown quantity and their intelligence service was certainly efficient. It was thanks to this that Paris had fallen in 1871.

Nonetheless, Melville must occasionally examine the French way of doing things, and sometimes in the context of a little spying of his own.

In 1904 we were very anxious to get the French bullet 'D' for the Lebel rifle. I sent several agents (Frenchmen) to France. They visited the various manufacturing centres but owing to supervision, chiefly in connection with the activities of German and Italian agents, they were unsuccessful.[36]

In December 1904 his Brussels agent, Hely Claeys, was supposed to set up a meeting with a disaffected soldier from the supplies division of the French war office who seemed ready to hand over samples of the new Lebel cartridges. On Christmas Eve it became evident that arrangements had been bungled, and Melville had to leave London for Brussels at once, thereby missing his traditional annual Christmas party at home. Thanks to him the Brussels meeting did take place, but not until New Year's Day. As it happened the cartridges were of the old kind, although the new kind could probably be got so the meeting was not entirely fruitless. In the end they were obtained in London 'and at a very low price'.

But Melville was disappointed at missing an annual family party that was so emotionally important and so unrepeatable. Perhaps this is what made him think he might be putting rather too much effort into this job than was merited by the reward.

He had only one yardstick to measure his salary by: Long, the other MO3 employee who generally worked abroad. But early in January while L was back in England Melville learned that the younger man was to take on an important undercover role in south-east Africa at a rate of pay twenty per cent higher than his own and with generous expenses.[37] Melville considered this; and he thought about former colleagues who seemed well off since they left the police; and he asked Davies for a rise in pay to £500 p.a.

It is thanks to this request that we have an estimate of his true value according to his superiors. Colonel Davies consulted Sir Edward Henry, the police commissioner, who wrote confidentially on 21 January:

> As you find him really useful might very reasonably recommend him for a rise from £400 to £500 by increments of £25 a year. I think it unlikely that for the same money you could get anyone

equally serviceable, trustworthy and experienced. Littlechild no doubt makes a good living – but it has taken him many years to get together his clientèle and he started private business when he was comparatively young. I should doubt Sweeney making anything like the income stated. Whatever he may have made will be swallowed up by law expenses and damages, the outcome of his amazing indiscretion in publishing memoirs.[38]

The advantage of spreading the rise over a few years is that during that period he cannot well press for further concessions – *L'appétit vient en mangeant*.[39]

Davies considered this and wrote to Sir Thomas Sanderson at the Foreign Office, whose department was ultimately responsible for paying the bill.

M has raised the question of his salary, and asks for an increase. He says that old subordinates of his, who have also left the force, are earning better incomes than he is. He quotes ex-Inspector Littlechild whom he states to be earning £1,500, ex-Inspector Sweeney, who only left two years ago and who he says is making £850, and ex-Sergeant Thorpe, who gets £450 from the *Russian* Government for reporting the movements of anarchists, and lastly he points out that Long gets £500, that is £100 more than he, M, does. This last is an unfortunate circumstance and one which I always hoped he would not discover, to which end I have always paid Long direct. I pointed out to Melville that he must remember that L can be at any time called upon to undertake duty which may lead him into a foreign prison, and that considering the risks he has often run, and will shortly run again, his salary is not so high as it seems. M admitted that L had to run risks, but it evidently rankled that a subordinate of comparatively little experience should get more than he does. He is also anxious about the security of his tenure, and fears that a change of Government might lead to his dismissal, as he has got it into his head that a Liberal minister might disapprove of anyone being employed on such work as he is doing.

His application is that his salary be raised to £500 a year, and that he is to be appointed for five years conditional of course on good behaviour.

I am glad to be able to say that in my opinion M has worked very satisfactorily, and I doubt very much if we could get anyone else for the money who would do as well. He is very resourceful, and has a great capacity for picking up suitable persons to act as agents. Further he has a really good working knowledge of French, which is uncommon in men of his class and is most useful, in fact almost indispensable. His accent would certainly appal you, but he is quite fluent and fully capable of transacting business in French; moreover he can write quite a decent business letter in French.[40]

Sanderson sent this on to Lord Lansdowne. His covering note remarks

This is an application from ex-Superintendent Melville (who acts as intermediary for communications with the agents employed by the Intelligence Dept.) for increase of salary.
I never supposed that he would remain content with £400 a year. He is a useful man, and I should be disposed to advance him to £450 with a promise of £500 after another year's service, and a year's salary in case his employment should at any time be terminated without any fault on his part.[41]

By the end of the month, Melville had exactly this, and had written 'a nice letter' to Colonel Davies expressing his pleasure at the outcome.

Davies himself was having trouble with a Prussian – another disaffected foreign war ministry employee, this time from Munich – whose demands were outrageous. His price seems to have oscillated between £150 ('I sent him £10 in a moment of weakness', admitted Davies) and the enormous sum of £7,500, which Davies saw fit to follow with *two* exclamation marks. 'I strongly suspect he is a fraud, and we shall lose our £10.'[42]

Finding trustworthy agents abroad was extremely difficult; Melville, since meeting the man in Brussels, was learning that all the French ex-soldiers who volunteered to impart secrets told the same story. He grew sceptical.

> I found them generally very logical, but brimming over with suggestion. They offered their services to us in consequence of bad treatment while in the army. In fact, it became a matter of revenge. It was noticeable, too, that many of them told the same sort of yarns. It looked to me as though they had been coached in this direction. Above all, I found their great desire was to learn what we wished to know. In the result, after due consideration, none of these volunteers were employed.[43]

Nonetheless, agents must be found. Davies's letter, in a mysterious postscript to the German story, mentions contacting the Japanese military attaché. The Foreign Office wrestled with questions about whom could they trust, and indeed where they most needed agents. In the autumn two memoranda were drawn up within the intelligence division. One was about 'Secret Service in the event of a European war' and the other 'Secret Service arrangements in the event of a war with Germany'. It seemed that in the latter case, 'the present is not a good moment for taking any active steps towards the organisation of a service – there is too much suspicion of our intentions'.[44]

It was mutual. Several times in his first few years of intelligence service Melville brought up the matter of German spies in England. Early in 1905, with a new Aliens Bill in the offing, the Home Office asked the Government to add a clause intended to put spies off. The Prime Minister was not convinced since, as Sir George Clarke wrote to Mr Chalmers at the Home Office in February

> …he doubts whether this could act as an effective deterrent. He thinks that it is desirable that these people should be watched by

the local police as much as possible. Could you take steps to carry this out?[45]

Like Melville, Mr Chalmers had no faith in provincial police. Unlike Melville, he could see no possible way to sharpen their perceptions. He foresaw little in any attempt to involve them except bureaucratic time-wasting, inter-departmental squabbles over who would pay the bill, and smart Germans running rings round a bunch of plods.

…The German officers can be watched, but there are some preliminary difficulties I must talk over with you. We could send down a Met detective because the Met police are under the Home Office. You must first tell us where the [German] officers are and then if a Met officer is not to hand we can discover whether they are in the jurisdiction of the county or borough police. In either event we have no control over the local police and can only ask as a favour that they will watch the Germans. Probably the Watch Committee (or standing joint committee) will want payment, in which case the Treasury will have to find the money.

As to sending a person to discover what can be found out, I think it would require expert knowledge… The Germans of course are military experts.[46]

It was a bleak conclusion but the matter arose again at the end of the year when one of Melville's reports made it to the desks of Lord Lansdowne, Mr Chalmers and Sir Edward Henry. Melville had spent several days in the middle of November investigating a German who had been staying at a Suffolk farm, having paid for a three-month course in agriculture. He made his way there – and to one fresh from Victoria Street, the place was in the middle of nowhere – and found that the German (a heavily built six-footer with sabre-cuts from duelling) had left only a week before.

Melville interviewed the farmer, Mr Smith ('a very intelligent man and by the way an Imperialist'):

Mr Smith noticed that Mr Hederich knew quite as much about farming as he did, and also that he paid little attention to it. Smith said that he had now no doubt that Hederich was a spy… he drove much around the country and always took the German with him. Latter was persistent in asking and learning the names of roads and where they led to, the names of parishes, churches and mansions. They generally went to Ipswich perhaps twice a week and there the German left him and went around the town visiting the park, the docks and the vicinity. At Ipswich Hederich also bought a map of the country and made a trip by steamer from latter town to Clacton and back.

When at home (Hall Farm) he always retired to his bedroom immediately after luncheon and remained there till dinner, but he never made any reference as to how he occupied himself in the interval… He informed the Smiths that he was an officer in the German Army, they thought in the cavalry.[47]

In view of Hederich's trips to nearby ports, Melville concluded grimly 'no doubt he has returned to Germany with a complete map and valuable information of that part of the country and coast and the fortifications at Harwich and in the vicinity'.

To be fair to the police, there was not much they could do about tourists sketching and measuring picturesque features of the shoreline. Without proof of 'intent to communicate… to a foreign state',[48] which was almost impossible to get, there was nothing illegal in it. But Melville would argue that this wasn't the point; the idea was to let potential spies know that their curiosity did not go unremarked and that the police were vigilant. It was the prevailing lack of guile, the open-faced innocence of ill intent, which was so English and so irritating.

On 21 November Melville wrote another report. In the course of the Hederich enquiry he had come across two other East Anglian farmers who had played host to young Germans anxious to learn, thereby introducing them in good faith to the local community. It didn't smell right.

Learning farming is out of the question as the Germans consider they are far ahead of Englishmen in that direction. No doubt they are; one has only to travel in Germany to see this.

While at Woodbridge I also learned that a volunteer Chaplain, the Reverend J. Garforth, had written to the *East Anglian Daily Times* warning the population of Suffolk as to the espionage being carried out by Germans.

Melville tracked down the Reverend Garforth, a former Army officer of sixty-five, quite quickly, and heard an astonishing story.

A friend of his had last summer been enabled to visit a military college in Germany and found that the thesis a number of students was working out was *Having landed an army at Hastings, give a sketch showing the characteristics of the country, the names of the roads, villages and towns to be traversed* en route *to London.* [49]

That this had been reported by 'a friend' does not seem to have rung warning bells. There was a party of extreme paranoia at this time – the Legion of Frontiersmen, who saw Prussians behind every hedge – and this is the sort of story they would have told, but Melville was not sceptical. Instead he put Garforth's account into his report and suggested that confidential instructions should go from the Home Office to the chief constables of all maritime counties pointing out that there was a problem and their men should maintain a discreet look-out.

Lord Lansdowne of course thought that was perfectly reasonable.[50] Mr Chalmers picked up his pen with a sigh. Of course the Home Office could write letters to County policemen, but

They would have to act through the village sergeant or constable I suppose.

There is a further difficulty. All the fortified places on the coast are under borough police who are under the borough (or city)

watch committee. The county police cannot of course act in the borough and the borough police are usually not high class. You would probably have some stupid muddle or row arising.

PS Some months ago we wrote to War Office to above effect.[51]

The Home Office probably assumed that little of importance could be learned by mere casual observation and notation of arrangements which were, after all, open for all to see. Melville would be spy-watching for a good while before action was taken.

Nor had he forgotten the Russians. It was perfectly all right for his former subordinate, ex-Sergeant Thorpe, to work for them against nihilists in London; Thorpe had retired from the Yard in 1900 and worked to the Okhrana agent in London, a Frenchman called Farce. Farce lived in Hammersmith and was married to an Englishwoman. But since the mysterious affair of Mitzakis in 1900, Melville was no longer prepared to believe that all Russian agents were of friendly intent and he put himself out to track their present movements.

In 1902 Rachkovskii had moved from his Paris headquarters at the Russian Embassy, 79 Rue de Grenelle, to Brussels where he appeared to have retired on a pension. Milewskii, who worked for Rataev, had died. Melville had met Rataev before he left Special Branch, when in Paris with the King. In November and December 1904 he made notes on all of them, and in May 1905 he filed notes from memory about the physical appearance of Okhrana agents in Europe including Mitzakis, Harting, Rachkovskii, Golschmann and Rataev.

In February of 1905 the matter of Mitzakis, the mysterious Russian with influential friends, arose yet again, and in that month Melville wrote a full report headed 'Russian Spies in London'. Mitzakis had long ago in 1899 moved into an apartment at 9 Drayton Gardens, South Kensington, before taking over the whole house and leaving it empty, apparently for occasional use by the embassy as a safe house. He now lived there again.

> He has been on the continent for two to three months, being home only about a couple of weeks. He is a director of the Chatma Oilfields Co. Ltd, the office of which is at 1 Charing Cross. This company was formed in November 1902. Its property is at Chatma near Tiflis in Russia, and consists of naphtha springs.

> The nominal vendor was a Mr Mathias of 67 Park Place, Cardiff, but Mitzakis was mixed up with the company's business from its inception and there is little doubt that he was the principal in obtaining the concession from the Russian Government. In June 1903, Mitzakis was appointed a director of the company. Among other directors are Lord Armstrong, Sir A. Noble, Bart., and Colonel W.A. Tufnell.

> There is no doubt that Mitzakis was, up to about two years ago, in the employ of the Russian Government as a spy and it may be assumed that he is still, and that when recently on the continent he was so engaged.

Melville's report has a page missing, but it concludes:

> He professes to be an LLD, is keen at business thoroughly unscru-pulous [*sic*], by nationality I believe a Greek and has all the cunning of his race.

> It is not unlikely that Mitzakis might have been mixed up with the Hull business as he speaks English fluently.

What 'the Hull business' was, we shall never know. Melville's memoir is silent on the subject.

NINE

SHIFTING SANDS

It was stated the other day, on Russian authority, that ex-Superintendent Melville, the famous detective, had joined the Czar's secret police. The Russian police, it was declared, are to have the benefit of Mr Melville's unequalled experience, and the alleged appointment was generally looked upon as the highest compliment that could be paid to a man of even his great reputation.

We learn that the report is unfounded. In a letter to the *Daily Express* Mr Melville says:

Permit me to state that I am still in London, quietly enjoying what, after thirty years of occasional excitement, I consider to be my well-earned retirement, and that now, like most people, I am content to follow revolutionary movements through the medium of my daily paper. Further, I may add that after an almost life-long and I hope honourable career in the public service, the assertion that I have entered the service of another Government, which service may at any moment bring me into conflict with my own country, is at once unfair and offensive.

Police Review, 19 March 1906 [1]

Mitzakis' revenge could have inspired the original story. Had any Russian agent chosen to discover, by simple surveillance, what Melville was up to in 'retirement', suspicions would have been confirmed if they saw an active man still in his fifties regularly alighting from the Wandsworth Town train at Victoria and disappearing into a warren of offices down the street. We know of no leisure pursuits other than a supportive interest in the London Irish hurley team. The Melville family had grown up. The three surviving children were doing well; James, the youngest at twenty-one, would be called to the Bar in June. He and Kate at least (we are not sure about young William) would move, around 1908, with their father and stepmother to 24 Orlando Road, Clapham, a tall and pretty semi-detached house near the Old Town.[2] Amelia Melville could console herself that her husband was no longer risking his life to protect the King. Otherwise he remained as much absorbed by work as ever.

In the early months of 1906 he discovered an entire cadre of German spies going about their business quite openly from a furnished house in Epping. It was near a pub kept by a local fellow called Spiegelhalter. Melville had responded to a letter to the War Office about a foreigner seen photographing a disused fort nearby. He found that the complement of men varied between seven and thirteen, and

> They all had either cycles or motor-cycles and invariably carried cameras. They also carried field glasses. They had apparently plenty of money… They left home regularly every morning at 9 o'clock, irrespective of the weather, on their bicycles or motor-cycles and armed with cameras. All took different routes.[3]

None of the locals (with the probable exception of Mr Spiegelhalter, who wasn't asked) knew where they went, since they'd never thought to enquire, but with Melville's encouragement they got into conversation and found that these Germans were all 'on holiday'. Each man was 'on holiday' for exactly three months and then went back to Germany 'to join his regiment'. After a while they melted away to different parts of England, but not before Melville had despaired of trying to convince the local police that these men were engaged upon espionage. They were deaf to his warnings. 'Argument was useless.' As for the spies,

> Their business, I should say, was to become thoroughly conversant with the routes from the sea coast to London, and thus to be able

to guide a German army landed in this country. These Germans frequently, to the surprise of some Epping people, told the number of miles even to very remote places on the sea coast. They knew the geography of the country by heart.[4]

Later, in the years leading up to the War, popular novels would inspire widespread nervousness about invasion by Germany. But invasion was not the aim of German pre-war espionage. Nor was sabotage, at least not immediately. The German Government simply wanted facts about British naval defences, armaments and shipping. Armgaard Karl Graves, who was a wild fantasist, describes how he was trained to recognise other nations' ships in silhouette, flag signals and uniforms, besides 'topography, trigonometry, naval construction and drawing':

> A Secret Service agent sent out to investigate and report on the condition, situation, and armament of a fort like Verdun in France must be able to make correct estimates of distances, height, angles, conditions of the ground etc... he must be able to make quick and accurate calculations using trigonometry, as well as possessing skill as a draftsman.[5]

If German intelligence was not all it might have been, this was at least in part because few if any spies were trained as thoroughly as Graves claims he was, certainly before 1909. And no disaffected Englishmen were recruited. The spies warned off by Melville's snooping in these years were either young soldiers on routine exercises unlikely to yield much of value, or immigrant or travelling Germans without technical knowledge who probably seemed more suspicious than they were. Steinhauer, who like Melville had shifted his professional attention to espionage and counter-espionage, wrote

> A spy is a man – or woman – whose business it is to obtain information of naval, military or political value. Such people must naturally possess infinitely greater technical knowledge and daring than the ordinary Secret Service agent, the individuals whose

work is confined to opening letters they have received from their employers, taking out the enclosures they contain – chiefly sealed letters – stamping them, and putting them into pillar-boxes to reach the spies for whom they were intended.

These agents were seldom used – at any rate by me – for anything else. Occasionally I might have utilized them to ascertain whether a certain person lived at some particular address, but that was about as far as I would trust them.

The work of the agents outside London, say those living in naval localities, was a trifle more difficult. Questions were put to them, mainly dealing with changes that had taken place in naval or military matters, but even then there was nothing especially secret about the whole business.[6]

Part of the trouble was money. Steinhauer never had a budget adequate for the purchase of principles or imagination or expertise. Yet if he got no results at all and the German Chief of Admiralty Intelligence happened to be replaced by somebody unsympathetic to 'the anti-English party', his work would falter to a complete halt. In his budgetary problems he was not alone.

Back in Victoria Street, Melville had cause to feel rather glum. A Liberal Government had taken over at the turn of the year and the new regime was scrutinising expenses. He had been right to assure himself of compensation in case of redundancy. Hely Claeys, his Brussels agent, was the first to find himself surplus to requirements. His story indicates how precarious, and risky, a spy's job could be.

He was a man in middle age, Belgian by birth, a naturalised British subject, and had been reporting, through Melville, to Colonel Davies. Now he visited London and appealed to Colonel Charles A'Court Repington, ex-Military Attaché in Brussels and presently military correspondent of *The Times,* to save him from penury. In the six weeks since Intelligence dispensed with his services Claeys had struggled to support himself, his wife and teenage daughter on a meagre income from journalism. All he wanted, he said, was a small retainer and he would go anywhere and do anything, with or without his family. He spoke three languages and his wife eight, but in view of his career history it had proved impossible to find work. His wife and daughter did not even know he was anything but a journalist. He must go back to Belgium on Saturday; he needed an answer.

Repington was sympathetic and asked him to put something on paper that he could show to his superiors. That afternoon Claeys sat down at his boarding house near the British Museum and put his case in a letter. He had originally been hired – by Repington – in 1898, to assist with enquiries around the Fashoda incident. In those days Claeys was stationed at Cherbourg. Fashoda was a Nile port under Anglo-Egyptian rule which was seized by the French General Marchand. Kitchener was able to seize it back, but diplomatic relations between England and France were sour for a few months. Claeys provided good information at Cherbourg but was unfortunately over-zealous, as a result of which he was arrested, fined 1,000 francs and jailed for two years. Upon his release he was deployed at the Cape, and his family accompanied him there. ('Sir E. Bradford saw after his being sent off to South Africa though I found the money', noted Repington.)[7] He was there from June 1901 until June 1904, around the time when the young 'commercial traveller' Henry Long was despatched to work in South Africa. Claeys had since been employed in Brussels by the Intelligence Division, reporting to 'W. Morgan' at 25 Victoria Street, until 2 February 1906. And here he was, with a prison record, cast upon the labour market in his fifties.

It is not economy cancelling my work on the continent in time of trouble. Double and treble is to be paid for bad work as an agent just arrived does not feel at home. Economy consists in paying not too much but a fair salary... I tried my best, as they told me to do, to get another situation. I did not succeed. If the Admiralty, the War Office or the Foreign Office cannot employ me now I beg to ask for a waiting salary of £10 a month with residence in Brussels as being the cheapest place to live in. If you cannot help me I do not know what will become of me. I am without means.[8]

Claeys was paid out of the 'Secret Account', funds that came from the Foreign Office, so Sir Charles Hardinge had to make the decision. The new masters were still figuring out exactly what the Secret Account was for. Hardinge asked Sanderson, his predecessor, for advice, and received the following:

He is, I believe, a good man for his particular business but whether he is worth retaining at a sinecure salary of £120 a year is another question. In any case I strongly advise you to have nothing whatever to do with him directly. I think that if you answer A'Court Repington at all, it would be prudent to tell him that you never have any dealings with agents of this kind. Perhaps you might add that that was also my rule.

There are some papers in the safe or in the press about the man of which I can point out the whereabouts next time I look in at the FO…[9]

Sir Charles took the advice about maintaining a lofty distance, and wrote to Repington in the manner suggested. Repington would have known exactly what was going on: no one in Government dared leave a trail of evidence that he had ever been in contact with espionage agents. In 1919 Repington admitted in his own published memoir to having been in the Secret Service at the time of Fashoda, but certainly not when he was in Brussels; heaven forbid he would have known such a person as Claeys there. He wrote primly

My view is that the Military Attaché is the guest of the country to which he is accredited, and must only see and learn that which is permissible for a guest to investigate. Certainly he must keep his eyes and ears open and miss nothing, but Secret Service is not his business, and he should always refuse to take a hand in it.[10]

Repington was being economical with the truth. He probably knew Claeys in a Secret Service capacity in Brussels. They worked for the same War Office and he seems to have felt to some extent responsible for him.

Undoubtedly, as Steinhauer sagely remarked, 'A discarded spy – like a discarded mistress – is dangerous for any man'.[11] There was a happy ending for Mr Cleays. Sir Charles's assistant dropped a line to Major G.K. Cockerill, who worked safely below the parapet at the War Office, forwarding the correspondence 'in case you should think it desirable to do anything about it'.

Gun-running had been a preoccupation from the start. During the Knox D'Arcy enquiry, Melville had known about the smuggling of arms into Persia, which was of particular concern. He also kept an eye on guns entering ports mainly in Africa and South America. In his memoir he names Rudolph de Paula and Carling and Co., both based in the City of London, as arms dealers he investigated. 'Colonel Davies's Separate Account', the secret Foreign Office fund from which Melville and Long were paid, provided one-off sums to diplomats and agents in ports all over the world to facilitate enquiries about this kind of thing. Davies' accounts for the spring of 1906 include receipts from Cairo:

I, Mansfeldt de Cardonnel Findlay, acknowledge to have received from Sir Edward Grey, Baronet, His Majesty's Principal Secretary of State for Foreign Affairs, the sum of twenty-five pounds (£25) for the purposes of His Majesty's Foreign Secret Service, and I do hereby solemnly declare that the said sum has been disbursed faithfully and according to my best judgment for those purposes...

while from Malta, payable to the agent in Genoa of the *Navigaziione Generale d'Italia,* came:

For one first class passage to Benghazi and return, via Canea (25%
reduction), £9 14s 1d

and *Señor don Arturo Peel*, Chargé d'Affaires in Montevideo, submitted quite a little pile of receipts in February and March. They
included a large one listing '*Champagne, Vino, Whisky, Licor*' and
another from the

Confitería y Café Jockey-Club
CASA ESPECIAL
Para el Servicio de Banquetes, Soirées y Lunch

Arthur Peel seems to have refurbished the Legation with new
carpets and sofas and potted palms and held quite a few *banquêtes*
and *soirées* at Secret Service expense but no doubt it was all to
some long-forgotten purpose. The bills are filed with Davies's
accounts. In a tight, neat, little hand are monthly listings such
as 'Major Thwaites (journey to Brussels: £6 9s 1d)' and 'Pay of
agents at Overburg, Baku, Petrovsk and Kimel for January, £156'
and 'Capt. B-S for HDL (paid into Parr's Bank) £150'. Henry
Dale Long was still in Africa, about to leave. 'Kimel' was Samara.
B – Byzewski, an Austrian, the third permanent agent besides
HDL and M – transferred funds to agents in the Central Asian
cities from his base in Berlin. RBT (Richard Tinsley, who later
became a permanent agent in Rotterdam) received £19 4s 0d
for 'plans of Dutch forts'.

The Secret Service account also paid for repatriation of
'unprotected British subjects' such as, in 1906, 'Miss Ashe and
Miss Stegwell' ('on the recommendation of the Chaplain'),
and 'the Freed family'. What with the potted plants and the
unprotected spinsters vying for funds with Byzewski, Long and
Melville, full-time operatives who produced useful intelligence,
it was rather a catch-all arrangement. But there was no other way
of accounting for these mostly *ad-hoc* items which were better
kept out of the public eye. In November of 1906 Major Cockerill
wrote to Sir Charles Hardinge at the Foreign Office:

I have lately been enquiring into every item of Secret Service expenditure with a view to possible reductions. We do not think it is any longer necessary to keep an agent at Samara, and I have accordingly arranged that he shall not be retained after the 1st January next. This will effect a saving of £380 a year commencing from that date. I have searched in vain for any further means of reducing expenditure. All our other expenses seem not only justified but indispensably necessary.[12]

Among the justified and indispensably necessary items, Melville notes:

During the early part of 1906 I succeeded in obtaining in London particulars of the system prevailing in Germany re mobilisation of the army in peace or war. Also the various punishments meted out to deserters in peace and war; the conditions under which reservists are allowed to leave Germany and their action in foreign countries; and how they keep in touch with their authorities. Also the same information re members of the Landwehr.[13]

The War Office needed to know this but there was no point in hoping the War Office could pay for it; it was all too awkward to be absorbed by a department whose expenditure often came under close parliamentary scrutiny. The Foreign Office had been paying since 1886, and must continue to do so. By 1908 Mr Byzewski had his contact in Samara back on the books.

In 1905, letters from a 'C. Werner', a Hamburg import–export agent, began to fall into Melville's hands. All referred to the importation of arms to South Africa.

These letters were marvellously well written and were masterpieces of detail and perfectly logical. Names and addresses were given in Hamburg and South Africa.[14]

Yet something wasn't right; despite shipping details, even markings on the packing cases, being mentioned in the letters, these boxes never appeared on any ship's manifest. So in June of 1906, with the letters still coming and the Foreign Office scrutinising every penny, Melville accepted his £50 expenses and set off for Hamburg to get to the bottom of it. In this he was assisted by Gottlieb Goerner, Long's old contact in Hamburg, who became a friend. Goerner was an interesting character known to the German authorities. He told Melville that the German Colonial Minister had approached him in 1904 to run a fake import-export business in Fernando Po, a Portuguese colonial possession in the Atlantic, with the ultimate aim of starting a diplomatic incident which would result in a German seizure of the island. He objected reasonably enough that, were he to be shot, the Berlin Government did not guarantee to look after his family. He refused to go, and the whole plot came out in the *Reichsrat*, causing quite a stink at the time.

Goerner probably gave Melville all sorts of useful information, for, according to Michael Smith in *The Spying Game*,

> Melville proved his resourcefulness by blackmailing the city's Chief of Police into helping him find the mysterious 'Herr Werner' who, along with a known gun-runner called Otto Busch, was allegedly behind the conspiracy. Melville investigated a number of different Werners, conning them into providing specimens of their hand-writing which he then compared with intercepted letters from Herr Werner. The main suspect turned out to be 'not a man as originally assumed, but a woman with whom Busch is believed to have had immoral relations'.[15]

Goerner had known (and sued) Busch in South Africa, but could shed no light on the letters. Once again Melville drew a blank. To sum up, the Hamburg addresses existed but, except for Busch, the people and businesses didn't. Maybe, since these were German steamers allegedly used for transport, the guns destined for South Africa were being smuggled ashore somewhere along the West African coast and forwarded overland to the Transvaal? Sometimes the letters gave details of Werner's own travels, yet when the passenger list was checked, Werner wasn't there.

Inevitably, the plug was pulled. There would be no more money. Mr Haldane, now at the War Office, thought this chase after Werner was all a waste of time.

Melville passed the letters up the line to Haldane, who read them and revised his opinion. Suddenly it was all on again. One of the letters provided intelligence of an important Boer conference, to be held at a given time and place in Carlsbad.

It didn't happen.

By now this farrago had been going on for over two years. Melville was on holiday at Ramsgate in October 1907 when the London office informed him by letter that Werner was due to call at Dover the following morning aboard the SS *Eliza Woerman, en route* for Hamburg. Durban officials had instructed a passenger on board called J.W. Brown to point out Werner to Melville.

This was exciting news, but how would Melville recognise J.W. Brown?

> I was on Dover Pier the following morning in good time. All was ready for the arrival of the *Eliza Woerman*, the buffet was open, and the pier men at their posts. Suddenly I noticed a man on the pier evidently saturated with alcohol. He had three or four lots of whisky in the buffet. He then sat down on the pier and took off his boots and socks. I went to him and said 'Going to have a swim?' He replied 'No, I'm just warming my feet to the sun. They're as cold as ice.' I said 'Excuse me, but is not your name Brennan?' To which he replied 'No sir, my name is George Brown, and I've come here to meet my brother, J.W. Brown, who is arriving by this ship from Durban.' I said 'I know him too!' He said 'Then you must be one of his wife's people.' I said 'Yes.'[16]

There were over 500 passengers on board the SS *Eliza Woerman*, which would drop anchor at Dover Harbour for just fifteen minutes, so it would be helpful to have Mr Brown pointed out. Melville left the pier and discovered that the ship was delayed by fog far south-west down the Channel. It would not arrive until 9.00 p.m. He kept clear of the drunken brother all day, but at

9.00 p.m. both George Brown and Melville were on the tender that drew up alongside the big ship when it arrived. Hundreds of excited people crowded above them on the upper deck.

'There is my brother', said George Brown to me, 'him with the straw hat.' I looked up and called out to J.W. Brown, who thought I knew him, that I was coming up.[17]

Melville shinned up the ladder. Unfortunately J.W. Brown had not been approached by anyone at Durban, was mystified by any reference to Werner, and in his bewilderment handed him a passenger list. It showed no such man aboard.

Back in London, Melville was now the sceptic while his superiors, previously lukewarm, were all for offering a £1,000 reward in South Africa for anyone detecting the smuggling of arms. He persuaded them to delay this plan for a week, in which he wrote a report. The whole thing, he insisted, must be a hoax. Not a hoax with any point to it; just a meaningless time-waster. He listed his reasons, which could be summed up as a trail of red herrings which he had been following for far too long. And besides, the letters when minutely checked against the facts did contain inaccuracies.

The substance of this report was cabled to South Africa, and as a result a number of men were arrested. Somebody had been paying them ten pounds per letter. Exactly who this was remains unclear; Steinhauer, in his memoir, makes no reference to it and Michael Smith in *The Spying Game* says it was 'a freelance' making work for himself. The person had succeeded in wasting a good deal of British intelligence time.

Melville remained convinced that local police, the postal authorities and the coastguards should be alerted to suspect foreigners. Unlike the Home Office he did not see insurmountable legal and operational difficulties. He doggedly submitted reports suggesting at least an awareness-raising round robin, and the Home Office just as doggedly made objections; they had no authority over

police or coastguards, they could not legally allow mail interceptions, the police outside London would make a mess of it, and so
on. So these cases kept frustrating Melville, usually because he was
told about them long after the protagonists had moved on.

There were, for instance, in 1907 three Germans at Hartlepool
photographing gun emplacements and railway viaducts and the
coast at high and low water. They always took their film to Mr
Walburn, a chemist in the town, to be developed. These were
holiday snaps, they told the incurious chemist, for their friends
in Germany. After a while they were joined by another man
who sent some of the pictures back to be redeveloped. One
day the four of them had an argument, in German, in the shop.
Unnoticed by them, an Irishman was listening. He had lived
in Germany for years and after they left, he told Mr Walburn
that the men were spies, one of them being a superior officer
who was annoyed with the other three for having failed to get
a decent shot of a certain gun near a lighthouse. Mr Walburn
thought it over and later offered this information to the *Standard*
newspaper, who told the War Office. Melville visited the area.
But the Germans, and their photographs, had long gone.

Many times he found himself pursuing lines of enquiry that
had gone cold or been mishandled. In Trearder Bay, North Wales,
somebody told the coastguard that a couple of Germans staying
at Roberts' Hotel had hired a boat and a boatman and were
out every day taking soundings. Whoever reported this had the
wit to understand that depth soundings were useful to anyone
investigating submarine access to the bay.

Had Melville received this information, he would probably
have got aboard as a substitute boatman and watched and obtained
written proof before having his suspects arrested. The coastguard,
meaning well but completely uninstructed in these matters, put
on dress uniform before proceeding to the landing stage, where
he waited proudly decorated with badges and braid in full view
of the incoming party. The Germans saw him, panicked, and
told the boatman to turn around and sail along the coast, or go
wherever – just not here. He ignored their instructions, and when

the officer strode sternly aboard to question them they said they were taking scientific soundings of the temperatures of various waters. Then they scuttled off. Melville was disgusted.

> For the few evenings that those Germans were at the Roberts' Hotel, their demeanour was typically German. They overshadowed everyone in the dining room. But on arrival there, after seeing the naval officers, there was a marked change in their conduct. The other visitors noticed it. They ate their dinner in silence and sneaked away like mice. Evidently they were in mortal terror of arrest. Their names were never taken at the hotel.[18]

It was all highly unsatisfactory. The old MO3 was reinvented in February 1907 as 'MO5 – Special Duties Section, Interior Economy'[19] with a brief to assume 'duties of an executive nature' (i.e. breaking and entering, shadowing and eavesdropping as required) but it was still a tiny department operating partly in contravention of the law, in the interests of national defence, in an international political climate which the Admiralty and the Home Office, at least, did not seem fully to comprehend.

It was in this year that wheels seemed at last to be creaking into motion; at least, Prime Minister Asquith insisted that the Committee for Imperial Defence must enquire into the state of military preparedness for a German invasion. As things stood, forewarning seemed to be left to chance. A group of concerned civilians led by Colonel A'Court Repington had told Balfour, now leader of the opposition, that nothing systematic was being done. In Repington's view, mobilisation for an attack could be swift and unseen. German forces on land and sea were in such a state of readiness that movements of transport and men were familiar and could be explained away, and a big fleet was often concentrated in one place; and in an emergency Berlin could take a strong grip on communications.

The committee enquired, and did not agree. Germany could not mount an offensive out of the blue. Nonetheless, there was cause for concern, as the Admiralty had no effective espionage network abroad. Naval intelligence relied upon consuls or naval attachés for information and the only relevant British representation was at Hamburg. The Foreign Office (*Arturo* Peel notwithstanding) disapproved of the services' independent use of consular staff as spies. It followed that more agents must be actively recruited in the German ports.[20]

Colonel Edmonds, Kell's superior officer, was a fan of, indeed a friend of, the novelist William Le Queux. History has judged Le Queux a conspiracy theorist and a dreadful writer and he had his detractors at the time, but his books, such as *Spies of the Kaiser* and *The Invasion of 1910*, set off a whole new spy-paranoia bandwagon. They were popular in the decade before the outbreak of war and the *Daily Mail* encouraged the moral panic.

In his batty way, Le Queux was right. There were German agents at work in British ports. Steinhauer ran the network and managed to move around British coastal towns in the guise of a commercial traveller visiting them. He could pass for an American and at least once, according to Melville's memoir and his own, narrowly escaped arrest in England. But where Le Queux imagined thousands of fiendish Huns just biding their time before arising, like the dragons' teeth of legend, to slay the peaceful British, the real agents were numbered in tens. With few exceptions they were a sorry lot, desperate for the pittance they got in exchange for information that required sneaking, rather than skill, to obtain. Edmonds probably exaggerated the cunning of their masters too; Steinhauer, whose opinion of his military superiors was disparaging, opined that even intelligence officers in Berlin were selected because they were not bright enough for the army.[21]

Le Queux and the *Mail*, despite their outraged xenophobia, were right in another respect. Public fear of a threat from Germany reflected a perceptible shift in international relations between 1906 and 1909. Traditionally the British Empire had been safe thanks to a small, expert, professional army for deployment when required in the colonies, and an overwhelming navy that no other nation could match. The Germans had treaties with the Austrians and Italians, a big, well-armed and determined army, the Schlieffen Plan to mount a defensive line against the French in the west, and a comparatively insignificant navy. Nonetheless they felt encircled and threatened by the increasing *rapprochement* between the British, French and Russians.

When the British launched the first Dreadnought battleship in 1906 it was so much faster and better equipped than anything else that many in the Admiralty must have felt the British Navy was invincible. In fact it had set a new standard, so that Germany soon began building Dreadnoughts of its own while Britain was lumbered with the world's largest fleet of out-of-date ships. For the first time Germany was turning itself into a formidable naval power. Germany was also starting to pick fights, mainly with the French in North Africa.

Le Queux knew both Steinhauer and Melville; he had known Steinhauer for years. Ironically, the one English spy who did supply the Germans with useful information throughout the prewar years had been spotted in Chatham Dockyard in Steinhauer's company long ago in 1902,[22] and it was Le Queux who saw them together. Perhaps it was something about Steinhauer's false beard that alerted him. He hot-footed it to the police. Had he taken more notice of Steinhauer's companion, he could probably have saved Melville a good deal of trouble later. The man was Frederick Adolphus Schroeder, alias Gould, and he would remain undetected until the first months of 1914.

From 1907 onwards military and naval intelligence began, if not to collaborate, at least to talk to each other. Efforts were made to find new agents. Within a year agent R appears in the accounts. He is based in German south-west Africa; there are others named E and D. In 1908 a man called Rué, who worked for Courage's brewery in Hamburg, undertook to provide information for £250 a year for British intelligence. He took on the job under subtle pressure from his boss at the brewery in London.[23] There was another new man, H.C. Bywater, a British subject, naval expert and sometime *Daily Telegraph* correspondent, spying for the Navy at Kiel.[24]

It was time to get a feel for the territory. Mr and Mrs William Melville left for New York from Liverpool in the *Carpania* on 9 January 1909. They returned across the Atlantic not to England but to Hamburg. While in Germany Melville is said to have recruited a 'retired officer of the army of a friendly power' at £600 a year.[25] Melville also deployed one of his agents from Russia to join Byzewski in Berlin. The Navy organised a system whereby correspondence was sent by cipher from Germany via Holland to a London office, almost certainly Melville's.[26]

The network was far stronger, yet the fundamentals had not changed. The Navy faced the greatest threat, and had just £500 a year from the Treasury for Secret Service.[27] The army ran the espionage and counter-espionage service with meagre Foreign Office funds; the Foreign Office disapproved of consuls spying for the services ('Any further act of spying such as taking photographs &c of guns and forts would be treated as a breach of discipline,' wrote Sir Charles Hardinge fiercely, on discovering that a vice-consul had been paid direct by the Admiralty[28]) – while paying, for instance, a regular £1,000 p.a. for its own Secret Service to the Constantinople Embassy alone.[29] On top of this, the Post Office was not officially allowed to intercept letters; and only the police could make arrests. This shambles could not be allowed to continue.

Edmonds worked through Major-General Ewart to impress upon Viscount Haldane, Secretary of State for War, the need for a well-financed, co-ordinated system.[30] Haldane was a Liberal Imperialist. He was not an alarmist, but grasped the point that British defences were inadequate. He had instigated the Territorial Army which, if war broke out, would become part of the British Expeditionary Force, and his efforts would be wasted if swift military action depended on under-resourced, chaotic intelligence about what the enemy was up to. Under his influence the Committee for Imperial Defence decided, late in 1909, upon reform.

Melville and the overseas agents would remain within MO5 under Major MacDonogh, but would be part of a secret and unnamed 'Secret Service Bureau' answerable to both the Admiralty and the War Office through the Directorate of Military Operations. SSB (as it will henceforth be called here) would continue with counter-espionage efforts while paying more attention to active recruitment of agents abroad. The structure appears to have grown out of a report submitted by Edmonds. He had spent two years with the Committee on Imperial Defence compiling a history of the Russo-Japanese War,[31] and was already working with Melville. In the file is a document dated 8 October 1908 which sets out his ideas:[32]

1. System required:

(a) in Germany, based on a centre [*sic*] in Switzerland, Denmark and Poland, to watch army and report concentrations and deployments
(b) in England, to mark down spies and agents in peace and to remain in German lines and spy on troops if they land.

(a) may be carried out by paid agents gradually collected; (b) by police, post-office officials, custom-house officers &c with a few paid agents. Co-operation of the civil authorities is essential, and authority for this must be obtained…

4… It is probably best to employ a first class detective under direction of an officer to collect and work agents abroad.

He noted that the Official Secrets Act must be amended. 'At present we cannot arrest a spy or search his habitation without consent of Attorney General which takes any time to obtain.' Vernon Kell, like Vincent thirty years before, had already done enough creative research to take on this new post and drive it forward. On Edmonds's recommendation the head of counter-espionage in Britain ('b' above) would be the multi-lingual, half-Polish Vernon Kell.

SSB's recruitment of an agent network overseas ('a') would be the responsibility of a retired naval officer called Cumming. The credibility of the entire system depended on his finding good local, preferably indigenous, agents, for while the Foreign Office paid, Sir Charles Hardinge remained adamant that no espionage must ever be traceable to British embassies or consulates abroad.

That was the theory. In fact Cumming took a while to settle in, not through any fault of his own but because he had been set an impossible task. He and Kell were to share an office in Victoria Street, on the north side at No.64; the front man there (who unlike Melville was rarely present, but merely rented the place) was a retired police inspector called Drew, also known as Sketchley or D. From the start Cumming was unhappy with the restricting, nine-to-five implications of this. As for foreign agents, perhaps the naïve majority on the committee assumed that MO5 would cheerfully hand Cumming the list of contacts and leave him to get on with it. To understand how unlikely this was, we have to remember Jenkinson. Rule one: a case officer does not reveal the identity of his agents.

Cumming came aboard late in October 1909. By this time several new agents had been recruited. One of them, initially paid for by the Admiralty, appears as 'HC' in the accounts of August 1909 and, like E, V (presumably Rué, generally called Verrue), M, L, B and D, is receiving regular payments.[33] HC *could* have been Hely Claeys but in asserting that it was H.C. Bywater, this author defers to Alan Judd:

> There are diary references on 2nd March 1910 to the recruitment
> and debriefing of HC (Bywater's initials)[34]

The diary is Cumming's – payments six months before would seem to contradict the assumption about HC's identity, yet H.C. Bywater almost certainly was the man at Kiel, for

> In his little-known book, *Strange Intelligence* (Constable 1931) he
> gives convincing descriptions of his penetration of German dock-

yards during 42 months of spying (although not claiming in that book the experiences as his own, there is strong evidence that they were…)[35]

In November of 1909 it was agreed that the Admiralty would henceforth submit its bill to the War Office and both sets of accounts would be amalgamated in advance of submission for payment by the Foreign Office. This would avoid duplication. The SSB was in business.

TEN

THE BUREAU

Information may hibernate in our minds for decades until the moment comes when we can retrieve it to our advantage. On the other hand, an inescapable fact from the past may arise unbidden and unwelcome, representing a threat.

In 1902, when Melville was in his last eighteen months of office as Superintendent of Special Branch and the Boer War was drawing to a close, the Home Office was approached by the German Embassy with a request for information. In March of that year Melville filed a report on the object of their enquiry, Farlow Kaulitz. Kaulitz was a journalist born of a German father and English mother, and brought up in Germany. He had spent three years in a Prussian prison for *lèse majesté* and being rude about Bismarck in the *Basler Nachrichten* and had been expelled from France in 1898 because, as that paper's Paris correspondent, he challenged the French Government over the Dreyfus affair.[1] Interviewed by police at Victoria Station on arrival, he seems to have been perfectly frank about all this, and was allowed to go about his business. He took furnished rooms at first in 25 Bessborough Street, Pimlico, and worked as a journalist. Quite soon he had set himself up as a continental press agency. He employed a couple of assistants to hang around Fleet Street from 8.00 p.m. until 4.00 a.m. getting items from the wire services and newspaper offices – especially concerning the war in South Africa. When a newsworthy item became available Kaulitz's man would hand it to his assistant, who would leap onto his bicycle and race back to Bessborough Street with the wire.

This early information gave Kaulitz a good start and pretty soon he was able to take a whole Pimlico house at 31 St George's

Square and install an expensive Exchange Telegraph Column Printing Instrument. This meant simultaneous transmission direct from a big agency and Kaulitz had prospered ever since; so much so that by the end of 1901 he had moved into 44 Temple Chambers, Temple Avenue, on the City borders. The building backs onto King's Bench Walk, within the enclave of Temple, a foundation of ancient origin where barristers from two Inns of Court (the Inner Temple and the Middle Temple) have their chambers.

It was Special Branch practice to intercept mail or telegrams which might be of interest, and since the German Embassy wanted to know about Kaulitz, Melville instructed his officers to get hold of any messages to or from South Africa. He was interested to discover that normal GPO deliveries excluded Temple Chambers. Messages in the immediate vicinity were instead received and distributed by the Eastern Telegraph Company of Electra House, Finsbury Pavement. Inspectors Quinn and Walsh called at the company's offices only to be firmly informed by the Assistant Secretary that 'no information could be given respecting telegrams or those who send or receive them'.[2] Since Special Branch was in no position legally to demand access to another person's mail, that was that. The War Office, to which Quinn next had recourse, informed him that it was improbable that Kaulitz could be getting cables direct without attracting the attention of the military authorities. There the trail ended, and whether or not the Government passed on all the information to the German Embassy is unknown. Melville noticed the security of Temple, however, and retained it for future reference.

In 1906 his son James set out upon the path which would lead him to political prominence. After an unpromising start (he had left school to join the Eagle Insurance Company like his siblings) he had worked for several years for the rising barrister Douglas Hogg. Now, still only twenty-one, he was called to the Bar of the Middle Temple. The buildings of this Inn are slightly west of the grassy square, shaded by majestic trees, that is at the heart of the Inner Temple.

In October of 1909 Cumming noted at a meeting that Edmonds and MacDonogh 'said they were going to keep M (the best man we have at present) in an office of his own, to which letters could be addressed'. Melville's friend at the Royal Mail, Henry Freeman Pannett, whose two future sons-in-law had been witnesses at Sidney Reilly's wedding, retired in 1908. From now on, how sure could Melville be that his own correspondence would not be tampered with?

After five years at 25 Victoria Street, the office of W.G. Morgan moved to the more discreet environment of Temple Avenue in December 1908. Temple Avenue was not isolated by its postal service alone. Only yards from the bustle of Fleet Street, it was close enough to the gates of Temple itself to be frequented mainly by lawyers who kept regular hours. Unfamiliar faces were remarked by beadles.

In October also, Melville's old acquaintance Sidney Reilly paid the first of several visits to London from St Petersburg where he was now based. 'Based' is the word to use. Reilly was one of those rare people for whom everywhere is a jumping-off point to the next opportunity. Reilly was staying in Rachkovskii's favourite London haunt – the extremely grand Hotel Cecil next to the Savoy, a few hundred metres along the river from the Temple. He took advantage of his temporary residence to regularise the change of name by deed poll which he had begun before his precipitate departure from England in 1899. He also re-formed the Ozone Preparations Company, which would be run from an office above Saqui and Lawrence, the jewellers, at 97 Fleet Street.

Two days after he filed the deed poll application from his temporary address at the Cecil, it seems that there arose, unbidden and unwelcome, a face from the past. A young woman called Louisa Lewis had been working at the Hotel Cecil for four years. On the evening of 25 October 1908 she was seen, dressed in outdoor clothes and hat, at the bottom of the hotel's imposing marble staircase speaking to a man.

Later, when a search was mounted and the authorities notified, it would have gone unnoticed that Louisa Lewis was the daughter of

Alfred Lewis, manager at the London and Paris Hotel, Newhaven; or that she had been working there when the Reverend Thomas was found dead, and had met 'Dr T.W. Andrew' who signed his death certificate. Neither the death nor the young doctor would easily have been forgotten by a young woman.

The man at the foot of the stairs answered Sidney Reilly's description perfectly. Louisa Lewis was never seen again.[3]

The Ozone Preparations Company, managed in Rosenblum's (Sidney Reilly's) absence by his partner William Calder, ran for three years and was wound up in 1911. The choice of Fleet Street for its office may be significant; like Farlow Kaulitz earlier in the decade, Sidney Reilly understood that early knowledge can be converted into hard cash. He was at this time working for the St Petersburg agent for Blohm and Voss of Hamburg; in the course of chasing contracts he would place information, and mis-information, in a St Petersburg newspaper. The English wire services at the time physically received news at Fleet Street offices and hardly anywhere else.[4]

The British Secret Service was also aware how much the slant of international news could influence diplomatic, as well as commercial, events. A 1909 letter to the Ambassador in Peking proves that the Foreign Office subsidised Reuters' office there in order to offer an alternative source of information to the German news going in and out of China.

Technically the Secret Service also had to keep up with the quickening pace of change. In 1906 Colonel Davies had been a delegate at an early international conference on wireless telegraphy. MacDonogh, besides being a former barrister, was a qualified engineer, and in the years leading up to the war would make it his business to understand advances in the field. Fortunately for Melville, the spy network he would eventually discover made little use of the new technology. Before the First World War, agents put it all down on paper.

Melville was unchallenged as Chief Detective of the new SSB. At one of Cumming's first meetings with Edmonds and Kell in November of 1909 he noted that D – Drew – was already out of favour, to be used as little as possible as a matter of policy. Edward 'Tricky' Drew ('time was when Edward Drew was the handsomest man in the Criminal Investigation Department of Scotland Yard', sighed a biographer[5]) had probably found it hard to adjust. A lifetime in the Metropolitan Police did not necessarily make a man suitable for secret work. For one thing, he might keep on gossiping to his old cronies down the road. Melville never had that problem because he had made professional discretion a habit throughout his life; it had helped him maintain his authority. Nor could an ex-policeman necessarily understand the political and diplomatic niceties of counter-espionage work – unless, like Melville, he had already become familiar with highly placed civil servants and the everyday international intrigue of people at the top. And then, an SSB detective needed to be something of a self-starter; he needed to know when to show initiative, and when to hold fire and consult a senior officer. A lifetime in a hierarchy can undermine independence of thought.

Cumming noted two other policy decisions made at the same meeting. No other detectives were to be employed just yet. And M was to be present at all meetings with 'rascals' (suspects), presumably because his years of experience in dealing with criminals gave him a nose for them. Cumming had not yet met M. He would not meet him for some time. When an appointment was arranged (at Edmonds's house) Melville failed to turn up – 'disappointed to find on my arrival that a note had been left for me saying that the authorities had decided that the meeting had better be postponed' wrote Cumming.[6] MacDonogh was determined that Melville should not tell Cumming who the existing foreign agents were.

This unwillingness to share information was indicative of a deeper awkwardness afflicting the infant SSB. The Navy was sidelined, and Cumming with it. Although Kell and MacDonogh appeared friendly enough they were united in treating Cumming (who had been quietly working for naval intelligence for some years) as a junior partner. Worse: Cumming was older than Kell, and stouter, and up from the country (he had spent the past decade working on boom defences in the Solent). Where Kell was multilingual and thirty-six, Cumming was fifty and – although he spoke French – was only now beginning to learn German. Where Kell was urbane, impatient, and his talents obvious, Cumming was original, modest, patient and a clever engineer whose overriding enthusiasm was for new boats, planes and dirigibles. They were the hare and the tortoise.

The military men held onto their contacts. Bearing in mind point 4 of Kell's report,

> It is probably best to employ a first class detective under direction of an officer to collect and work agents abroad.

Kell's chief operative, Melville, should have been working equally for both of them. His experience in many respects was unmatched by any senior officer and this is acknowledged by his gradual re-invention not as mere M, but 'Mr M', as Long and others came to call him. There is affectionate respect in their attitude to him.

Melville had personally sanctioned most of the MO5 agents overseas who were now supposed to be handed over to Cumming, but Cumming waited in vain; MacDonogh was playing power games. And naval intelligence had no counterpart network of civilian spies to offer him, because the Admiralty had been employing consular staff. But that policy had decisively changed following a rap over the knuckles from the Foreign Office.[7]

In the first months MacDonogh was inappropriately controlling, expecting Cumming to be ever-present at Drew's empty Victoria Street office where nothing happened and there were no records or facilities. Unsurprisingly, Cumming was soon agitating to be permitted to move from Victoria Street to a headquarters of his own (six months later, in March 1910, he briefly relocated to Ashley Mansions in Vauxhall Bridge Road prior to a more permanent move to Whitehall Court). In November of 1909 he was allowed to meet his first foreign agent, B – Byzewski, who was already working in Berlin – but was only reluctantly permitted to pay him.[8]

Long, who had been valuable abroad, was back in England working for Melville. Again, this was all about the War Office maintaining control. In the August of 1910 the Admiralty showed that it was just as capable of petty behaviour when it prohibited coastguards from communicating with Kell.[9] Yet over the years the SSB did become a more collaborative service, albeit one that eventually evolved into two separate services, headed respectively by Kell and Cumming, dealing with home and foreign intelligence. That it did so owed more to Cumming's patience, sharpness and determination than to any unprompted generosity on the part of Kell or MacDonogh.[10]

With no espionage network so far uncovered, yet a certainty that systematic spying was going on, Melville's investigations had to start from a wide base and narrow their focus to likely individuals. Kell had no problem with this; he was an orderly fellow who dealt well with card indexes and lists and his report had recommended

11. The registration of aliens which was enforced by Act of Parliament in 1798 and 1804 must be revived.

Conveniently, spies in Britain before the First War seem almost without exception to have been foreigners. If they sounded British and looked it, they usually turned out to have (exactly like Kell himself, as it happened) foreign parents. Inconveniently, the information-gathering must be unofficial because Parliament had not given the go-ahead for a register of aliens. So when Kell set out to compile his register of immigrants, rather than visitors, to Britain, he cast his net extremely wide. Nearly all of them would be safe. But among them would be people with something to hide – people subject to blackmail by the authorities in their own country; or people who would do anything for money; or (rarely) genuine patriots of another country. Most often, the tasks demanded of them seemed so harmless that the people themselves cannot have realised what terrifyingly deep water they might be stepping into.

It would be Melville's task to investigate individual foreigners who, in his judgement and Kell's, were up to no good. This represented a new departure because most of his work to date had been about investigating suspicious visitors and scaring them off. If he did uncover a network, in his view he should do exactly what he had done with the anarchists of the Tottenham Court Road: make them nervous without letting them know what he knew, then leave them alone so that he could learn more about them if he wanted to and pick them off if need be. This approach made efficient use of scant resources. It had worked for the Deuxième Bureau and Special Branch twenty years ago, and it would work again.

Kell kept memoranda of his activities in the first summer of SSB's existence. M, L, and K (as Kell was known) met quite regularly at the Temple Avenue office. Melville's plan for a round-robin was bettered, for in June 1910, Kell himself made a tour of chief constables to impress on them the need for vigilance. Henry Dale Long was encouraged to join the Legion of Frontiersmen to find men who would supplement the post-office and police authorities as the 'few paid agents' of Kell's report, which at this stage remained the blueprint for activity. M hopped across to Ireland to investigate the sister of a deceased soldier called O'Brien (she was trying to sell plans of Portsmouth), and reported on a German who seemed to frighten all the foreign waiters around Folkestone. At Harrow School a drill instructor called Greening was under surveillance.

On the evening of 10 July 1910, a Sunday, M was to meet naval Captain Roy Regnart in Brussels. Regnart had been set to work with Cumming on the orders of Admiral Bethell, head of the Department of Naval Intelligence. There was evidently a 'traitor' in that city. The word is in inverted commas in Kell's memorandum. The information had come to Kell via Cumming, whom Kell did not yet take entirely seriously, only slowly perceiving that Cumming's preoccupation with dirigibles and other transport wizardry might be more to the point than it appeared. (The first plane had flown the Channel exactly a year earlier.)

If the Brussels lead proved genuine and Melville required an arrest to be made while they were in Belgium, Superintendent Quinn was on standby to provide a detective at short notice. On Wednesday 13 July everyone was back in England and Kell noted:

> Meeting with C and Regnart in C's room at 11am. Regnart gave a full account of the Brussels affair, which ended in a fiasco.

The following day:

> Met M in his offices at 10am and he gave me an account of the Brussels affair. He seems to think they were taken in by Rouveroy and that no more confidence should be reposed in him. I told M to send in a written report.[11]

They would discover that in Brussels

> …there were two very dubious agencies… which make a business of prying into the military secrets of all the big powers and selling information to the highest bidder.[12]

They would use them, too; but they needed their own man on the spot. Henry Dale Long, now working to Melville, would be relocated to Brussels for a second time in 1911. A continental posting was what Regnart wanted for himself. He was a trouble-some colleague although he held Melville in high regard. In the course of his absence for the 'fiasco',

> Cumming discovered yet more examples of his having given to agents addresses of his own for communications that should have been sent to Cumming. The trip, meanwhile, was disappointingly inconclusive but in one respect surprising: Regnart formed a high opinion of Melville and his methods, the tactical subtlety and pen-etration of which may be gauged by the following: 'He [Regnart] says M is much bolder than he when dealing with strangers. He goes right up to them and peers in their faces.'[13]

It would become apparent that for Cumming's purposes, spies in the inland capitals of Europe were less important than people who could survey the north German coast with an expert eye. This coastline of shifting sands was almost impenetrable of access from the sea without recent intelligence of sandbanks, mines, harbour works and submarines. The Admiralty were particularly interested in Borkum as a possible landing place because it was sufficiently distant from the *Hochseeflotte*'s base at Wilhelmshavn. Unfortunately, in August of 1910 the Germans would scent British interest in Borkum when a couple of amateur spies, Brandon and Trench, were caught snooping and taking pictures in the area. They were naval officers doing some inept detective work for the Admiralty (not SSB; Regnart acting on his own initiative) while on leave, and they were jailed in Germany.[14]

As this embarrassment must be followed by a tit-for-tat arrest, the first alleged spy to make headlines was a cheerful German soldier cadet who probably meant no harm. His capture had nothing to do with Melville at all.

In the summer of 1910 Lt Siegfried Helm, at twenty-one a very junior engineer officer of the 21st Nassau Regiment, visited England for a month. One of his friends had already been to London and had enjoyed a brief flirtation with a Miss Wodehouse. Helm wrote to her at her London address; he would appreciate her company on his visit to the capital. The reply that reached him in his Tooting boarding-house (the only people there were old ladies, he had complained, 'from 45 to 70 years old') came from Fratton. Miss Wodehouse had moved there with a family she was working for.[15] Helm had told her he wanted to see Chatham and Aldershot and Portsmouth while he was in England. She told him Fratton was very close to Portsmouth, so he came to stay at the house next door for a few days.

Miss Wodehouse, probably missing her former beau, was impatient with Helm from the start. He sketched everything – forts, ships, anything he could see around Portsmouth – showed her the pictures and then said winningly 'You won't tell, will you?' Miss Wodehouse did not find this romantic, or even

interesting. He was an overgrown schoolboy. However, she probably wanted to enlarge her circle of male acquaintances locally
and Helm unknowingly represented an opportunity. Following
a tedious afternoon in his company she walked, emboldened by
self-righteousness, right into the local barracks and spoke to a
senior officer. He and a colleague watched Lt Helm in the days
that followed and saw more sketching and some behaviour they
interpreted as furtive. They stopped him and asked questions, and
Lt Helm was detained for a couple of days in the Officers' Mess
at Fort Purbrook, where everyone was very hospitable, according to an anxious note he wrote to his betrayer. His capture
seems to have been made with embarrassed good humour; the
officers did it because they had been told to be vigilant rather
than because they saw much harm in the young man.

Meanwhile, they applied for permission to charge him. ('Captain
Bonham Carter came up from Portsmouth with all necessary
evidence and documents about Lt Helm's espionage', wrote Kell
sternly in his diary.)[16] The War Office permission, granted with
alacrity in view of the Brandon and Trench fiasco, was implemented by Inspector Abel of the Hampshire police. Lt Helm was
driven to Fareham Police Station by Lt Salmond, 'the police following close behind in a trap'. He was charged with attempting to
take a plan of Fort Widley for communication to a foreign power,
a felony under the 1889 Official Secrets Act, and appeared in
court in the second week of September 1910.[17] News of his arrest
was leaked to the *Daily Express* before the court appearance; the
Admiralty were highly displeased and summoned Kell to explain
himself. He told them airily that '…it was an excellent thing that
the arrest should become known as soon as possible as it might
have a soothing effect across the water'.[18] After the first court
hearing, the conservative German *Kreuz Zeitung* said indulgently
that 'the temptation was great, during his free time which was not
devoted to the study of the English language, to practise technical
drawing from nature' and fancied the young man reclining idly in
the grass drawing, quite by chance, picturesque naval installations.
The writer then pulled himself together to face facts: 'two real

British spies' were in German custody, so Helm would probably be in for the high jump. The *National Zeitung* pronounced the arrest 'less of a mistake than a somewhat malicious revenge'.[19]

Helm, 'a young man of soldierly appearance', appeared a couple of times at Fareham Police Court to packed houses, with admission by ticket only.[20] The prosecution insisted that the sketches could be 'worked up'. Chief witness Miss Wodehouse accused a newspaper reporter of tricking her into giving an interview by claiming to be from the War Office. The German Embassy had engaged the famous barrister Travers Humphreys to put Helm's case: that he was just a young pup, keen on playing soldiers, and obsessively keen on putting things down in his notebook. These included a description of a vicar on a train and measurements of the distance between his chest of drawers and the bed. There were also poems and stories. For the prosecution, Colonel Twiss of the General Staff sneered that he would omit translating the poetry to the court. The public gallery tittered. A former officer from the boarding house at Streatham had heard from Helm about his impending trip to Chatham. The evidence was mounting up strongly on the defence side, and when Helm was bailed to appear at Winchester Assizes the more serious part of the charge, about intent to communicate to a foreign power, was dropped; he was now charged with a misdemeanour only. His appearances at Winchester in November resulted in a guilty verdict and a binding-over. He was free to go back to Germany. The judge told him he hoped he would leave with a good impression of British justice.[21] No doubt he did, although Colonel Twiss may have put him off keeping a notebook for ever. Kell travelled back to London in the same railway compartment as Helm and his father and noted that they did not say much to each other.

Thanks to Helm, the weaknesses of the 1889 Official Secrets Act had become apparent. Work to amend it had begun, but had not passed through Parliament before the first genuine spy was unmasked. He was working for Steinhauer, known to him as 'R.H. Petersssen', in Rotterdam, but he was barely more professional than Helm.

His name was Dr Max Schultz.[22] He was a thirty-one-year-old doctor of philosophy claiming (falsely) to be an officer in a German Hussar regiment, and in the summer of 1911 he took a houseboat at Plymouth, hoisted the German flag, and proceeded, with another man as companion, to entertain young naval officers. The wine flowed freely and quite a little social scene developed, although the sailors preferred not to talk shop. One of the guests was a local solicitor, Mr Duff, who arrived with his friend Mr Tannen. They enjoyed Schultz's company, although he often turned the conversation to matters of naval defence. Finally Schultz took Duff and Tannen aside. Schultz was a correspondent for a continental 'Government' newspaper, he said; it would pay well for accurate and specific information on naval topics but he couldn't very well collect this himself. As a German, he could hardly approach his young English officer friends because they would think he was spying. But an English solicitor – now he would be answered freely enough. How about it? He would like Duff to submit reports from here in Plymouth and Tannen from Chatham, Portsmouth and other ports along the South Coast. The monthly retainers offered were extremely generous: £60 to Duff and £50 to Tannen. As to the material, he emphasised again that accuracy was paramount.

Duff and Tannen promised to think about it, did so, and sensibly approached the police who alerted the War Office. Kell and Melville proceeded in the time-honoured way. They told the helpful solicitor and his friend to go ahead and accept, and to keep them posted. Duff signed a 'contract' with the 'newspaper' which Schultz forwarded to a Mr Neumann (one of Steinhauer's postbox addresses) at Walthamstow. Duff then received long lists of queries such as

What ships of the 3rd and 2nd divisions of the Home Fleet were put out of service on July 25, or about the end of July, or have reduced their crews, and the reason for so doing? How many officers and men are still aboard, and why is the programme altered?[23]

Kell and Melville allowed the correspondence to continue while feeding Duff with duff information. At the end of August Kell, supported by a posse of policemen, approached Schultz on the houseboat and identified himself. Schultz was found in possession of a cypher, incriminating letters, and banknotes sent from Germany. He was charged with attempting to procure Duff to commit an offence against Subsection 2, Section 1 of the Official Secrets Act of 1889;[24] at the beginning of November he was found guilty at Exeter Assizes and sentenced to twenty-one months' imprisonment.

The case is interesting for several reasons. It was the last major case under the old Official Secrets Act, which required proof of *intent* to spy and warrants to arrest and search which must be signed by the Attorney General himself. And as usual the press reports indicated that only the police were involved. A detective sergeant was credited with intercepting the mail. This was Secret Service policy so that Kell, Melville, and War Office interference with the Royal Mail could remain undercover.[25]

Most importantly, Schultz's correspondence provided proof that a German network was in existence. Kell had been following leads on this for a long time, and most of them led nowhere. In his diary for 27 July 1910, over a year before the Schultz trial, Kell had noted:

Called on the Home Office and saw Sir E. Troup, who said he would get the necessary warrant signed as soon as possible for watching the following addresses:
1. FA, 74 Poste Restante Berlin C25
2. Berlin. C Postlagernd C 25
3. F Keldermans 98 Boite Postale Aix-la-Chapelle.

The warrant was signed the same afternoon.

'Watching the following addresses' meant the interception of letters to those places. A couple of weeks later MO5 required copies of further letters and telegrams. The terms were minutely scrutinised before the GPO would accept responsibility. They were within their rights to insist, under the old Act, upon a specific warrant signed at the highest level.

> I took the matter over to the Home Office in the afternoon, and Mr Churchill being on leave I left the warrant with Mr Byrne, who said he would ask Sir Edward Grey to sign it that afternoon.[26]

The 'Neumann' address used by Schultz was that of a German barber called Kronauer whom Steinhauer had recruited to receive mail and post it onward. Soon afterwards came the discovery of a second clearing-house for mail run by another barber, an Englishman born in Hoxton to German parents whose name was Karl Gustav Ernst. There are at least two versions of how the network was revealed and both are probably true. The first is the official version compiled at some time after 1931 from SSB files. It was released by the Public Record Office in November 2002 and reads in part:

> In August 1911 Francis Holstein, proprietor of the Peacock Hotel, Trinity, Leith, received a letter from Germany, asking for information about the feeling of this country with regard to a war with Germany and its preparedness for such a war. This letter was discussed in a railway carriage in the presence of an officer of the security service. Enquiries were made, and it was discovered that Holstein had received two previous letters of the same nature in June and August 1909 and that they were signed 'F Reimers, [an alias of Steinhauer] Brauerstrasse, Potsdam.' This name and address were put under special censorship on the 14th September 1911, and by this means the ramifications of Steinhauer's organisation were brought to light.[27]

On the other hand, why was the officer sharing a railway compartment with a German hotelkeeper, and presumably at least one other German, unless the man was already under surveillance? Leith is the port for Edinburgh, opening onto the Firth of Forth.

A different account has a German naval officer in the entourage of the Kaiser being watched at a London address.[28] Late one evening this man drove away in mufti from the house where he was staying. He was followed, again by an unnamed shadow, to 'a small shop, already closed for the night' where 'the side door opened as soon as the car stopped, and he went straight in without knocking'.[29] This was at 402a Caledonian Road, where Ernst was getting a regular £1 a month from Germany.

Armed with a warrant to copy all incoming and outgoing mail, Kell and Melville could collect the names of correspondents in England who were in contact with Steinhauer's cover addresses abroad. They could also manipulate the intelligence trickle from Ernst and Kronauer however they wished.

As it turned out, Ernst's shop would gain some traffic after the 'Neumann' (Kronauer) address was exposed by the Schultz trial. Ernst's fee would rise to £1 10s a week, plus expenses and an occasional 'honorarium' of £5.

Soon afterwards there came a third lead, this time to a friend of Ernst and Kronauer called Kruger living in Mountain Ash, a small town far inland in South Wales. Steinhauer generally had no interest in Germans outside the main ports and London, but through this contact he succeeded in recruiting Kruger's nephew – a serving British naval officer called Ireland. By now SSB were aware, thanks to mail interceptions, that Steinhauer was in Britain:

A report dated December 1911 states that a German officer was found to be travelling through various counties and devoting much attention to maps and plans, but that he returned hurriedly to Germany before sufficient evidence could be collected to justify his arrest. Evidence that this was Steinhauer is to be found in the 'Reimers' letters. He evidently came to London and saw Ernst and Kronauer and then went north. On 30th December he wired to Kronauer from Rothesay under the name 'MacMillan', telling him to keep his letters until his return, and he wired again from Glasgow on 2nd January saying he would be in town on the third. He wrote to Kruger from Germany on 13th January saying that he expected to return before the end of the month, and to Kronauer on 22nd January he stated that he had left in a hurry as he feared he was being shadowed.

On 23rd February 1912, after the arrest of Ireland, Steinhauer wrote
to Ernst, urging him to be very cautious in communicating with
Kruger, who would be watched...[30]

Steinhauer used not only Reimers and Peterssen as aliases, but
also Stein, Schmidt, Reimann, Tornow, Torner, Dinger, Tobler,
Fritsches and others. He also used disguise, and would dress up as
an elderly solicitor from the continent ('big round glasses, black
suit and a hand bag beyond suspicion') bearing information
about a huge inheritance owed to lost German relatives in an
English port. There he would accost a local policeman.

> It was easy for them to get a list of the foreigners in the town,
> and just as agreeable – with the reward in view – to meet me an
> evening or two later in the corner of some restaurant with a bottle
> of whisky and a few nice cigars to help along the discussion.[31]

This, before about 1910, led him into the British homes of a
number of people who were afterwards persuaded, by a cautious
follow-up letter, to work for the Fatherland. Kronauer had been
on his books since about 1908 and Ernst since 1910.[32]

Kell fitted in. If he needed a signature or a decision he could
wriggle swiftly upstream through the bureaucracy to the highest
level because he had been to the right schools, came of the right
class. (It has been suggested that he may have known Churchill
at Sandhurst.)[33] His predecessors in military intelligence, Davies
and Trotter, had both moved on and were generals now. He, however, would never willingly release the reins of the Secret Service
Bureau. It was a fascinating job, although he was frustrated by
officials who were not, as he was, professionally vigilant. When,
for instance, in October 1910 he discovered that the Lepel Wireless
Company employee at Slough who habitually sent messages to
Berlin was also able to intercept wireless communications from the
Admiralty, he pointed out the security risk to the GPO Wireless
Officer who 'did not think any harm could arise'.[34]

Kell owed a great deal to Melville. The older man, lacking the social background required for acceptance into the Edwardian mandarin class, taught him tradecraft and discretion, patience and wariness. Melville also had a sense of proportion that Kell seems sometimes to have lacked: mostly, as Kell's journal shows, his reports on 'suspects' were negative.

Kell, however, had an agenda that transcended petty issues of guilt or innocence. He was busy grinding down opposition to a register of aliens. Since this was not so far permissible he made do with an alien returns form of his own devising, which was circulated to chief constables in the winter of 1910-11. There were a few grumbles and raised eyebrows; but this, with other lists compiled from regional or professional records (for instance, German zinc-workers in Hartlepool) and individual reports from members of the public, formed the basis of an index that held up to 30,000 names by the start of the war.[35] The idea was sound, given the political circumstances, though the form it took seems somehow less so.

The Central Registry was a card index in which the subjects were classified on a bizarre scale that ran from AA for the least dangerous to BB for the most. AA was Absolutely Anglicised or Absolutely Allied, denoting somebody who was definitely supportive of the British cause. A was Anglicised or Allied, i.e. supportive. AB was Anglo-Boche —allegiances unclear, but probably pro-British. BA was Boche-Anglo – allegiances also unclear, but probably pro-German. B was Boche, i.e. hostile. Where a subject's hostility to the British cause was not in doubt, he or she was graded BB, or Bad Boche.[36]

Extra staff were gradually being brought on board. And then there was the technology.

Last week I asked M to look out for a good pocket-camera, which I think is indispensable for our work. M now writes that he considers the *Ensignette* camera (with an extra good lens) is the best for

our purposes. I went to the Stores to inspect one and I quite agree.
I have therefore authorised M to get one, price £3 10s.[37]

Expenditure for a second typewriter was sanctioned (in the
new year of 1911, there would be 'a lady type-writer', Miss D.
Westmacott, at £5 a month)[38] and a telephone line was installed
for SSB purposes at Melville's home in Clapham. The Bureau
was becoming a force to reckon with.

In January 1911, Kell joined Melville on the City borders.
Cumming was now working out of his wife's flat at Ashley
Mansions in the Vauxhall Bridge Road.[39] Kell and his assistant
Captain Stanley-Clarke would henceforth work from 3 Paper
Buildings, just a stone's throw from Melville's office and within
the security of the Inner Temple. As an empire-building ploy the
Central Registry was a work of genius. After all, it would take not
only bigger better offices but an awful lot of M's time to investigate
30,000 people. But the need for dozens of underlings does not
seem to have occurred to Kell at first. It was March before he had
a long talk with Melville and 'impressed upon him the necessity
of our being more energetic in the future, and that I expected
him to think out new schemes for getting hold of intelligence'.[40]
The slightly panicky call to action is unsurprising. An important friend of Kell's had recently informed him that there were
20,000 German agents in Britain ready to arise within twenty-
four hours.[41] Four more days passed, reason prevailed, and he
suggested to Melville that pressure of work demanded two more
detectives. Melville wasn't keen. Detectives talk to each other, he
pointed out, 'and consequently all our business would become
common property at the Yard'; and it would be almost impossible
to find men with 'knowledge and experience of the world, and
full of discretion and tact'. He talked Kell into looking, instead, for
retired men not above the rank of sergeant. In June, only weeks
before the Schultz investigation began, the first man was hired: his
name was Regan. He was to be known as R.

The law was about to be adjusted in SSB's favour. July 1911
was the month of the Agadir crisis, when a German gunboat

off Morocco made German hostility towards France only too apparent. Taking advantage of the nervous mood, Viscount Haldane (whose briefing material included a report by Kell) spoke on the Amendment to the Official Secrets Act in the Lords on 25 July:

> The main change which the Bill made was a change of procedure. In order to convict anyone under the Official Secrets Act of 1889 it was necessary to prove a purpose of wrongfully obtaining information… That was often very difficult to prove.[42]

The Amendment represented more than 'a change of procedure'; under its provisions someone sketching a fort, for instance, would have to prove his innocence – for guilt could legitimately be deduced 'from the circumstances of the case or his conduct or his known character as proved'.[43] Haldane pre-empted criticism by citing a precedent for this in the Prevention of Crimes Act 1871: 'loitering with intent'. Objectors could have pointed out that treason and espionage were capital offences in time of war, and therefore different in degree, but such arguments would not wash when the threat of invasion seemed so vivid. Haldane also asserted that currently

> the places which were barred from public access were too few… Therefore it was proposed to widen the definition of those places and to give the Secretary of State power to be exercised in times of emergency to proscribe other places.[44]

Finally, if the Bill were passed, warrants for search and arrest would be available from a magistrate – not only from the Attorney General as at present and as still pertained during the Schultz case. The Amendment went through in due course. In the following year at the Newington Sessions William Melville took the oath as a Justice of the Peace for the County of London.

ELEVEN

Drift to War

James Melville was a surprising young man. He was an impressive barrister, well liked, and interesting work came his way.

Like his father, he was proud of his Irish background. Unlike his father, he had an ambivalent relationship with the Establishment. This extended beyond his professional life. It was true that Sarah Tugander, the girl he was seeing, was private secretary to the next leader of the Conservative party, but she was neither Irish nor Conservative; she was the daughter of Russian Jewish immigrants and both she and James Melville were, of all things, Fabian socialists. Twenty-five years before, his father would have been lurking outside their homes making notes in a little black book.

James was beginning to find work through his left-wing contacts, and he was part of the legal team that defended two refugees accused after the Houndsditch Murders. The murders, in December 1910, had been followed by a pursuit that ended in the Siege of Sidney Street. This notorious siege, despite its political overtones and the newsworthy presence of Winston Churchill at the showdown, appears to have been a City Police and Special Branch affair in which the infant SSB played a comparatively minor role. Years later, MI5 wished it had paid more attention.[1]

Special Branch was still headed by Melville's old colleague Superintendent Patrick Quinn. The public believed it to be Britain's only, and rock solid, line of defence from insurgents of all kinds, be they German spies or striking miners. Kell and his superiors liked it that way; they wanted SSB to remain unknown. After all, there was not much use in a Secret Service that wasn't. So Special Branch handled arrests, court appearances, and statements to the press in cases that SSB had in fact investigated and brought to the point where charges could be preferred.

Special Branch retained a separate internal political role of its own. It kept an eye on suffragettes, Indian nationalists and trade-union agitators and watched the few remaining 'anarchists', although these last were now more likely to be anarcho-syndicalists, breakaways from socialist or communist groups, disapproved of by the majority but nonetheless dedicated to empowering the working class by force if necessary.

The Siege of Sidney Street originated in an ordinary police investigation, when, as Harold Brust, a former Special Branch officer, gasped:

...a strange concatenation of circumstances spewed to the surface the dregs of London's Underworld, when police and soldiers armed with rifles battled with infuriated alien gunmen, when Mr Winston Churchill, as Home Secretary rushed to the scene of the fight to direct in person the operations of the Scots Guards and artillery.[2]

The facts were these: on 16 December 1910, at a jeweller's shop in Exchange Buildings, Houndsditch, which had been closed for the night, some robbers were disturbed. They ran away and holed up in a house close to the scene of the crime. The police surrounded the house; there was a shoot-out; the men fired, killing two police constables and accidentally wounding one of their own party, who later died.[3]

In the ensuing confusion several suspects escaped. A man-hunt was mounted to find anyone who had been in the Houndsditch house and survived. Witnesses reported having seen a man carried, wounded, through the alleyways of the quarter. Girlfriends were questioned. Two men in their early twenties, Yourka Dubov and Jacob Peters, were among those taken into custody. Special Branch files showed that both were political refugees from Latvia (then under Russian rule). Dubov was a member of the

Lettish Social Democratic Party who had come to England less than a year ago; Jacob Peters was a fellow member, as well as belonging to the British Social Democratic Federation and the Working Men's Federated Union.[4] They remained in custody over Christmas and the New Year.

That these young men might be politically involved refugees was nothing new: crime was a favourite way of raising money for the desperate underground back home in Russia and the occupied lands of the Baltic. The local (H Division) Metropolitan Police did not necessarily take the political angle seriously. In 1931 one of them, Frederick Porter Wensley, reminisced:

> Nothing… that I learned during or after the investigation has ever led me to think that there was any political significance about the affair. The Houndsditch plot was hatched and carried out by a bunch of foreign thieves who happened to find the so-called Anarchist Club in Jubilee Street − which was simply a meeting-place for foreigners, some of whom, no doubt, held revolutionary opinions − a convenient rendezvous.[5]

He was right in a way; yet there was a political background to the affair and documents found at the Houndsditch hide-out, and retained for many years in the files of the City police, confirm this. 'Most of the documents found consisted of letters, accounts, or in the case of Gardstein, recipes for manufacturing explosive'.[6] Houndsditch was still occupied mostly by immigrants from eastern Europe, swelled after 1905 by Russians fleeing from retribution after the attempted revolution. Lenin's Bolsheviks, desperate for funds, had proclaimed a readiness to seize funds from 'the enemy, the autocracy'. This was discussed at the 1906 Stockholm Congress. One result was a drift towards violent anarchy on the part of a renegade group from the Lettish Social Democratic Party in London.

Following the rise to power of the Bolsheviks in 1917, MI5 (as MO5 had subsequently been renamed) opened reconstituted files on Sidney Street and Jacob Peters. In the files is a letter from a man who was part of the Whitechapel émigré community at the time; by 1932 he was interested in being naturalised and was perfectly happy to help MI5 in any way he could. Having enumerated eight separate groups of Russians, Poles, Jews and Letts, he goes on:

> Besides these fractions there were several groups of anarchists with their headquarters in Jubilee Street, London E.

> Although discussions about general political changes in Russia between these various groups took place daily, the fractions worked more or less separately, especially the anarchists who worked in groups of three or four persons, but as their tendency was leaning towards expropriation of other people's property, they did not get any sympathy from the Social Democrats and Revolutionaries and generally speaking they were looked upon as social outcasts and expropriators.[7]

The little group that included the robbers was only about a dozen strong. The police were hunting especially for an anarchist (as distinct from a Social Democrat) known as Piatkov, or Peter the Painter.

On 3 January 1911, some other members wanted for questioning about the Houndsditch affair were traced to nearby 100 Sidney Street. The police surrounded the house but the occupants held their ground. The Home Secretary Winston Churchill arrived; so did journalists, photographers and troops. The house was fired upon by the overwhelmingly superior body of soldiers and set alight. Cruelly the observers allowed it to burn to the ground. Two charred bodies were found. One dead man was Fritz Svaars. He was a cousin of Jacob Peters, the man in custody. The other was Jacob Vogel, also known as Sokolov. Of Peter the Painter there was no sign.[8]

When the case against Peters, Dubov and the others opened at the Guildhall on 23 January, the Prosecutor asserted that Gardstein, the man who had been injured and later died, had been responsible for the death of the first policeman on 16 December. But at committal in March and at the Old Bailey in May, Peters and Dubov were charged with murder. A witness appeared who swore to having seen them, before the Houndsditch shoot-out, with pistols.

Neither their association with socialist political views, nor their foreign-ness, would play well with an English jury: they were on trial for their lives. Peters claimed that he was an ordinary, hard-working man, not an armed robber at all, who had been mistaken for his notorious revolutionary cousin. Indeed Svaars, Peters' dead cousin, had borne such a strong resemblance to him that the case rested on unsatisfactory evidence. Melville was eloquent in pointing out, also, that both Peters and Dubov had assisted the police since their arrest.[9] They were acquitted. Peters, ironically echoing the gifts of the Tsar to William Melville, in his gratitude gave his young barrister an inscribed cigarette case. [10]

James Melville made news again in March of 1912, when he defended some printers and a writer from *The Syndicalist* against charges of incitement to mutiny. They were remanded on bail and their sureties (who were in court) included George Lansbury, Will Thorne and Josiah Wedgwood. The accused men had published an article purporting to represent a call from working men to servicemen. It began:

> Boys! Don't do it! Act the man! Act the brother! Act the human being! Property can be replaced! Human life never!

The prosecution was led by the chief Treasury Solicitor, Mr (later Sir) Archibald Bodkin. Bodkin would appear for the Government at every pre-war spy trial; his brief would come directly from Kell and would include detective work by Melville. The Okhrana had a comprehensive file on the Sidney Street affair that included material supplied by and to Melville, and gives the strong impression that he knew a great deal more about the case than came out at the time. Among the

surveillance reports are several on Piotr Piatkov, the gang leader
known to posterity as 'Peter the Painter'. These include reports
from Riga, Irkutsk and Mitava (1910) and from London and
Paris (1911).

MO5 was concerned, not just with spies, but with subver-
sion by 'the enemy within'. Melville had always been good at
snooping on outfits like *The Syndicalist* and following up suspicions about where their money was coming from, and Kell was
ever-vigilant in case dissidents were being funded from abroad.
The Government was particularly suspicious of pacifist and
trade-union organisations from about 1910 onwards. Late that
year a series of strikes, persisting through the summer of 1911,
led to civil disorder and a few rioters were killed by troops in
Liverpool and North Wales.[11] Syndicalist unionism, should it
get mass support, would make a dangerous alternative power-
base. In case of war the dockers, transport workers and miners
acting in unison could paralyse the country. And such a syndicate of unions could ultimately make common cause with the
working classes abroad. Workers of the world would unite. This
would undermine nationalism, imperialism and everything the
Government stood for.

So in August 1910, when Mr and Mrs William Melville took
their holiday at Ilfracombe, it was probably not coincidental
that their fellow guests at the hotel included Mr & Mrs Will
Crook, the Labour MP for Woolwich and his wife. Woolwich,
with its arsenal and docks, was key to the new arms race and
would be crucially important in wartime. Melville would have
found it useful to hear Crook's opinion of the state of labour
relations.[12]

Two years later James Melville would defend *The Syndicalist*. He
was unsuccessful; the syndicalists got six months' hard labour.[13]

1911 was the turning point: after Agadir, well-informed men
no longer said 'if' war comes, but 'when'. Churchill, as Home
Secretary in 1910 and 1911, was avoiding delay and serenely
disregarding the protection of civil liberties by signing 'general

warrants' – warrants to examine the correspondence of listed
individuals.[14] The list was updated from Kell's alien return forms
whenever anything suspicious was reported.

Steinhauer, in the English version of his autobiography, insists
that he quickly discovered that mail to and from the Caledonian
Road and Walthamstow addresses was being opened because
a postman told Ernst it was.[15] His strategy after that was to
send misleading information through the post. This does not fit
the facts. Although most of his network remained in place and
under surveillance, some spies were informed upon, arrested and
charged before the war and incriminating letters to and from
Steinhauer came up more than once in evidence. He does not
appear to have understood the extent to which his communications must be penetrated. If he did, he would surely have dropped
the whole set-up and started again.

The first man to be tried under the new Official Secrets
Act of 1911 was Heinrich Grosse, masquerading as merchant
marine Captain Hugh Grant. He was an ex-convict who had
been given a ten-year sentence in Singapore in 1898 for forging
banknotes. Steinhauer, as Richard H. Peterssen, had hired him
in Brussels.

Grosse had persuaded Steinhauer into giving him the job,
but that was a minor hurdle; when he got to Portsmouth, he
had no idea how to obtain the information that was wanted. In
desperation, he decided to pay for it. He saw an advertisement
placed in a local paper by 'William Salter, Inquiry Agent', and
invited the man to visit him at his lodgings. When he arrived
Grosse introduced himself as the Captain of a merchant ship
who needed information about how much coal was in the
dockyard at Southsea. As there was a strike in the offing, he
explained that he was hoping to find a market in England for
German coal.

As the case officer was pretending to be someone he wasn't,
and so was the spy, it was only fitting that the inquiry agent
should be a fraud too. William Salter was in fact a retired Chief
Petty Officer trying his hand at detective work for the first

time (and as it turned out, the last). When Grosse next asked him to find out how many men were stationed at the Royal Naval Barracks at Portsmouth, he became suspicious and told the police. They referred him to the Admiral-Superintendent of Portsmouth Dockyard, who told the Admiralty. SSB was approached; the Bureau provided information so that Salter could string his client along. As in the case of Schultz, duff information was provided and coded letters to 'Peterssen' in Hamburg intercepted.

By November of 1911 Melville had been snooping in the district. When the case came up at Winchester Assizes there was evidence from local people about stories Grosse had told them. To one he had said he was in Portsmouth on a fishing trip, to another that he was writing a book, to another that he needed information about the Navy to settle a bet, and so on; these variant accounts did not inspire confidence. Grosse was arrested and appeared at Winchester Assizes in February.

> Grosse stepped briskly into the dock. He was smartly dressed in a dark suit and a black overcoat with velvet collar. His strong-looking face was quite stolid at first, but as the charges were read out an expression of anxiety overcast his features.[16]

As well it might. The charges included conspiracy (with Peterssen) which carried a seven-year sentence. He maintained his plea of not guilty at Winchester Assizes, but was sent to jail for three years.[17]

At about the same time an even odder character was jailed. This was Dr Armgaard Karl Graves, the self-mythologising 'doctor' ('he was never a spy of mine', growled Steinhauer.)[18] He later claimed he had been a spy since the old days in Port Arthur, when his masters in Berlin had barked that

> You must abstain from intoxicating liquors. You are not permitted to have any women associates. You will be known to us by a number. You will sign all your reports by that number...

That was before he got there and found himself ankle-deep in wine and surrounded by slappers from four continents (see Chapter 8).

Most newspaper reports of the 1912 Graves case have been destroyed, so we are mainly reliant on his own account which was published in New York in 1914. It deals with his entire career and is written in a somewhat narrow-eyed style, typically

> Slowly inhaling the smoke of my excellent Mejideh, I fell into a sort of contemplative reverie while waiting for the Prince...[19]

His 'mission' on this occasion was particularly dangerous, for the new Official Secrets Act was 'so elastic and convenient for convictions that a judge could charge a jury to find a man guilty on suspicion only'. [20] He was risking seven years' penal servitude – in England, 'plain hell'. However, duty called from Berlin, so he set off to Edinburgh posing as an Australian doctor engaged in postgraduate work at the University. He was looking for information about Scapa Flow, and claims to have struck up an acquaintance with a keeper of the Forth Bridge and through him the 'waterguard' (coastguard?) who knew the Firth of Forth well. He filed his intelligence but he had already aroused suspicion: the landlady let searchers into his room, and he was followed. He confronted the local police chief who knew nothing about any searchers. But he moved to Glasgow to be on the safe side.

In Glasgow he paid for, and claims that he obtained, plans of naval guns then being manufactured by Beardmore & Co. But it was all wasted effort; his support staff let him down. He was using fake Burroughs & Wellcome envelopes and according to him, the people at the mail-drop misdirected his reports to the real company, who called the cops. His account of his arrest by four burly, plain-clothes men is quite gripping; one is impressed that he was ready to inject himself with deadly poison, obviously, but the circumstances were inappropriate. And the police did not behave like gentlemen.

The Inspector seemed to me to subsequently try and get a lot of publicity out of my arrest as if he himself had detected the whole concern, instead of having it thrust under his nose by the London chemical company.

He was sentenced to eighteen months, spent some time incarcerated in Bairlinnie, and was released when the British realised what they were missing.

In the fifth week of my imprisonment I was taken to the office of the Governor of the prison. As I entered I saw a slight, soldierly looking English gentleman of the cavalry type – (a cavalry officer has certain mannerisms that invariably give him away to one who knows).

They were left alone by a deferential Governor, and 'Robinson' began to make casual conversation.

'Is the confinement irksome to you?'
'Naturally.' I looked him straight in the face. 'I am a philosopher. Kismet, Captain.'
'Oh – ho', he exclaimed. 'You address me as Captain. Wherefore this knowledge? We have never met.'
'No', I replied. 'But I have associated too long with various types of army officer not to be able to detect a British cavalry officer. Formerly of an Hussar regiment, I take it?' [Kell was in the South Staffordshire Regiment]
He laughed for some time…

How could Graves stay inside after this? It would be like keeping Sherlock Holmes banged up. They immediately reached a gentlemen's agreement and Graves changed sides. The following day the Lieutenant-Governor escorted his distinguished prisoner by train to London and handed him over to 'Captain Robinson'. Graves stayed overnight at the Russell Hotel before keeping a luncheon appointment with Robinson at Morley's Hotel in Trafalgar Square.

There another gentleman joined us – a Mr Morgan, whom I easily judged and afterwards knew to be of the English Secret Service. Presently Morgan told me that I was to drive with Captain Robinson to Downing Street that afternoon.

'One of our ministers wishes to see you', he explained.

There follows a highly unlikely interview with Sir Edward Grey.

It is all preposterous. Graves got out of jail early, as all model prisoners may, and did, as he says, go to America. Whether or not anyone, either German or English, thought of employing him on a 'mission' there is doubtful. According to Steinhauer, 'most of the letters and telegrams he sent from Glasgow contained nothing but requests for money, which is always the way with these swindlers'.[21] And an SSB 'List of persons to be arrested in case of war' drawn up in July 1914[22] contains his name, marked 'in America'.[23] But by 1914 he, at least, knew or had been told about Mr Morgan.

In the summer of 1912 Melville was on the trail of a Royal Navy gunner who would later be charged with 'communicating information prejudicial to the safety or interests of the state… useful to an enemy'. Warrant Officer George Charles Parrott, aged forty-five, was in charge of the rifle range at the Naval Gunnery School at Chatham, where he lived with his wife in a private house at Alexandra Road, and was officially stationed on HMS Pembroke further along the coast at Sheerness. According to his commanding officer, he was 'an exceptionally smart man'.[24] Some time before, he had become friendly with a language teacher called Hentschel from Sheerness. Parrott, ace marksman, boasted also what was then called 'a keen eye for the ladies'. He began an affair with Mrs Hentschel, an Englishwoman *née* Riley. Later his defence was that Hentschel had told his wife to seduce him so that he could blackmail Parrott into spying.[25] If this was true, Parrott risked jail and dismissal from the service after twenty-seven years rather than have Mrs Parrott discover his infidelity. It seems unlikely. Whatever his motive, he agreed to provide Hentschel with information, and did so from 1910 onwards.[26]

Eventually the two spies fell out over money. Parrott claimed that he was being cheated. Maybe Mr Parrott's ardour for Mrs Hentschel was cooling too. Anyway, he began freelancing direct to Germany, and Hentschel, annoyed, communicated anonymously with the British Admiralty.

In July of 1912 Parrott obtained leave to visit Devonport. A Warrant Officer was not allowed to leave the country without permission, which he made no attempt to obtain. He set off from Sheerness Dockyard, accompanied by a lady, on the train to Sittingbourne, where she disembarked. He carried on to Dover. At Dover he was stopped as he tried to board the Ostend boat. At first he claimed to be a civilian. Then, confessing his identity, he explained that he had to meet a lady at Ostend at 8.00 p.m.

The person he was really going to meet was either Steinhauer, or another officer of the German Secret Service; it was all pre-arranged by an intercepted telegram from 'Seymour' (Parrott) to Richard Dinger in Berlin. Steinhauer used that name, and on the matter of the actual trip to Ostend the German *Meisterspion* may be less than trustworthy as his account of Parrott's trip to Ostend is pretty much identical to the one Melville gave in court. However, Steinhauer claims to have been in Dover, shadowing Parrott to the continent in case he was really a double agent:

Shortly afterwards the detective let him go aboard the steamer. Parrott did not notice what I had already seen – something that told me his fate was sealed. I had been hanging around – easy enough with a big crowd of people such as travel by the Ostend boat in summer-time – when I noticed, behind a pillar in the waiting room, a quiet, keen-eyed man who followed Parrott with his eyes and missed nothing.

Scarcely had Parrott gone up the ship's gangway than the detective went to the man behind the pillar and greeted him unobtrusively. The pair of them followed Parrott aboard and then, as I caught a good sight of the second man, I nearly fell backwards with fright. In spite of his excellent disguise, of which he was a master, who should I recognise but my former friend, the famous Superintendent Melville of Scotland Yard!

...I should have liked to warn him but it was utterly impossible. I knew too well that any attempt on my part would only make it worse, for the moment Melville caught sight of *me* any uncertainty they may have harboured about Parrott's guilt would have vanished *instanter.*

Steinhauer followed Melville and the detective, and Parrott, onto the boat. Months later at Parrott's trial, we find a retired, but unusually vigilant, former policeman appearing as a witness.

Mr William Melville, of Clapham, formerly a Superintendent of the Metropolitan Police, said that he was at Dover on July 13th, and saw the defendant go on board the boat. The witness also went, reaching Ostend about 8.30. On leaving the boat and passing through the railway station the defendant was joined by a man. There was no mutual recognition or handshaking; the stranger, evidently a foreigner, sidled up to the defendant. The foreigner was about 35 years of age. The witness thought that he was a German. They walked off together and went through various back streets into the fishing quarter of the town, finally coming out on the promenade. As they walked the foreigner looked round several times. They sat down on two chairs in a remote place where no one was about. At 9.25 several persons came along, and the defendant and the foreigner got up and moved about 50 yards to another retired position. They remained chatting until 10.15 when the other man got up and hurriedly walked away. The defendant remained sitting for a few minutes longer, and then he got up and walked away too. The witness followed him through various streets to the Place d'Armes, in the centre of the town, where the defendant entered a cigar shop and bought a box of cigars. There

he entered a café, afterwards going towards the Dover boat, which
he reached about 11 o'clock. The witness saw him on board but
did not travel by the same boat.[27]

It is the only post-Special Branch court appearance that we
know of by Melville, and it could well be that he had seen
Steinhauer on that boat and knew that Steinhauer had seen
him. If so, his appearance was a signal, almost a challenge to his
German opposite number.

Quite soon after the trip to Ostend, Warrant Officer Parrott
was sacked on Admiralty orders following an official inquiry.
He and his wife moved to Battersea, to Juer Street off Parkgate
Road near the Albert Bridge, and he began to send and receive
mail through a newsagent's shop across the river in Chelsea. He
made regular trips to Germany.[28] In October or November he
visited Hamburg. In November, the lodgings in Battersea were
raided. Bank books were found; as a Warrant Officer he would
have been paid around £20 a month, but there were records of
mysterious deposits to his account as well as proof of the trip
to Germany, and thirty-five guineas in cash in a writing desk.
The formidable Mrs P had a word with the searchers and the
guineas stayed put.[29]

Parrott, in the dock, underestimated the strength of the case
against himself. He came up with cock-and-bull stories about
who the man at Ostend was (someone apologising for the non-
appearance of his date, a lady picked up at the Palace Theatre)
and about questions he had promised to answer concerning the
Firth of Forth (for a newspaper article). Earlier he had told the
police that he met no one in Ostend, but he had been 'protecting
the identity of a lady'. The more excuses he made, the deeper
the hole he dug himself into. The jury took only half an hour
to find him guilty. Fortunately for him, the unlikely story of
the seductive Mrs Hentschel had seized the imagination of Mr
Justice Darling, who said 'You abused the trust which was placed
in you… Of any one in the service of the Crown it is impossible
to imagine a graver offence than that…' and then sentenced him

to four years, rather than the possible seven, of penal servitude because 'I think you were probably entrapped'.[30]

There was a sequel. Hentschel went to Australia and in Steinhauer's account 'for some time money was sent to him to keep him quiet'. Hentschel's contact in Berlin was Colonel Torner – Steinhauer himself. For several months German Secret Service funds leaked unproductively to Hentschel's antipodean hideaway; but one day in June 1913, an item appeared in a London paper stating that Colonel Torner, of the German General Staff, had been lost overboard in mid-Atlantic. Hentschel received a cutting in the mail. He wrote a threatening letter from Sydney to Berlin, to the effect that he was not born yesterday. His wife had had diphtheria; the medical bills were huge. He wanted either a stream of remittances, or 're-engagement under a different name, but the same salary'. If he didn't get either, he would go to the English newspapers or the English security services. And then 'Germany will have a startling row'.

It was not the most diplomatic way to approach an employer. His letter was ignored. In October 1913 Hentschel turned up at Chatham Police Station and surrendered himself as a spy. He wanted to be arrested, he said. They told him to push off. So he went to London and walked into the police station in Old Jewry where somebody took him seriously and he obtained an audience with concerned authority, probably Cumming and/or Kell. In exchange for money he was able, according to Steinhauer, to tell them all about 'his activities with Parrott from 1910 onwards'. He must have told them everything he knew, because when he appeared in court the prosecution – led, once more, by Archibald Bodkin – declined to pursue the case. Karl Hentschel and his wife, under her maiden name of Riley, remained on the list of persons to be jailed in case of war. At the outbreak of hostilities his address was listed as unknown and she was removed from the 'jail' list and marked 'search'. Hentschel, at least, had left to start a new life elsewhere.

By the end of 1912 Special Branch (which retained the power of arrest that MI5 officers did not have), Cumming, Kell and

Melville were established in separate offices within half a mile of each other, strung along the north bank of a bend in the River Thames. Special Branch was of course at Scotland Yard, on the southern end of Whitehall close to the Houses of Parliament. Cumming was based a few hundred yards further north, high in a Victorian Gothic warren of offices called Whitehall Court that overlooked the river, from which he ran SIS – Secret Intelligence Service – agents overseas. Beyond Whitehall Court, past Charing Cross, the Thames swings east and in the 1920s the old Adelphi building, with its vaults and passages, ranged along the riverbank. In September 1912 Kell moved a few hundred yards west of Temple to the third floor of Watergate House, York Buildings, Adelphi. MI5 mail was forwarded from 'Kelly's Letter Bureau, 54 Shaftesbury Avenue' (Kelly was a name he often used.) By the summer of 1913 he was a major with three captains working under him: Drake, Holt-Wilson and Lawrence. Drake was the one Melville would have most to do with. The other two gathered, filed and sorted information, but Drake was involved with action on known agents and counter-agents.

The German Secret Service officers, compared with the British, had a fatal flaw: arrogance. The glass ceiling of class was present in the SSB too, but Melville was respected. When, in 1909, an extra layer of management was introduced and his involvement with agents overseas diminished, MacDonogh took pains to include him in the new MI5 set-up; he knew the value of his broad experience and took his opinions seriously, and so did Kell. Melville was allowed to run his own show[31] in Temple Chambers, later with the help of Regan and, from 1913 onwards, another ex-policeman called Fitzgerald.

Steinhauer, on the other hand, bemoaned more than once the stupidity of his superiors in Berlin. The notorious strutting conceit of the Prussian military and naval top brass, personified in Kaiser Bill, seems really to have existed. Why else would German intelligence have refused to listen to the common-sense view of an experienced policeman like Steinhauer? They were completely taken in by Wilhelm Klauer: a puny, unqualified,

Portsmouth tooth-puller who lived off the earnings of his wife, a prostitute. He offered to spy for Germany. Steinhauer, having looked into the man's background and mode of life, advised against having anything to do with him, but Berlin went over his head and started sending him money. When Klauer (in England he was known as Clare) was asked for the results of the latest British torpedo trials, he asked his German hairdresser friend Levi Rosenthal to help. Rosenthal nodded wisely, appeared to go along with the plan, and told a friend of his – a town councillor – that he had been approached.

Not only had Rosenthal a sharp eye for a dangerous situation, but he was unable to read and write; Klauer could not have picked a more unsuitable partner in crime. Acting on instructions, Rosenthal strung him along; Klauer was watched by Melville & Co. and led into a trap. He got five years' hard labour.

Steinhauer, by his own account, had no idea that Klauer had ever been hired, or arrested, or jailed; so when he went to Portsmouth to check up on him out of curiosity in June 1913, three months after the trial and the publicity, he almost got arrested.[32]

Klauer was otherwise insignificant, but MI5's next major case was the most important spy the British had yet brought to justice. In Steinhauer's view Frederick Adolphus Gould 'was able for something like eleven years to forward to Germany more information on naval matters than all our other spies put together'. He was a tall, powerfully-built man who had spent twelve years in the German navy, and his real name was Schroeder. But he spoke English like a native, for his mother was English. According to Steinhauer, Gould had worked for the German Secret Service in the 1890s and stopped, and had then been reintroduced to them by an Englishman of dubious motive called Stevens. Stevens worked for France and Russia and around 1902 obtained some British naval information which he induced Gould to offer to Germany. Steinhauer claims that he frightened Stevens into the background by tricking him into thinking that Melville and

Special Branch were onto him, waited a while and then turned his own attention to Gould. It was Gould who had been showing Steinhauer around Chatham Dockyard in 1902 on the occasion when Le Queux spotted the German policeman.

Walking boldly into the enemy's lair, so to speak, was typical of Gould. He was just a little too reckless. But his material was reliable and informative, and in 1908 he persuaded the German Secret Service to set him up as landlord of a pub at Chatham. This was the Queen Charlotte, from which he passed on tidbits of gossip from the naval ratings who were his customers until the end of 1913.

According to Steinhauer, Schroeder worked with Stevens all along, and his decision to leave the Queen Charlotte came when their partnership was dissolved. Stevens's involvement begs questions, but at any rate Gould's recklessness now proved his downfall, because the pub's incoming tenant found incriminating documents in the attic and informed the authorities. The papers included maps and a letter to 'Dear St' (Steinhauer) asking for money.

If Schroeder had indeed parted company with Stevens he was continuing in business on his own, because at his new address at Merton Road, mail was still passing to and from the German Secret Service. Through an intercepted telegram it was learned that Mrs Schroeder would soon be delivering material to 'Schmidt' (a Steinhauer alias) in Brussels. She was arrested at Charing Cross Station.

In her possession were found an English Admiralty chart of Spithead, a gunnery drill book, and certain confidential drawings dealing with the engine rooms of battleships which had clearly been obtained by someone connected with espionage.

Schroeder, entirely ignorant that his wife was in custody, was also arrested shortly afterwards. When the police came to search his house they discovered more fatal documents. Valuable as he had been as a spy, he had been unutterably simple when it came to destroying traces of his guilt. The police found in his possession a paper containing a list of thirty-odd highly important questions relating to the English navy which no man in his sane senses would have kept about him.[33]

Steinhauer's account must be treated with caution as it was edited and given a decidedly pro-British, pro-Melville slant by Sidney Felstead seventeen years after these events. Felstead's account was approved by Basil Thomson, the jingoistic Scotland Yard Assistant Commissioner in charge of the CID from 1913. Readers were kept in ignorance of MI5 or the Special Section within it, as Steinhauer refers to Special Branch, and Melville, but never explains exactly who Melville is working for.

Steinhauer's MI5 file shows that Gould's capture was the most important so far.

In March 1914 after Gould's arrest, F Reimann [Steinhauer], a traveller in jute, wrote to William Schutte, son of Steinhauer's agent Heinrich Schutte, stating that he was coming to England and asking whether it was worth while coming down to Portland. The reply was to be sent to the Wilton Hotel, but on 29th March Reimann wrote to the hotel from Antwerp asking the management to forward letters to Hamburg, and it is doubtful whether he ever came.

His correspondence with agents here during the latter half of March shows that he was aware of danger in coming here. *The Times'* report on the Gould trial mentioned the following documents:

Incriminating letters signed 'St' dated 1904.
Friendly letters signed 'St' dated 1914.
A picture postcard photograph of Gould's correspondent dated 8th December 1913.
A Cabinet photograph on the back of which the words *London, February 1913* were written in ink.

The fact that this photograph represented a man in police uniform and was signed 'G. Steinhauer' was not reported.

On 4th April 1914 the *Continental Daily Mail*, also reporting the trial of Gould, referred to the search made by the British Secret Service to establish the identity of the agent who signed himself Schmidt, RH or CF, Peterssen, P, and Richard, aliases used by Steinhauer in the Gould, Grosse and Parrott correspondence.[34]

Steinhauer was being told in no uncertain terms via the *Continental Daily Mail* that SSB existed, was onto him, and had evidence to bring a case against him. On 26 March Steinhauer's photograph was circulated to Dover, Folkestone, Queenborough and Harwich and evidence submitted to the DPP. A solid case would also require proof that he had actually procured Gould to obtain information which might be useful to an enemy, and in support of this telegrams were produced in which Gould had asked for money for his services in 1912 and Steinhauer had sent it by registered post. There were also letters to Holstein. On 27 March an arrest warrant was issued.

Three months later, on 28 June, the Austrian Archduke Franz Ferdinand was shot at Sarajevo and, thanks to the network of protective agreements now in place, war between the super-powers was imminent: but when? Steinhauer was ordered back to England.

At the end of June, 1914… I found myself on the Belgian coast anxiously asking how I should get into England, in what guise, and more important still, how I could trick my old foe at the War Office in Whitehall.

I knew him, oh yes, and he knew me. Would he, or some of his men armed with my photograph, be waiting for me at Dover?

Well, yes. His book claims that he put the British off the scent with fake postcards to be sent via the Caledonian Road. Whatever he did, it worked; he did at least get to London unnoticed. There,

he claims that he went to Becker's Hotel in Finsbury Square
where a jumpy waiter called Albrecht wanted him gone because
Scotland Yard men were hanging around. Steinhauer moved on.
He visited Mrs Hentschel at Chatham but she

> ...was anxious only that I should be gone, for, as she said bitterly,
> the English people had given her a terrible time ever since the
> exposure of Parrott.

Another spy, a Sittingbourne photographer called Losel, was also
'very uncomfortable and anxious to get rid of me'.[35] It seems
that by this time fear was overtaking the network. Most of these
minor players recognised that war was coming and when it did,
they could risk long jail sentences or worse. They were sorry
they had ever got involved.

All this time,

> It would have taken more than my old friend, Melville of Scotland
> Yard – he had ostensibly retired from the police but still carried on
> his Secret Service activities – to have recognised me in Hendryk
> Fritsches, the Dutch manager of a Hamburg coffee merchant.

> Even Melville, whose cleverness in the case of Parrott I readily
> admit, might have looked more than twice before he discovered
> in the elegant Dutchman with the mutton-chop whiskers and the
> monocle his formidable adversary, Steinhauer.[36]

The facial hair, hats and bulky, ill-fitting tailoring of the period
must have assisted disguise. But was Steinhauer such a formidable
adversary? His vanity was colossal. It is impossible to imagine
Melville presenting an agent with a signed photograph. And as
the British file on Steinhauer laconically comments,

> In July 1914 it became known that a man named Fritsches, a travel-
> ler in jute, was in this country. This name was already known to the
> Security Service and was suspected of being an alias of Steinhauer.

Every effort was made to identify him and effect his arrest, but
without success.[37]

Again he eluded Melville, yet narrowly. He headed north, visiting
a series of nervous agents and telling them to leave for Germany,
and spent a week in the east of Scotland on a 'fishing trip' taking
depth soundings and hearing about troop movements. He got
out by the skin of his teeth, having aroused suspicion, at the
end of July.

The agents were less fortunate. On 4 August 1914 with the
declaration of war only hours away, twenty-one of the twenty-
two names on the MI5 list are said to have been rounded up
in towns and cities all over Britain. In fact, on 5 August, the
Home Secretary Reginald McKenna stood up in the House of
Commons and made a statement to the House that the operation had been a great success and that twenty-one German
spies had been arrested. However, much is still unclear in terms
of who the twenty-one spies actually were. The fact that three
separate lists were subsequently published by Kell's Bureau has
somewhat compounded the confusion.[38] While a list of twenty-
two targets was initially drawn up, it would seem that when the
Home Secretary made his statement, only nine (as opposed to
twenty-one) suspected spies on Kell's list had in actual fact been
arrested. However, the Director of Public Prosecutions reported
the following year that, '24 German spies were arrested at the
outbreak of war under the Official Secrets Act 1911'. Intriguingly,
not all the names on this list appeared on Kell's target list of
twenty-two. When, in 1921, the Bureau was writing its own
internal history of the war years, the list of twenty-one that
appeared did not correspond entirely with either the 1914 target
list or the DPP's report.

The solution to this conundrum seems to lie in the fact that the
1914 list was very much a 'wish list', while the DPP list reflected
actual arrests. By 1921, few in the Bureau had worked for it a decade
earlier, and those responsible for writing the internal history had
little or no direct knowledge of what did or did not happen in

1914. It would seem that their 1921 list was actually based on a July 1915 press report from the *Daily Chronicle* which summarised the DPP's report and listed twenty-four names – however, unknown to the internal historians, the *Chronicle*'s article actually contained a number of factual errors, due in part to inaccurately copying down extracts from the DPP report.

Most of those arrested in August 1914 were interned (held in custody without charge or trial) for the duration of the war. Karl Gustav Ernst, having been arrested with the rest, petitioned the Home Secretary on grounds that he was a British subject, and therefore could not legitimately be interned as an alien. As a result he was charged with treason and espionage: a capital offence. He was tried in November 1914 and imprisoned for seven years.

As the rolling-up of the network was handled by Special Branch, and there was now plenty of time to interrogate the internees, life at MI5 proceeded undisturbed. An unsigned internal memo dated the first day of the war, 5 August, advises that 'it is desirable to find out a little more about' a Mr Robertson, resident of the Salisbury Hotel and Secretary of the Neutrality League of 12 St Bride Street, who

…has been publishing articles in various newspapers calling upon Englishmen to do their duty! (This consists in stopping the war.)

Typed below is:

Mr M to enquire.

On 7 August Mr M submitted the following:

I have made enquiries and learned that the Neutrality League no longer exists at 12 St Bride Street. It was only at this address for a few days and got into an office there while the tenant was away. The people who came there respecting the league were a nondescript crowd of cranks, male and female – not at all numerous.

Dr Robertson the supposed Secretary is a fictitious name. The real name of the man was Mr Langdon Davis, of whom however nothing seems to be known at present.

The Salisbury Hotel people would have nothing to do with the League. The Neutrality League was really got up by Mr Norman Angell, 4 King's Bench Walk, and the defunct remnants have now gone to that address.

The raison d'être of the League was that some unknown person gave £200 for the purpose. It is not unlikely the German Ambassador knew something about it. This was the money which enabled the League to advertise, but the cash was soon spent. The persons frequenting the office were a needy-looking lot. A Mr C.E. Fayle was also connected with it.

This is pretty good detective work in two days, even allowing for the convenient proximity of the 'defunct remnants' right behind Temple Chambers in King's Bench Walk.

Melville's work proved that he knew what he was doing and his superior officers listened to him. Thanks to this, and Kell's meticulous inventory of facts about who was doing what and where, SSB was pretty much on top of home security when war began. Cumming too knew about the disposition and movements of the German navy thanks to sub-agents recruited on the Baltic and North Sea coasts. Further, his men abroad were technically adept as Steinhauer's were not. Bywater, for instance sent back reports such as this, describing his own memorisation of defences both existing and planned at Sylt...

In rear of the second coast battery was an armoured fire-control station with a very large range-finder; the base I estimated at 25 feet.

Here I may interpolate that the calibre of the guns in the batteries was ascertained, not by a direct inspection of the guns, but by observing ammunition being unloaded from railway trucks at

Emden for shipment to the island. Howitzer shells of 11 inches and gun projectiles of 9.4 inches were definitely identified...[39]

The Admiralty was concerned that von Tirpitz was working with Krupp to provide superior armaments. The arms race was on and the Germans were suspicious of snooping Englishmen. Yet Cumming was able to receive from Borkum items such as a sketch-map which

> ...showed the site of each battery with the number and calibre of its guns; the location of all magazines, bomb-proof shelters, and observation posts; the positions prepared amidst the sand dunes for the mobile 4.1 inch high-velocity guns which were to supplement the fixed defences and the narrow-gauge railway and paved roads that had been made for the transport of troops and material. Other details indicated were the main and emergency wireless stations, the secret telegraph and telephone cables leading from garrison HQ to the mainland – as distinct from the ocean cable lines which traverse Borkum – and indeed every feature of the entire defensive system.[40]

The British took pains to find out about the 'weaker' German navy; the Germans, over-confident in their own military superiority, had no up-to-date intelligence from the British army. Steinhauer lacked Melville's credibility with superior officers. Steinhauer also made mistakes which played in MI5's favour. He should have wound up the letter-drop network at the first suspicion that it was intercepted. He left it in place and played into British hands. When war began, German informants in England were detained and Berlin's flow of news stopped.

As a result, as late as 21 August the Germans did not know that the British Expeditionary Force was on its way. In concentrating on their enemy's maritime force, they had lost sight of their own weakest point: the vulnerability in the Schlieffen Plan that left them open to attack from the west as their mighty army wheeled south and east through Belgium and northern France.

TWELVE
G MEN

Karl Hans Lody was the first German spy arrested, tried and sentenced during the First World War. He was a former naval officer who, too impecunious to maintain the social expense of a position in the navy, had quit in his twenties to become a tour guide overseas. Now in his late thirties, he had travelled widely, spoke English with an American accent, and had lost nothing of his patriotic fervour. But as a spy, he was hopelessly unwary, trusting and untrained.[1]

Some writers have sought to explain away Germany's use of such a man with the excuse that, their English spy network having been silenced, they were desperate. In fact, in July of 1914 when Lody volunteered his services, the network was still in place.

He was provided with a genuine American passport in the name of Charles A. Inglis by the German authorities in Berlin less than twenty-four hours before a state of war was declared. A couple of weeks later he returned to Norway, where he had been working, in his new identity. From there he entered Britain (probably via Hull) as an American tourist. So far he had not incited suspicion. The war was, after all, not yet the Great War. It was a long-overdue trouncing of the belligerent Hun that would be over by Christmas. American visitors were routine enough.

From the time of his arrival in Edinburgh on 27 August things began to go wrong; not only because he lacked sense, but because nobody had prepared or trained him for the job. He hired a bicycle, and pedalled around naval installations taking notes and asking questions. He sent an uncoded telegram to someone with a German name in Stockholm. He sent another, and another. He left forwarding addresses and travelled to

London, whence he sent news of the defences of public buildings. He went to Liverpool, and wrote letters about the refitting
of cruise liners that was going on in the docks. Nothing was
encoded or written in invisible ink. Then he went to Dublin,
and it was decided that the evidence already intercepted was
enough to detain him. In Killarney he was arrested by officers
of the Royal Irish Constabulary.

Trotter, now a Major, sat on the Court Martial that tried
him at the Middlesex Guildhall at the end of October, Captain
'Blinker' Hall, from naval intelligence, was among the witnesses,
and Mr Bodkin prosecuted. The case against him rested more on
mail interceptions than anything else. Patriotism was his motive.
This was counted in his favour, but did not save him because
it was necessary to make an example of him. Lody was duly
removed from the court to the Tower of London where his
deportment was brave and courteous to the end. 'May my life be
honoured as a humble offering on the altar of the Fatherland',
he wrote to his relations in Stuttgart. Patriotism of this mystic,
quasi-religious type was normal in the officer class at the time,
and led Germany into a lot of trouble later. He was led into a
room at the Tower, seated in a chair and shot by an eight-man
firing squad on 6 November 1914.[2]

Under the Aliens Restriction Act, which was rushed through on
the first day of the war, 'enemy aliens' – Germans who had settled
in England and had English children, for instance – must register
with the police and were usually restricted in their movements
and activities. The Defence of the Realm Act of 8 August 1914
– 'Dora' – went further and pretty well imposed martial law
on everyone, including aliens from neutral countries. Thomson
of Scotland Yard insisted that 'It is necessary in the interests of
public safety that the police should be almost unreasonably cir-
cumspect in dealing even with [aliens] against whom nothing
specific may be known.' The powers of the State to 'defend the
realm' from the people by preventing them from moving or
communicating were wider than ever before.

MI5's anti-espionage section understood perfectly well that Germans were not necessarily spies and spies were not necessarily German. On the other hand, Berlin was more inclined to trust people of 'German blood' or neutrals, suspecting British agents of playing a double game. So suspicion fell particularly on foreigners communicating with the continent.

Lody was the first of many wartime spies whose arrests arose out of mail interception. Once war began, systematic examination of the mail could be acknowledged in court. This had been a more delicate matter before mobilisation, not least because it put the enemy on their guard. In wartime accused aliens were usually tried by courts martial, detailed evidence being unavailable to the press. Captain Lawrence's special section had been intercepting mail to and from the addresses of known spies abroad for some time, and during the war teams of postal censors were put in place. There were well over a thousand of them by 1918. Through them, the special section of MI5 fed Melville's detective section with a stream of names and addresses to investigate. By 1916 he had seven full-time 'shadowing staff' all believed to have been ex-Metropolitan Police officers.[3]

Kell's outfit was also re-designated – at least twice. From 17 August, a fortnight after war began, Melville and Regan and Fitzgerald, his first two detectives, became part of 'G Section' of MI5. A chart of October 1915 shows Lt-Col Vernon Kell (working to Cockerill who works to the DMO, Major-General Callwell) in joint charge of other MI departments, but in sole charge of MI5 E, F, G and H. MI5 G under Major Drake is responsible for 'Detection of Espionage'. Other specific tasks covered by E, F and H include administration of counter-espionage, military policy regarding aliens, organisation of counter-espionage at ports, and so on.[4]

Homeland security and military and naval intelligence abroad were fast becoming a huge, sprawling series of slightly differing fields of responsibility employing thousands of people, from military personnel to clerks and typists; keeping the security services secure must have been problematic, despite the obligatory signature of a declaration under the Official Secrets Act.

The natural division between Kell's counter-espionage, counter-insurgency people, and the interests of Cumming's SIS which
lay largely overseas, was finally rectified when MI1(C) and MI5
opened for business as separate arms of a new Directorate of
Military Intelligence in January 1916. Melville was still based in
Temple with his Detective Section or 'Special Staff', but it was
from then onwards part of MI5.[5]

Detective work arose from mail interceptions; mail interceptions arose from suspicion; suspicion arose from the Port
Police. And the public. Within months of the war's beginning
the British public, if Sidney Felstead is to be believed, were suffering from 'spy mania':

> Where is the man or woman who did not know a German who
> had a concrete gun platform built in his back garden?... And
> who... did not know of a fashionable restaurant patronised by
> naval and military staff officers where German spies disguised as
> harmless waiters were always found to be standing at the back
> of officers' chairs, carefully gleaning the conversation which was
> taking place?... The number of people who were reported to the
> police as signalling to Zeppelins ran into thousands: in practically
> every instance the culprit was either a careless servant girl or a blind
> flapping in the breeze... There was an unfortunate individual from
> whose house a light had been seen on the night of a particular raid,
> reported to the authorities as having been seen signalling to the
> enemy, who was raided first by the Competent Military Authority,
> then by the police, and lastly by the naval authorities, who drew a
> cordon round the house and then sent a bluejacket to swarm up
> the balcony and seize the culprit in the act.[6]

Felstead obtained his information from Basil Thomson of
Scotland Yard and, fortunately for Melville, these panicky
reports were normally rejected by the police at an early stage,
long before they reached the detective branch of G Section.

Melville – Mr M – had another job to do, besides detection.

In 1911 the British spies Brandon and Trench had been caught because they went about their business as stupidly as Lody did. They had gone into Germany without vetting by Kell, Melville or Cumming, but with the blessing of at least one Admiralty official who was as arrogant as any Prussian and should have known better than to send them. This must not happen again. The British had been getting valuable information from Byzewski, Bywater, Tinsley and others for some time before the war. None of importance except Max Schultz (a British Max Schultz working in Germany) had been caught and none but Rué had been turned. British spies vetted by Melville were skilled operators, usually resident, with good cover in the way of a job so that they fitted seamlessly into life abroad.

Now, in wartime Germany, anyone interested in Germany's conduct of the war would be automatically suspect and if they could not account for themselves they would be shot. Lody had been caught because he made the elementary mistake of underestimating his enemy. The same must not be true of anyone Cumming sent abroad, or of anyone Kell sent to infiltrate groups such as the Neutrality League at home. The right people must be picked, and they must be properly trained. Bernard Porter gives an account of a man who got into MI5 in December 1914, and

....was a medical doctor, taken in because MI5 reasoned that a doctor was 'the last person to be suspected of intrigue'. Together with him in that class of 1914 he later remembered 'ex-policemen, journalists, actors, ex-officers, university dons, bank clerks, several clergy, and to my knowledge at least two titled persons'.

That was at what he described as a Spy School, started up then to teach them all what today is called tradecraft. The training included lectures from ex-Detective Superintendent Melville on how to pick locks and burgle houses, followed by practical exercises; others on the Technique of Lying, the Technique of Being Innocent, the Will to Kill, and Sex as a Weapon in Intelligence; and (finally) Dr McWhirter's Butchery Class, which gave advice on how to top yourself if you were caught... If we can credit this account

Spy School clearly gave these new wartime recruits an excellent grounding, especially in practical subjects.[7]

It must have been quietly amusing for Melville, who knew his audience of university dons and titled persons would be goggle-eyed at the sight of a real, live criminal, to introduce the safe-cracking expert as 'a very experienced assistant who is out on a kind of compassionate leave from Parkhurst so he can put his shoulder to the war effort for a few days'.[8] He was probably a master locksmith from around the corner, but Melville was at pains to remind his class how foolish they would be to attempt an exercise of their new skills in peacetime. (Indeed, there was a – no doubt purely coincidental – rash of country-house jewel heists in the 1920s.) Melville was adept at getting in and out of locked rooms and had been much impressed, on meeting Houdini at the Yard in 1900, when this genius of escapology freed himself in a twinkling from some handcuffs.[9] The fascinated student also recalled Melville's advice that doors squeaked more in daytime, usually on the upper hinge.

Spy School took place every Tuesday and Friday at 5.00 p.m.[10] Melville was not the only lecturer. Others were Ewart, Cumming and possibly, interestingly, Douglas Hogg, the barrister James Melville worked for.[11]

On a day in January 1915, a small shivering crowd of refugees from Belgium landed somewhere on the North Sea coast of England. All of them were fleeing from the Germans who had overrun their country. They arrived unnoticed and scattered as soon as they reached dry land. One of them, a tall Russian who spoke many languages, had a respectable identity as a businessman and, unusually for a refugee, life insurance to protect his wife and children should anything happen to him.

Within a month, a letter to a Rotterdam address caught the attention of an officer of the special section. This Rotterdam address was known to be used by German intelligence and the letter, from L. Cohen at 22 High Street, Deptford, was incongruously inconsequential yet so affectionate; there were lots of kisses. Invisible ink technology being in its infancy, a hot flat-iron would reveal most messages written between the lines in, for instance, lemon juice:

> An iron was heated and, hey, presto! Out came as pretty a mass of information as any enemy could desire to possess. There were certain divisions of the New Armies training at Aldershot which would cross the Channel before long, certain ships building in the Clyde which would be a grave menace to the German submarines, and remarks to the effect that the *Moral* of the people was poor, and that the recruiting for Lord Kitchener's armies had died away to nothing.[12]

Melville and his detectives investigated. There was no L. Cohen at 22 High Street, Deptford. More flirtatious letters were read on their way to Rotterdam. They proved, when pressed by the flat-iron, to be demands for money. Finally one arrived which had a postscript: 'C has gone to Newcastle so I am writing this from III instead.' There was a III Deptford High Street, and it was occupied by a baker and confectioner called Peter Hahn. He was arrested.

> While waiting to take him away some of the police made a search of the back room where, much as they expected, they found a complete kit for writing in secret ink. There was the ink, special paper, wool and ammonia, neatly stowed away in a cardboard box. But of the actual spy himself no trace could be found.[13]

Local inhabitants provided a lead to a Russian who often visited Hahn; he lived somewhere in Russell Square. This tall, dark, middle-aged fellow was traced to Bloomsbury, and thence to Newcastle, where he was arrested. His accommodation was searched and his belongings confiscated, and he was taken to London.

Under interrogation he denied knowing any Germans; he said he hated them. He spoke English well with the slightest of accents. He had arrived on the refugee boat, but records showed that he had visited England at least once since August 1914 and the authorities were convinced that he had lived in Britain as a spy before the war and escaped detection. The place on the refugee boat had been bought for him.

He was identified as Karl Muller. He was a resourceful man who had bought and sold different commodities for different companies, who had run this enterprise and that, and served in the Turkish army; he was not well off, but he had made a passably good living. He could, in fact, claim to be Russian, for he had been born in Russian Poland. He said he had been living in Antwerp when the Germans invaded, and they picked him up as a likely spy.

The German Admiralty, since the Lody disaster, had improved their own spy school, and Muller had been trained to recognise ships by their silhouette. 'There are well-defined architectural lines to every group of ships in the British Navy, and these silhouettes I learned to know by heart before I was permitted to leave Berlin', boasted the liar Karl Armgaard Graves, and in this respect he seems to have known what he was talking about even if it didn't apply to *him*. Muller knew how to recognise battleships and use invisible ink. He was set afloat, and landed safely, and it was only through the vigilance and diligence of G Section that he was ever caught.

He was a tragic man, who wept bitterly for his wife and children the night before he met his end. (The life insurance provided by the German authorities, while no compensation at all, was nonetheless an improvement on the cold comfort offered to Gottlieb Goerner years before.) Muller and his baker accomplice had been found guilty in a civil court, for Hahn, born of German parents in Battersea, was a British subject and therefore qualified for a civil trial. Muller was defended, unsuccessfully, by Henry Curtis-Bennett, a barrister friend of James Melville from Middle Temple.

Hahn, the younger man who had written only once to Rotterdam at Muller's instigation, got five years. Muller was condemned to death. An appeal was lodged and rejected. When his time came he is said to have walked along the line of men who were about to kill him, solemnly shaking each one by the hand, before his eyes were bound and he bravely faced the firing squad on 23 June 1915.

Shortly after Muller's detection it was suggested to Kell, by the Special Section, that since the trial had not been reported, the Germans would be none the wiser if they kept on getting intelligence from their correspondent. Special Section officers therefore imitated his codes, his invisible ink and his handwriting:

> Among the falsified items sent was a faked description of the results of the Battle of Jutland, one bogus photograph which would later appear in a German newspaper indicating that it had been accepted as genuine. Another item successfully enticed a German U boat into the open in a bid to sink an important British steamer, only to be met by the guns of a Royal navy destroyer... money sent from Rotterdam for Muller enabled [MI5] to purchase a second, much-needed motor-car – promptly christened 'The Muller'.[14]

The war was grim and earnest now. The newspapers did not say how bad it was, but everybody could tell from the men who came back. There was no more false optimism. As the casualty lists lengthened, there was some bitterness, but also resignation; Germany was an aggressor, that much was proven; to most people the war must be right, and the 'top brass' must know what they were doing, and good would prevail. But when, exactly? Unsure of their future, people put their affairs in order. In this spirit Major James Melville, who would shortly be posted to Gallipoli, and Miss Sarah Tugander of Abingdon Mansions, Kensington, cast their cares aside and quietly married at Kensington Registry Office on 1 July 1915.

Sarah was part of the family, left behind in England to hope that James would return unharmed. She had been secretary to Mr Bonar Law, now leader of the Conservatives, for ten years, but as was usual even in wartime, quit her job upon marriage.

Melville had his occupation to distract him. He had dealt with the loss of a wife and three children by working, and with war raging and two sons at the front he would work still. From late May onwards, dogged detection followed up a series of cable and letter interceptions and revealed what the newspapers would call a gang, but which was really more of a loose espionage network. Fortunately, the load was spread over two extra men: Burrell joined early in May and Hailstone at the beginning of June.

Discovering spies like Lody before they had had time to do much damage was merely encouraging; finding that others had been getting away with it, and that their information could already have sent men to their death, was frankly worrying. Between 24 and 25 May, routine checks on telegrams out of Southampton had alerted the section to messages destined for Dierks & Co., cigar merchants of the Hague. They were orders for items such as '3000 cabanas AGK; 1000 Rothschilds K; 4000 coronas USB'. Scrutiny of these cables by a German speaker suggested *alte grosse Kreuzer* (big old cruisers) for AGK, *Kriegsschiffe* (battleships) for K and *Unterseebotten* (submarines) for USB. That was enough. When the order of 25 May was checked against ships in port, three cruisers (3000 AGK) had just *arrived* (cabanos), one battleship (1000 K) had just *departed* (Rothschild) and four submarines (4000 USB) were *stationed there* (coronas). Every recent telegram from ports up and down the country was now being urgently reviewed and Dierks & Co. in the Hague investigated; they were not the 'cigar and provision merchants' they were supposed to be. And more telegrams were still being sent out of Southampton.[15]

On 27 May a £25 money order came from Dierks & Co. payable to the man who had sent the cables, Haicke Marinus Petrus Janssen. His location could now be discovered and the damaging cables stopped.

He was a thirty-two-year-old Dutchman, and he was arrested on 29 May in the presence of detectives from G Section. In his room there was evidence of communication with Dierks as far back as March, cigar samples and lists of tobacconists. But the company's price list was somewhat odd, with inexplicable notes on it indicating a code. There was also a current copy of Jane's *Fighting Ships* and a puzzling collection of items including eau-de-cologne (which he was not wearing), custard powder, liquid gum, pens, nibs and a mapping pen.

Other cables had gone to Dierks and Co. this month. There had been two from Edinburgh on 17 and 18 May and another on 25 May which was followed by a £25 remittance from Dierks. The sender in Edinburgh, another Dutchman called Willem Johannes Roos, had left the city. He was traced to Aberdeen; then to Inverness and, finally, on 2 June, to London where he was arrested by Herbert Fitch of Special Branch at a commercial hotel in Aldgate.[16] When he came into the country on 14 May, he had claimed to represent Dobbelmann's of Rotterdam, a legitimate cigar trader; but there was no evidence of that. A search of his room by G Section detectives revealed Dierks' stationery and cigar stock lists, and recent hotel bills, which were the only indication that this man might be a commercial traveller for Dierks as he now claimed. However, he did have a magazine article about F.E. Jane of *Fighting Ships* fame, some notes on ships he had seen, custard powder, pens, and a letter from Janssen.

The men were held in custody and interrogated, probably by Drake and Cumming. Janssen, protesting his innocence, said he was a former merchant seaman who had even received a medal from the Board of Trade for rescuing British sailors from a sinking ship. It had been awarded to him at Liverpool in February. This was interesting, for although it was true, further investigation showed that he also travelled to Cardiff, Hull and Edinburgh on that occasion. This time he had entered the country via Hull on 13 May and immediately wired for the funds that did not arrive until 27 May at Southampton. He had been to other South Coast ports in the meantime. He had visited no tobacconists and obtained no orders. He claimed that he had never heard of Roos.

The cigar lists smelled of scent and there was secret writing on them, which a forensic expert said been made with eau-de-cologne and a talc fixative. But Roos had more codes on his, respecting ports in the north and east, as might be expected. Roos had to admit that he knew Janssen, because he had a letter from him, but said that Janssen didn't work for Dierks. Janssen insisted he knew nothing of Roos; this went on for some time even after they were brought into the same room. It was pretty tragic stuff because the more they talked the more they denied the obvious. They were not legitimate cigar traders, they knew each other, and they were communicating salient facts to the enemy.

They were tried at Westminster Guildhall and found guilty. Major Drake presented convincing evidence. At some stage both realised that the game was up, and separately wrote to their wives giving the same address to which to apply for a pension. Janssen, after the court martial, talked resignedly about spying. Information came out of England every day, he said; sometimes messages were hidden in the spines of books. He informed on a naval inspector called Hochenholz. Roos said nothing further, but is said to have tried to cut his own throat in prison.[17] The two Dutch sailors were shot in the Tower on 30 July.

Thanks to the watch on mail to Dierks & Co., Melville and his detectives were already working on the next case. On 25 May a letter addressed to the firm had been sent from London by a George T. Parker, who could not be traced. Then

The Censor forwarded from Holland a telegram of 30th May 1915 announcing the despatch to Reginald Rowland, c/o Société Générale, Regent Street, London, of £30 on account of Norton B Smith & Co., New York.[18]

On 3 June came another letter from the mysterious Parker, this time addressed to H. Flores in Rotterdam. Both of Parker's letters referred to a female accomplice called Lizzie. From the context investigators deduced that this might mean the liner *Queen Elizabeth*. In Holland, Tinsley and his agents were quietly checking all the Dutch contacts.

On the same day, Scotland Yard received a report about a woman called Mrs Wertheim who had been asked to leave her hotel at Inverness. Something about her behaviour, her general throwing around of money and nosiness and getting herself driven about the local naval installations, had alerted the hotelkeeper, who called in the Chief Constable, who visited this lady and told her to get out of town; she apparently left for London.

At least one lead could be pursued: sooner or later Mr Rowland would collect his £30 in Regent Street. He proved to be a thin, blond, young man of about twenty-eight, rather highly strung – as he would be in the circumstances. He had a German accent with an American twang and claimed that he was a naturalised American. The detectives searched his accommodation. They found hotel bills establishing part of his movements; cards of Norton B. Smith and a letter showing that he represented the firm; Jane's *Fleets of the World 1915*; a phial of lemon juice; pens and a tin of talc; a code not unlike that used by Janssen and Roos; and a receipt for a registered letter, sent to L. Wertheim in Inverness. His handwriting looked just like Parker's. Upon investigation, they found that L. Wertheim was Lizzie, that George Parker and Reginald Rowland were one and the same, and that Scotland Yard had already received a report on Mrs Wertheim.

Rowland/Parker was using an American passport in the name of Reginald Rowland which was a fake, and yet Reginald Rowland did exist; he was an older man who had deposited his documents with the authorities in Berlin for just one hour earlier in the year. So who was this man with the false passport? Rowland/Parker was saying nothing.

And now, on 4 June, the day of Rowland's arrest, came another wire from Dierks & Co. This one was addressed to a Fernando Buschmann, and mentioned Flores. Buschmann, a young Brazilian, was picked up on 5 June. He seemed to be connected with a German naval inspector called Grund. The list of suspect names was lengthening. Postcards addressed to Flores, and to Grund c/o other suspects, were detected at once; they came from a man called Roggen.

Melville's Special Staff were almost overwhelmed. They were still looking for Lizzie Wertheim. She had apparently been in Edinburgh before Inverness, having travelled from London in the company of an American woman called Knowles-Macy. It being wartime, Miss Knowles-Macy should have brought her passport to register with, but did not, and was turned away from the Edinburgh hotel. This had left Mrs Wertheim to continue her Scottish tour alone.

Patient detective work uncovered relations of Lizzie Wertheim in Hampstead. They did not want anything to do with her. But by 9 July enquiries led them to the house of another acquaint-ance, a Miss Brandes in the Hammersmith Road. She had turned Lizzie Wertheim out two days before. Finally, on 9 June, they traced her to the house of Miss Knowles-Macy at 33 Regent's Park Road. She was arrested there. 'When the police went to search her room, she entered the maid's room, tore up a letter from George T. Parker and threw it out of the window.'[19]

Reading between the lines, she was an annoying, self-drama-tising, selfish woman. Her papers were circumstantially, rather than substantially, incriminating; besides the scent and talc of the regulation spy kit were evidence that she had recently been in Berlin and had been in touch with German prisoners of war, a letter from Parker, an envelope addressed to Rowland, an Irish railway guide and Irish money, £115 in banknotes, and all sorts of correspondence and addresses linking her to suspected persons, notably one 'Dr Brandt' in Amsterdam. There was no technical data, no evidence that all the touring around Ireland, Fishguard, the Isle of Man, the South Coast and elsewhere looking at naval installations had provided the Germans with anything they could otherwise not have guessed. But she must have given them useful information, because she had been earning more money from them than she was used to having (she had started taking cocaine; even in 1915, nature's way of telling her she was overpaid).

Incarcerated in Brixton on remand, and knowing that Wertheim had been arrested, Rowland decided the game was up. He told the full story. He was George Breeckow, a Russian born in 1884, whose father had lost money and taken the family to live at Stettin when George was a child. George Breeckow was brought up speaking German and at some stage was in the German army. He earned his living playing the piano for five or six years before the war in America, and although he took out naturalisation papers the process remained incomplete when he returned to Europe in 1914.

He was engaged in Antwerp in March of 1914 'to act as imperial courier between Germany and America' but his first assignment was to go to England. He had £45 for Mrs Wertheim and a mission to persuade a Mr Carter of Southampton to work for the Germans; this the man declined to do. It was all downhill from there onwards. Lizzie Wertheim spent a few days with Breeckow in Southampton and proved to be a trying companion, determined to draw attention to herself. When she left for Scotland, he travelled to Ramsgate with a male friend and sent information to Germany. He then returned to London, and was arrested.

Mrs Wertheim was a Pole whose mother lived in Berlin. She had British citizenship by marriage but had been separated from her husband since about 1911. She was defiant to the end. They were tried at the Old Bailey on 20 September and Breeckow was sentenced to death. He appealed against the sentence. Wertheim got ten years' penal servitude because she was a woman. Kell was angry, saying that this would encourage Germany to send more female spies in future.[20]

Fernando Buschmann, arrested shortly after his arrival in June, was convicted on the scant evidence of intercepted communication under the Defence of the Realm Act. Buschmann was a Brazilian of German descent and his motive for spying was never clear. Roggen had time to travel around a little before he was caught; like Janssen and Roos, he had arrived with a cover story that did not bear the most cursory examination. He was supposedly a Uruguayan farmer on the look-out for horses to buy, but knew nothing of Uruguay and did not buy horses but arrived in Scotland for 'fishing and his health' to stay just a couple of miles from a torpedo testing site. Documents and circumstantial evidence linked him with Breeckow. He, and Buschmann, were tried by court martial in September and shot in October 1915.

Not long after MO5 was renamed MI5 in 1916, James Melville's friend from the Middle Temple, Henry Curtis-Bennett, was informally approached by Sir Archibald Bodkin and

> Without further explanation, he took Curtis-Bennett by the arm and led him to offices at the corner of Charles Street, Haymarket. It was the headquarters of the Secret Service, nerve centre of the British counter-espionage system.

Curtis-Bennett joined in November 1916. His biographers say he found that

> German agents who came to England were given all the rope they needed, provided eventually they hanged themselves. He took to this strange game of bluff and double bluff with enthusiasm… He was the man of the world among the soldiers, sailors and police-men with whom he was now working, and they used his supreme ability to read character and motive to great effect.[21]

From 1917 onwards Curtis-Bennett became part of the triumvirate who interrogated suspects. One of the three was always a military man like Drake or Kell and one was Basil Thomson; Curtis-Bennett was the other. Curtis-Bennett at least occasionally found himself overwhelmed with remorse when the questioning was successful, for the evidence thus produced would almost inevitably send the man to his death. There were, increasingly, exceptions. Sharing a cell with Buschmann had been a middle-aged Dutchman called Joseph Marks; he, like so many, had been let down by props (in his case a stamp collection) and a cover story that did not bear examination by a detective.[22] But unlike the rest, Marks confessed and provided information about his spymaster in Holland. He received a five-year sentence and was deported after the war.

In 1916 German intelligence began to take the likelihood of detection more seriously. A man called Vieyra came under observation from May onwards because Richard Tinsley, in Rotterdam, had heard that he was a German spy. Vieyra was also known as Pickard, and lived in Acton with a woman called Mrs Fletcher. He had run a midget troupe before the war and had then got into the film distribution business, which took him to the continent and America. He came back from Holland in May, went about his business, and apart from the odd bank deposit from overseas, nothing was noticeably strange. His letters and business were ordinary. Enquiries on the continent, however, revealed some mysterious correspondents, an untraceable 'partner' and a mistress whose testimony, while not exactly incriminating, was not reassuring either.

The Vieyra case is interesting for several reasons. For one thing, Tinsley according to the records had access to the services of a Dutch police sergeant; for another, some of the correspondence to and from the untraceable 'partner' must have travelled via the diplomatic bag of the Dutch Consulate in London. Vieyra's letters, when they were finally developed in a three-stage process taking several days, showed not only that he was spying, but that the Germans had invented a new kind of invisible ink. Vieyra was also the first spy to be condemned to death and then have his sentence commuted to life imprisonment. In this way his testimony could continue to be of use in future cases.

Over a five-month period starting at the end of the year the British security services detected a sophisticated spy network which, if its full ramifications were to be understood, must be kept in place.[23] The first suspect was a man called Denis, who in September 1916 was under observation by Richard Tinsley in Holland. On 20 September George Vaux Bacon, an American journalist newly arrived in England from New York, wrote to Denis from London. On 22 September Bacon went to Holland where he stayed throughout October; his letter, however, was not intercepted until 29 September and not read until 9 October, so its late arrival at Denis's address in Holland naturally aroused Bacon's suspicion. This was compounded when, in October, Tinsley's agent Mauritz Hyman approached Bacon rather clumsily.

On 2 November Bacon returned to England. Tinsley watched him leave Rotterdam, and saw a couple of other suspected spies see him off. Mail interceptions had thrown up their names and connected them to people called Sander and Wunnenberg in New York. Instructions to the Port Police at Gravesend were that Bacon was to be 'searched but not alarmed'.

In London, Melville's men watched him. He deposited £200 with the American Express Company and stayed at the Coburg Hotel in Bayswater. This was new; before the war, German spies had put up at a predictable range of hotels – the Bonnington and the Ivanhoe in Bloomsbury, the Wilton at Victoria.

On 14 November there came a breakthrough in Rotterdam. Tinsley was approached by a man called Graff, a metal merchant who was on the British blacklist but wanted to be taken off it for the sake of his business. He told Tinsley that he had been approached to join the 'imperial messenger service' of the German admiralty and showed a couple of sheets, apparently blank but containing secret messages, which were destined for New York. This was what Breeckow would have been doing had he not been caught, but Graff had been invited to be a courier for what had obviously become a much more secure service. He described the instructions and props he had been given. He had been told to observe specific things while in transit through England, and to obtain answers to questions such as 'What is the English end of a submarine cable from Alexandrovskii on the White Sea?' He was also given a sock impregnated with a solution which, when dunked in lukewarm water, would yield invisible ink; a palpable advance on the old talc-and-eau-de-cologne method. Graff was told to go along with Germany's plans for his deployment, and duly went into action.

Curtis-Bennett was with the Bureau now, and it was in the middle of collating an entire ring of spies. Many names were gathered by 23 November thanks to translation and development of Graff's documents and associated mail interceptions from England and Holland. A number of American journalists and some business people were linked and all communicated with Sander and Wunnenberg in New York. A week after Graff's visit to Tinsley, Bacon in London filed an article to America and sent a letter. Both were intercepted and read. By the time a decision had been made to call him to Scotland Yard for an interview that would frighten him off, he had left for Ireland. A message went out to all ports to review neutrals, especially those coming and going via New York.

Bacon travelled around Ireland between 25 November and 8 December, when he returned to London to find a letter from Basil Thomson awaiting him. It was an invitation to attend Scotland Yard for an interview. He was detained on admitting that he had been in touch with Denis. Meanwhile, a suspect American journalist called Hastings had landed in Rotterdam and had been spotted by Tinsley with other suspects. The ramifications of this spy ring seemed to spread almost beyond the capacity of the Bureau to deal with it. Information came from Germany to the effect that 'reports satisfactory in the highest degree had been received from three sources in Ireland'. In December Tinsley obtained material from an anonymous informant which confirmed that Hastings, along with Rutherford and Cribben who had seen Bacon off on the boat to England, were part of the ring. Graff confirmed this with damning proof against Bacon and Rutherford in February.

It was time to wind this operation up: 'A search of radiograms fell through owing to the labour and expense involved' and Graff's proof was enough. Bacon made a full confession on 9 February. On 28 February he was tried and condemned to death.

However, he was put to better use still. On 20 February the American Senate passed an anti-espionage Bill which, once enacted, enabled the arrest of Sander and Wunnenberg. Bacon was released on licence and sent to America to testify against them. They were both jailed. Those other American spies who escaped appear to have scattered, never to be of concern to the authorities.

We do not know when Melville stopped working. There is a record of him in action in Bloomsbury in May 1917, when he was staying at an hotel in Tavistock Square and watching a young Norwegian journalist who had borrowed money from the Vice-Consul in London and was waiting for more from home:

> Instructions were given to the General Post Office to forward the telegram and not to stop any reply to it but to send a copy to MI5... Meanwhile Mr Melville had made friends with Hagn at the hotel, had ascertained that the Dagblad had another correspondent in London, that Hagn did a good deal of writing in his bedroom [and] left the hotel at 11a.m. returning in time for dinner. By going out with him Mr Melville had managed to let him be seen by three members of the Special Staff and agents were watching to see whether he posted any letters. On the 12th, Mr Melville had secured from a glass-stoppered bottle in Hagn's bedroom some white liquid which on being tested proved to be, in MI9 nomenclature, C ink.[24]

Information that Alfred Hagn was a German agent had come from the police at Christiania. He was jailed for life but released after the war on compassionate grounds.

The wheel had come full circle. Melville had started like that, snooping in an hotel bedroom in Bloomsbury and uncovering a shirt marked 'Kent'. Now he fell ill. In the late summer of 1917, suffering from a kidney complaint, he had an operation and at the end of the year, in Bolingbroke Hospital, Wandsworth, he decided to retire.

> Chief Inspector Heat was very positive, but cautious.
>
> 'Well, sir', he said, 'we have enough to go upon. A man like that has no business to be at large, anyhow.'
>
> 'You will want some conclusive evidence', came the observation in a murmur.
>
> Chief Inspector Heat raised his eyebrows at the black, narrow back, which remained obstinately presented to his intelligence and his zeal.

'There will be no difficulty in getting up sufficient evidence against him', he said, with virtuous complacency. 'You may trust me for that, sir', he added, quite unnecessarily, out of the fullness of his heart; for it seemed to him an excellent thing to have that man in hand to be thrown down to the public should it think fit to roar with any special indignation …But in any case, Chief Inspector Heat, purveyor of prisons by trade, and a man of legal instincts, did logically believe that incarceration was the proper fate for every declared enemy of the law. In the strength of that conviction he committed a fault of tact. He allowed himself a little conceited laugh, and repeated:

'Trust me for that, sir.'

Joseph Conrad, The Secret Agent, 1906 [25]

Was Melville 'Chief Inspector Heat'?

Was he a 'purveyor of prisons', who sent innocent men to jail? He had cooked up the case against Deakin and the rest.

Asked by Counsel whether he had paid Coulon any money as a police spy, Inspector Melville declined to answer and the judge over-ruled the question on grounds of public policy. Counsel for the defence remarked that his object was to show that all which was suspicious in the case was the work of Coulon; in fact that it was Coulon who had got up the supposed plot.

Would he beat a man up to get a confession? Was he intolerant? Was he not called in court a 'notorious liar'?

London, Jarvis, 12th December
At the Trafalgar Square meeting last Sunday Malatesta got two black eyes, and Agresti had his left cheek smashed up, by Melville's men.

London, Jarvis, 12th December
…Melville wanted to close down the Lapie bookshop, but was dissuaded.

Would he do a deal with a criminal? Did he get

> ...that satisfactory sense of superiority the members of the police
> force get from the unofficial but intimate side of their intercourse
> with the criminal classes, by which the vanity of power is soothed,
> and the vulgar love of domination over our fellow creatures is
> flattered as worthily as it deserves?

He let Sidney Reilly escape arrest over the counterfeit roubles
and he must have known the man was a murderer. And yet,
by dealing with Reilly, who was a different class of informer
altogether, he was surely placing his head in the lion's mouth.
A 'satisfactory sense of superiority' is not something that serves
the lion-tamer well.

William Melville was not Conrad's Chief Inspector Heat.
Unlike that sly and mean-spirited character, he had a sense of
humour and its necessary obverse, a sense of tragedy. The Walsall
case was indefensible, and so far as we know he never did anything like it again.

He was tight with information but generous with his staff: he
had the gift of inspiring respect unaccompanied by fear. In later
years, at any rate, he seems to have mellowed out of his intoler-
ance; there is much in his professional reports to indicate that
he recognised human frailty, as well as human viciousness. He
loved his family and they loved him. James, his younger son, was a
protégé of Ramsay Macdonald and became Solicitor-General in
the 1929 Labour Government. He was of a different cast of mind
from his father but so far as we know they came to accommodate
one another's opinions. James died at forty-six, never having fully
recovered from serious injury sustained at Salonika. William, the
elder son, married and settled in New Zealand after the First
World War. Kate became Mrs Clifford Rainey.

In 1913 Melville wrote his will.

> I bequeath to my son William John Melville the gold ring which
> I usually wear the scarf pin presented to me by King George the

scarf pin presented to me by Queen Alexandra the cigarette case presented to me by the German Emperor the cigarette case presented to me by his Excellency Monsieur Gorymikine Secretary of State for Russia the silver cigar case presented to me by Princess Henry of Battenberg the tantalus presented to me by my colleagues on my retirement and also the sum of two hundred pounds which bequest I make to him inasmuch as he showed no desire as a youth to enter any profession and consequently spared me the necessary expenses in connection therewith. I bequeath to my daughter Kate Mary Madelaine the ring presented to me by the Emperor of Germany and the ring presented to me by the Shah of Persia. I bequeath to my son James Benjamin the cigarette case presented to me by the Czarewitch the sleeve links presented to me by King Edward the scarf pin presented to me by the King of Spain the gold watch presented to me by the Emperor of Germany together with the gold chain and appendages thereto which I wear with the said watch. Decorations I have received from King Edward and from foreign powers the combined scarf pin and stud received from Lady Pirbright the presentation tea and coffee service received from my colleagues on my retirement. I would like my wife my daughter and my son James Benjamin to live together as long as possible and I desire that during the widowhood of my wife and while she and my said daughter and son continue to live together they shall have the joint use of my plate linen china glass books pictures prints furniture…[26]

On it goes, the palpable proof of a successful professional life whose prosperous, liberal-minded end arguably justified the sometimes cruel means.

Melville's attitude to policing was revolutionary in its day and it was he who passed on this attitude to the Secret Service. He was focussed to the point of ruthlessness, discreet to the point of secrecy. He had begun work in the days of the hansom cab and the street-sweeper; he had seen the first motor cars and speaking tubes; he had come to recognise telegrams and morse code, cryptography and fingerprinting and forensic analysis, as the tools of his trade. When he lay in the Bolingbroke Hospital dictating his memoir in the latter half of 1917, Zeppelins had already dropped bombs on London. It was a new, fearful century, and his great days were behind him.

He died of kidney failure on 1 February 1918, just one month after acknowledging that he would never work again:

> In leaving the Branch now, it is to me a very great personal satisfaction that I cannot remember a single enquiry or mission on which I have been engaged, which was not carried out in a satisfactory manner. Another source of satisfaction is that I have always felt I had the support and confidence of my Chiefs, and never had a wry word with any of them.
>
> I wish the Department all good luck.
> (signed)
> William Melville,
> 31st December 1917

APPENDIX

DOCUMENTS

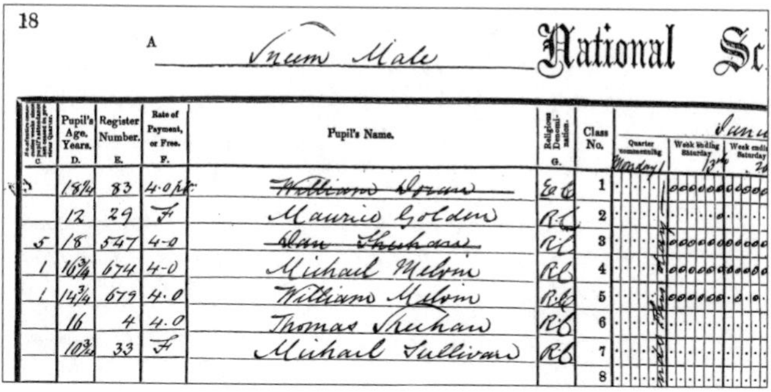

18 A Sneem Male National Sc

Pupil's Age, Years. D.	Register Number. E.	Rate of Payment, or Free. F.	Pupil's Name.	Religious Denomination. G.	Class No.
18¾	83	4.0 pk	~~William Doran~~	E.C	1
12	29	F	Maurice Golden	R.C	2
18	547	4-0	~~Dan Sheehan~~	R.C	3
16¾	674	4-0	Michael Melvin	R.C	4
14¾	679	4.0	William Melvin	R.C	5
16	4	4.0	Thomas Sheehan	R.C	6
10¾	33	F	Michael Sullivan	R.C	7
					8

Fig. 1 Melville's last year at school (school register)

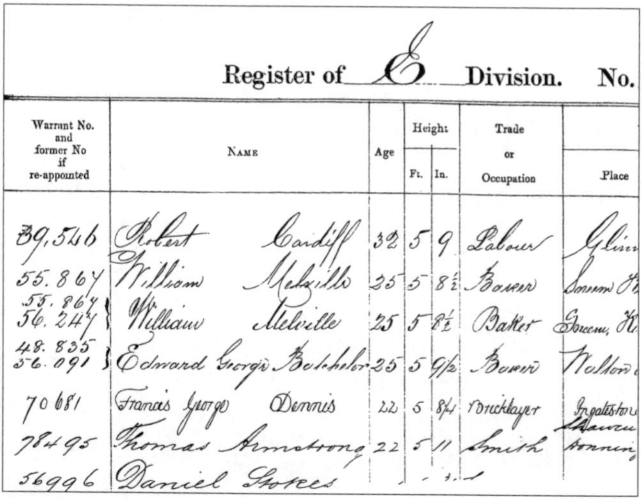

Register of E Division. No.

Warrant No. and former No if re-appointed	Name	Age	Height Ft.	Height In.	Trade or Occupation	Place
39,546	Robert Cardiff	32	5	9	Labourer	Glin
55.867	William Melville	25	5	8½	Baker	Sneem K
55.867 56.247	William Melville	25	5	8½	Baker	Sneem, K
48.835 56.091	Edward George Batchelor	25	5	9½	Baker	Walton
70681	Francis George Dennis	22	5	8¼	Bricklayer	Ingatestone
78495	Thomas Armstrong	22	5	11	Smith	Donnin
56996	Daniel Stokes					

Fig. 2 Melville joins the Metropolitan Police, 1872 (E Division register)

B 2840 G

W B & L (x)—43812—1000-10-94

METROPOLITAN POLICE.

CENTRAL OFFICER'S }
SPECIAL REPORT. }

CRIMINAL INVESTIGATION DEPARTMENT,

NEW SCOTLAND YARD,

SUBJECT *Petrick &*
Kuback, alleged
Bohemian Anarchist

23rd day of January 1895.

REFERENCE TO PAPERS.

I beg to report having
made enquiry and find
that Alois Kubalck, tailor
lives at 134 Wardour Street
W.C. and J. Petrick, clerk,
lives at 48 St James Road
N. It is highly probable
these are the two men
referred to. But they have
not hitherto been known
to Police, as having any
connection with the Anarch.

DATE.	NAME.	ADDRESS.
Jan 15th	M Merriman	Rozellgnarm
"	J Mortimer Dudman	— " —
"	C Dflasri	Alhambra Theatre
"	Harry Houdini	New York
"	E C Pickering	Alhambra Theatre
"	G Clown	Hassocks
	W. Robertson	Leytonstone
	Miss Ronald	Harbert
	E. Dunlop	Leytonstone
18	Col. W. F. Rideaux	St. Lawrence-on-Sea

RETIREMENT OF SUPERINTENDENT MELVILLE.—
A correspondent writes :—" Superintendent Melville,
Chief of the Political Department, Scotland-yard, has
resigned his position after 25 years' service in the Metropolitan Police Force. The resignation will deprive Scotland-yard of the services of the most celebrated detective
of the day. Mr. Melville, who is known as the King's
detective, has been responsible for the safety of many
monarchs and potentates, and he has been the recipient of
many foreign orders as well as English honours, including
the Royal Victorian Order, bestowed upon him by the
King. For 20 years Mr. Melville has been connected with
the special branch of Scotland-yard known as the
Political Department, and, while much of his work has
become public property, the full extent of it cannot for
obvious reasons be disclosed. He first came into prominence during the dynamite scare of the early eighties. It
was he who directed the operations which resulted in the
police of every country keeping a close observation on
every known Fenian, and it was he who, in conjunction
with ex-Detective-Superintendent Black, of Birmingham,
succeeded in capturing the ringleaders and effectually
stifling the most exciting political plot of modern times.
In stamping out Anarchism, too, Mr. Melville accomplished a great task. He had his agents in every capital
in the country, and it is said that there is scarcely a single
known Anarchist whom he could not put his hand upon at
a moment's notice. He has been instrumental in personally capturing some of the most dangerous Anarchists,
and as the result of his system of espionage gangs of
political plotters have been broken up before the danger
point could be reached. During the later years of Queen
Victoria's reign Mr. Melville was responsible for the
personal safety of her Majesty, and since her death he has
been performing similar offices for the King. He also
acted as bodyguard to the German Emperor and M.
Loubet when they paid visits to this country."

Fig. 3 opposite above Melville report on anarchist suspect, 23 January 1895

Fig 4. opposite below Harry Houdini's signature in Scotland Yard
visitors' book, June 1900

Fig. 5 above Melville 'retires' 1903 (*Times* hail him 'most celebrated detective of the day')

Fig. 6 top Business card of W. Morgan, General Agent (aka M)

Fig. 7 above Business card of H.D. Long (one of M's first agents)

Fig. 8 opposite M seeks a pay rise (letter, 23 January 1905)

WINCHESTER HOUSE,

ST. JAMES'S SQUARE,

S.W.

23·1·05

Dear Sir Thomas,

M. has raised the question of his salary, and asks for an increase.

He says that old ~~colleagues~~ subordinates of his, ~~too~~ who have also left the force,

S.190/2

8th April 1904

Dear Sir

I beg to inform you that Long left for Hamburg on 30th ult. But he had first to proceed to Brussels re obtaining some introductions if possible.

I gave him full instructions how to act & of course many suggestions. Everything is to be done in a commercial way. To this end he will present attached card which explains itself. I received a telegram from him yesterday from Hamburg stating that his address is Hotel Glaesner, Neuer Jungfernstieg.

✳ He will do all possible to get in with some employés in the firms of Busch ✳/c & Gottlieb Goermer, both mentioned in precis of reports

Yours obediently
W Melville

Fig. 9 *above* Report written by Melville, 8 April 1904 (re Long's mission to Germany)

Fig. 10 *opposite above* Secret Service accounts for December 1908 showing agents' salaries

Fig. 11 *opposite below* Service record of Col. Vernon Kell

December, 1908.

DATE.	EXPENDITURE.	£.	s.	d.
December				
2nd	Capt. G. B. Pretoria for R. (for Dec.)	40	-	-
14th	For B. from 1·12·08, & 28·209 (Admin. exp.)	170	-	-
22nd	For M. (pay & ex for Dec. & ½ for rent)	74	17	7
"	" L. (½ pay for Dec.)	20	16	8
"	" B. (for Dec.)	124	5	-
"	Minor expenses	1	-	-
29th	For C. (rent)	5	-	-
31st	For E. (½ quarter's pay in adv. (& Admiralty))	25	-	-
"	For D. (five months' pay in arrears)	62	10	-
		523	9	3
	Balance = £	287	9	2
	TOTAL. £	810	18	5

Surname **KELL**   Full Christian Names **Vernon George Waldegrave**   Present Rank **Lt.-Col.**

Full pay, half pay or retired? **Ret.**   Pension? **Yes**   Reserve of officers? **Yes**   £50.2.5☓☓ G.S.O.1 1.3.1

Record of Service

Rank	Regiment	Date
2/Lt.	S.Staffs	1894
Lieut	"	1896
Capt	"	1901
Major	Res of Off	1913
Lt Col	Temp	1914

Staff and extra-regimental employment or Regimental Staff Service

A.D.C. to Brig-Genl, Wei-hai-Wei 1900
Spec. Service. China Exp? 1900 - 8
Staff Capt. Hd. Qrs. 1904 - 7
Imperial Defence Committee 1907 - 9
(Historical Section)

Date of retirement **1909** on appointment t.M.O.5

War Services **China, 1900. Relief of Tientsin**   War Medals **Medal + Clasp.**   Other decoration, including Foreign Order:
Knight 2nd class Order of St. Olav
(Norwegian)

Staff College?   Languages   Write | Read | Speak   Other qualifications
Certificates? **Various.**   German   Interpreter
Russian   colloq. do —
Chinese
French   — passed. —   Travels in overseas Dominions or foreign countries
Date of joining this Section **1.10.09**   Italian   Reading —   Russia, Germany, France, China
grading before the War?   Japan. U.S.A. Canada. Switzerland
Holland. Belgium. Siberia.

> In leaving the Branch now, it is to me a very
> great personal satisfaction that I cannot remember a single
> enquiry or mission on which I have been engaged, which was
> not carried out in a satisfactory manner. Another source
> of satisfaction is that I have always felt I had the support
> and confidence of my Chiefs, and never had a wry word with
> any of them.
>
> I wish the Department all 'Good-Luck.'
>
> *Melville*
>
> MMC.   31st December, 1917.

1. Rummenie.	A.J.F.	London.	(See III,1108).
2. Stubenvoll.	Karl.	Newcastle.	(See III,1106).
3. Meyer.	Karl,	Warwick.	(See III,1094-1096).
4. Kuhr.	Johann.	Newcastle.	(See ----)
5. Buchwaldt.	Oscar.	Brighton.	(See 349 - 354).
6. Hemlar.	Karl.	Winchester.	(See III,1105).
7. Apel.	Fred.	Barrow.	(See II, 771-791).
8. Laurens.	Max.	London.	(------- -).
9. Lozei.	Franz.	Sittingbourne.	(See 171 - 180).
10. Hegnauer.	Thomas.	Southampton.	(See III, 1109).
11. Schneider.	Adolf.	London.	(See 142-145)
12. Von Willer.	Karl.	Padstow.	(----------)
13. Kronauer.	Marie.	London.	(See. 114 - 123.)
14. Rodriguez.	Celso.	Portsmouth.	(See II,882-915).
15. Diedrichs.	Fred.	London.	(See III, 1075 - 1080).
16. Klundor.	August.	London.	(See 135 - 141.
17. Heine.	Lina.	Portsmouth.	(See III,864-889).
18. Schutte.	Heinrich.	Weymouth.	(See 181 - 206).
19. Sukowski.	Fred.	Newcastle.	(See III,1104).
20. Kruger.	Otto.	Abercynon Mountain Ash.	(See 399 - 422).
21. Engel.	Johann.	Falmouth.	(See 274 - 287).

SENIORITY LIST AND REGISTER
OF PAST AND PRESENT MEMBERS
DECEMBER, 1919

NOTE.—The names of those not employed by the Service at the date of publication are printed in *italics*.

The names of those ranking as Officers and Officials of the Service are printed in capital letters, and of the Clerical and Auxiliary Staffs and Employees, in ordinary type.

Name	Date Joined		Date left		Remarks
MELVILLE, W., MVO, MBE.	1 Dec.	1903	18 Dec.	1917	Chief Detective (dec.)
KELL, Col. Sir V. G. W., KBE, CB, late Capt. S. Staffs. R. ..	9 Oct.	1909	*June 1940*		Director G.S.O.1.
Westmacott, J. R.	14 Mar.	1910	*1921*		Chief Clerk.
CLARKE, Capt. F. L. S., Suff. R.	1 Jan.	1911	30 Nov.	1912	
Westmacott, Miss D.	16 Jan.	1911	*1912*		Clerical Staff.
OHLSON, Comdr. B. J., R.N.R.	10 May	1911	12 Nov.	1914	
	2 July	1916	18 July	1917	
Regan, J.	7 June	1911	13 Aug.	1916	Detective (dec.)
Strong, Corpl. F. S., R.A.S.C. ..	18 Sept.	1911	26 July	1916	Clerk.
Newport, Miss H. M.	27 Oct.	1911	*1921*		Clerical Staff.
DRAKE, Major R. J., DSO, N. Staff. R., R. of O.	1 Apr.	1912	. 1 Mar.	1917	
Sumner, Mrs.	1 Oct.	1912	4 Aug.	1916	Caretaker.
Fitzgerald, H. I.	1 Nov.	1912	*left*		Detective. *left*
HOLT-WILSON, Lt.-Col. E. E. B. CMG, DSO, late Capt. R.E. ..	20 Dec.	1912	*June 1940*		Dep. Director G.S.O.2.
BOOTH, Capt. F. B., Gen. List	1 Jan.	1913	..	..	Joined as civilian.
LAWRENCE, Capt. K. E., late R.M.L.I.	31 Jan.	1913	31 Mar.	1914	
Holmes, Miss S.	27 Feb.	1913	31 Dec.	1918	Clerical Staff.
BRODIE, Capt. M., Gen. List ..	1 July	1913	*left*		Joined as civilain.
Strong, Stanley, late Cpl. R.A.S.C.	10 July	1913			Clerk.
FETHERSTON, Capt. J. B., Gen. List	1 Jan.	1914	*left* .	..	Joined as civilian.
Bowie, Miss D.	7 Jan.	1914	5 Dec.	1918	To Paris. (Clerical staff)
	20 June	1919			
HALDANE, Lt.-Col. M. M., late Capt. R. Scots.	22 Apr.	1914	*left*		Asst. Director G.S.O.2.

Fig. 12 opposite above Melville's farewell, December 1917

Fig. 13 opposite below MO5's list of the twenty-one spies arrested August 1914

Fig. 14 above MI5 Seniority List/Register, December 1919 (M is top of list)

BILL FITZGERALD INTERVIEW

Shortly after the publication of the first edition of this book in October 2004, I had the good fortune to meet and interview Bill Fitzgerald, the grandson of Harry Fitzgerald, a close colleague and confidant of William Melville's. The interview was originally published in Eye Spy *Magazine in February 2005:.*

We sip afternoon tea in a wood panelled room off the main lobby of London's Russell Hotel. After nearly fifteen minutes of small talk, Bill Fitzgerald takes off his glasses and slowly begins to relax. He had seemed slightly reticent when he arrived, but is now chatting away as if we're old friends. If it wasn't for the fact that I'd found his birth certificate some months earlier at the Family Records Office, it would have been difficult to guess that Bill was only a year and a few months short of his 75th birthday.

As interesting as his anecdotes about policing London's East End just after the last war are, it isn't his police career that we've met to talk about, but that of his grandfather, Harry Fitzgerald. In particular, Harry's tales of a superior he had referred to only as 'Mr M'.

According to Bill, Harry 'had known Mr M when they worked together at Scotland Yard' at the turn of the last century. Like Harry, he was a Londoner of Irish birth. One day, some years after Mr M's retirement, the two had met again at the wedding of a mutual friend, and Harry had been let into a confidence. Apparently, Mr M hadn't really retired at all, but was now working for the War Office in what Bill's grandfather described as a 'hush hush job'. Not only that, but Mr M was looking for an assistant and wanted Harry to join him. Although this would mean leaving the police force, Harry was assured that he would be 'well looked after' and would suffer no loss in earnings. So far as the neighbours were concerned, Harry was now working as an investigator for 'a small insurance office not far from Temple Underground Station'. The hours could be a little irregular, but insurance fraudsters didn't always work nine to five either.

In reality he was now an employee of the Secret Service Bureau, which had been set up in 1909 and would later evolve into what we know today as MI5 and MI6. I was able to tell Bill that Mr M was in fact William Melville, who had previously been Head of Scotland Yard's Special Branch in which capacity he had been described by the Times as 'the most celebrated detective of the day'. The blank look on Bill's face told me that this was the first time he had heard the name. This was not really surprising, given the fact that Melville's role as 'M', the Secret Service spymaster remained a closely guarded secret for the best part of a century, giving credence to the view that the most accomplished spies are those whose cover was never revealed or exposed during their lifetime.

The reason I had suggested that Bill and I meet in Russell Square was that it was just around the corner from an address that figured in a story Bill had partly alluded to when we spoke on the telephone two weeks earlier. During our brief chat, Bill had told me that his grandfather had been involved in tracking down an accomplished German spy in the First World War who had posed as a Russian. He and Mr M had 'searched high and low' for the spy, and had eventually found him in a town 'some-where up north'. I asked Bill if there was anything else about this story he had first heard as a young boy that he could remember. When he told me that the spy had a partner who was a baker and that he had somehow managed to escape the firing squad, the case of Karl Muller immediately sprang to mind.

Nearly two years earlier while reading through a set of MI5 case files on German spies arrested during 1915, I had been particularly intrigued by Muller's. A Russian born German, Karl Muller had, before the war, run a successful marine engineering business in Antwerp. Following the occupation of the city by German troops he was recruited for espionage work, given a basic training and put on a boat with a party of Belgian refugees which left Rotterdam for England on 9th January 1915. Little did he know that the Rotterdam PO Box number he had been given by German Intelligence to send his reports back to was already known to the British Secret Service. They had been intercepting all mail sent to that address for some time and had been testing the notepaper for secret ink. Several of Muller's reports had been posted from Deptford, south London, and were intercepted shortly after his arrival. Copies in his case file suggest that he was particularly interested in troops movements; 'today I visited Hampstead in London where the quarters of the Australian troops are. Saw 600-800 men, mostly recruits who will require training.'

According to Bill, Harry had been involved in a raid 'on a dirty little room above a baker's shop in Deptford High Street', where a supply of secret ink had been discovered, along with envelopes and writing paper which matched those that had been addressed to the Rotterdam PO Box. The baker, Peter Hahn was arrested, but no clues as to the identity and whereabouts of the letter writer were found. Mr M, who seemed to relish the opportunity of going under cover, decided to move into a lodging house a few doors away, where he befriended a number of his fellow tenants. A man they described as a Russian had been seen in Hahn's company on several occasions of late and had been drinking with him in the local pub. Apparently the Russian had lodgings near Russell Square and had been particularly noted by the other drinkers for the lingering odour that seemed to accompany him. Armed with a description, Mr M had then scoured the lodging houses and hotels in the Russell Square area until he found his man.

Not long before Harry Fitzgerald's death he recited the story of the spy's capture for the last time to his grandson, on this occasion referring to a few details he had not told him as a child. Apparently Mr M had been put on Muller's trail by 'a madam who ran a brothel in Bloomsbury'. The girls remembered Muller as a particularly ugly man with an unpleasant odour. Mr M had told Harry that a lot of useful informa-tion came out of brothels and after all, 'didn't the bible tell how Joshua had a spy in Jericho who was a prostitute?'

Muller was 'away on business' when Mr M, Harry and a posse of police officers came calling at his lodgings. As a result, information was obtained that led to his arrested in a Newcastle hotel room the following day. Four months later, in June 1915 he was tried, found guilty and condemned to be shot at the Tower of London. When his time came he apparently walked along the line of men who were about to shoot him, solemnly shaking each one by the hand, before his eyes were bound and he bravely faced the firing squad.

Had Muller managed to evade detection, his file makes clear that he would have represented a serious threat to British security; intelligent, well educated and person-able he spoke English with only the faintest of accents and was highly convincing in his guise as a Russian travelling salesman.

With a new pot of tea on the way, Bill's story was drawing to a close. 'Muller's trial and execution were never announced in the papers' Harry had told him. So far as his German controllers were concerned, Muller was still alive and at liberty. His death was followed by one of the first recorded 'double-cross' operations employed by the Secret Service. Experts from the Bureau's Imitation Section perfected his handwriting and continued to file reports containing false intelligence to his chief in Rotterdam. The case officer writing the reports even managed to negotiate Muller a pay rise, which was duly paid into Secret Service funds along with the regular money orders made out to Karl Muller that arrived from Rotterdam each and every month. According to the case file, there was soon enough money for the Secret Service to purchase a much needed second hand motor car, which was "promptly christened 'The Muller'".

According to a 1919 list of MI5 staff recently released to the National Archives in Kew, Harry Fitzgerald left the Secret Service before the war ended, which I found puzzling. I wondered if Bill knew anything about the reasons surrounding his departure from the service. Bill gazed into the distance, almost as if he hadn't heard the question, and then shrugged his shoulders. "All he ever said was that things were never the same after Mr M died, when that was I haven't a clue". On that point I was able to volunteer that Melville had died of kidney disease in a south London hospital on 1st February 1918. What precisely happened to the 'Special Staff' section of the Secret Service he had headed so successfully is still somewhat of a mystery. It seems clear, however, that its independence as an autonomous entity did not long outlive its creator. At some point during 1918 it became a victim of administrative re-organisation. Those hand picked men who worked under Melville, like Harry Fitzgerald, may well have coveted the idea of succeeding him, and no doubt greeted such developments with some despondence.

Harry Fitzgerald clearly felt that Melville's death changed things for the worse – he certainly didn't leave to improve his prospects. According to Bill, he went into the licensing trade, where he failed to make his mark. He died fifteen years after the end of the war, with no police pension and barely enough to his name to pay for his funeral.

Melville's legacy, however, lived on. His attitude to policing was nothing short of revolutionary in its day and it was he who passed on this attitude to the Secret Service. He was focussed to the point of ruthlessness, discreet to the point of secrecy. He had begun work in the days of the hansom cab and the street sweeper; he had seen the first motor cars and speaking tubes; he had come to recognise cryptography, fingerprinting and forensic analysis as the tools of his trade. He had also seen the potential of telephone tapping and mail interception and had determinedly lobbied the Government to create an effective counter-intelligence service that utilised these approaches. Today MI5, the organisation he strove to create, is a household name and one of the world's leading intelligence agencies.

ABBREVIATIONS USED IN NOTES AND BIBLIOGRAPHY

ADM	Admiralty
APP	Archives de la Préfecture de Police (Paris)
BL	British Library
BT	Board of Trade
CAB	Cabinet Office
HO	Home Office
FO	Foreign Office
GARF	State Archive of the Russian Federation
MEPO	Metropolitan Police
MO3	Military Operations 3
MO5	Military Operations 5
MI1c	Military Intelligence 1c (see SIS)
MI5	Military Intelligence 5 (The Security Service)
NID	Naval Intelligence Department/Division
PRO	Public Record Office (now TNA – The National Archives)
SIS	Secret Intelligence Service (MI1c, now MI6)
SSB	Secret Service Bureau
TCD	Trinity College, Dublin
TNA	The National Archives (Kew)
WO	War Office

NOTES

Chapter 1: The Man From Kerry

1   Memoir of William Melville MVO MBE, 31 December 1917, (TNA KV1/8).

2   For this and other points about the village and its history, I am indebted to T.E. Stoakley's *Sneem: The Knot in the Ring*, Sneem Tourist Association 1986.

3   M From Sneem', by Dan Downing and Ferrie Galway, 1999 edition of *Sneem Parish News, incorporating Sneem Past and Present*, p.6.

4   Summarised from the diaries of Father John O'Sullivan, later Archdeacon of Kenmare, quoted in Stoakley, ibid.

5   Primary Valuation of Tenements 1852, Parish of Kilcrohane, village of Sneem; The pub/bakery is today known as the Blue Bull in South Square, Sneem. Years later it was named after a line in Synge's *Playboy in the Western World*, in Act III of which there is a reference to 'my blue bull from Sneem'. See Stoakley, ibid.

6   Registration Office, Births, Deaths and Marriages, Southern Health Board, Killarney, County Kerry; Correspondence between the author and Father Patrick Murphy (Parish Priest, Sneem) 8 January 2004, 18 January 2004, 19 March 2004. On early documents and records, the family name appears as Melvin as opposed to Melville.

7   Sneem National School Roll Book. The school operated a six-day week and membership of the class was allowed by ability rather than age, which varied in this case between ten and eighteen.

8   *Police Review* 26 September 1896.

9   The story about William and his disappearance at the railway station was first published in the 1999 edition of *Sneem Parish News, incorporating Sneem Past and Present*, p.6. It is from an interview with Val Drummond, a village elder who heard it from Winnie Hurley, whose family ran the Blue Bull when it was known as Hurley's. The Hurley family took over the pub from the Melville family in the 1920s and ran it until the 1950s.

10 London's population in 1871 was 3.89 million. B.R. Mitchell, *British Historical Statistics*, Cambridge University Press 1988, Ch.1 Table 6.

11 Register of E Division, No 310, Metropolitan Police.

12 Family Records Centre, 1871 census. RG 10/657 ff 6-11.

13 Gathorne Hardy's remark to Disraeli quoted p.81 of Christy Campbell, *Fenian Fire: The British Government Plot to Assassinate Queen Victoria*, Harper Collins 2002.

14 Information on the police strike of 1872 from Martin Fido and Keith Skinner, *The Official Police Encyclopaedia*, Virgin Books 2000.

15 *The Times* 25 September 1876 p.12 col. a (Lambeth).

16 www.met.police.co.uk.

17 *The Times* 18 Dec 1877 p.11 col. c (Lambeth Police Court) and *The Times* 8 January 1878 p.11 col. f (Surrey Sessions).

18 PhD dissertation by Lindsay Clutterbuck of Special Branch, 'The Methodology of Police Operations', p.167.

19 *The Times* Monday 3 Feb 1879 p.12 col. a (Southwark).

20 This is Littlechild's version. It is one among many, all of them slightly contradictory but emerging at the same point: the admitted corruption of Detectives Meiklejohn and Druscovitch. Sir Basil Thomson's much later account (Thomson headed the CID before the Second World War) does not mention Littlechild at all. Basil Home Thomson, KCB, *The Story of Scotland Yard,* 1935. John Littlechild, *Reminiscences of John George Littlechild,* Leadenhall Press, 1894.

21 S.H. Jeyes, concluded by F.D. How, *The Life of Sir Howard Vincent,* George Allen and Co. 1912.

22 Quoted in Jeyes, ibid.

23 Jeyes, ibid., p.65.

24 Jeyes, ibid.

25 Ibid., p.69.

26 Patrick McIntyre in *Reynolds' Newspaper,* 14 April 1895.

27 George Dilnot, *The Story of Scotland Yard,* Geoffrey Bles, 1930.

28 *The Times* Thursday 8 Jan 1880, p.11 col. e.

29 File on Tarn's Department Store at the Southwark Archive.

30 *The Times* 29 September 1880, and *The Times* 22 October 1880 p.9 col. 9.

31 *The Times* 21 January 1882, p.4 col. f.

32 *The Times* Tuesday 19 Dec 1882, p.5 col. f.

Chapter 2: Dynamite Campaign

1 Major Henri Le Caron (Thomas Miller Beach), *25 years in the Secret Service: Recollections of a Spy.* Reprinted from 10th edition of 1893 by EP Publishing Ltd, Wakefield, Yorkshire, 1974.

2 Sir Robert Anderson KCB, *The Lighter Side of My Official Life,* Hodder and Stoughton 1910.

3 Sir Robert Anderson, ibid.

4 Sir Robert Anderson, ibid.

5 Quoted in Christopher Andrew, *Secret Service: the Making of the British Intelligence Community,* Heinemann 1985, p.17.

6 A memo marked 'secret' from Sir Robert Anderson dated 6 May 1882. 'My belief… is very strong that should these events avail to induce the Parliamentary leaders of the LL to abandon their irreconcilable attitude, they will rapidly produce a complete breach between the LL party and the Fenians. The result of course will be a revival of Fenianism pure and simple before the close of the year, and a demand probably for special powers to enable the Govt. to deal with it.'

7 Christy Campbell, *Fenian Fire,* Harper Collins 2002.

8 As told by Littlechild to a reporter from *Cassell's Saturday Journal,* quoted in Stewart P. Evans and Paul Gainey, *The Lodger,* Century 1995.

9 Bodleian Library Special Collections and Western MS, 4 April 1883.

10 *The Times* 12 May 1883 p.14 col. b and *The Times,* Thursday 14 June 1883 p.3 col. a

11 Entry 111, Register of Deaths in the Registration District of West Ham in the County of Essex, 3 July 1883, Margaret Gertie Melville.

12 Christy Campbell, ibid., pp.129–132.

13 Letter from Jenkinson to Earl Spencer, 3 April 1884. Spencer Papers, BL.

14 Sir Robert Anderson, ibid.

15 Sir W. Vernon Harcourt to Sir Henry Ponsonby, 21 November 1883. Bodleian Library Harcourt Collection, WVH691.

M: MI5's First Spymaster

16 26 February 1884 TNA HO 144/133. Square brackets indicate gaps where the original has been destroyed.

17 R.C. Clipperton, HM Consul, to Lord Granville, dated Philadelphia 3 March 1884. TNA FO 5/1928.

18 Letter from HM Consul 3 March 1884, ibid.

19 R.C. Clipperton, HM Consul, to Sackville West at the Legation in Washington, dated Philadelphia 4 March 1884. TNA FO 5/1928.

20 Edward Jenkinson to Earl Spencer 12 April 1884. Spencer Papers, BL.

21 Memo of 6 March 1884 from Jenkinson TNA HO 144/721.

22 Memo from Jenkinson, ibid.

23 Littlechild's account of the incident is on p.185 of Stewart P. Evans and Paul Gainey, *The Lodger,* Century 1995.

24 Edward Jenkinson to Sir William Vernon Harcourt, 2 June 1884. Bodleian, Harcourt Collection.

25 Edward Jenkinson to Earl Spencer 15 December 1884. Spencer Papers, BL.

26 Edward Jenkinson to Earl Spencer 15 December 1884. Spencer Papers, BL.

27 5 May 1894 report from the police in Cherbourg, to M. le Sous-Préfet in response to a query about the presence of British police there.

Chapter 3: Plot and Counterplot

1 Sir A. Liddell to his counterpart at FO, Whitehall 4 March 1884. TNA FO 5/1928.

2 Christy Campbell, *Fenian Fire,* Harper Collins 2002. See also TNA MEPO 3/3070 'Police at Ports' which shows that Moser was assisted by Sergeant (later Superintendent) Frank Forest.

3 Consul General Bernal to FO, Le Havre 17 Dec 1884.

4 Lord Sackville West to Sir Julian Pauncefote, 8 April 1885, TNA FO 5/1931.

5 In a memo dated 9 March 1886 Jenkinson acknowledged that there were, from the RIC, 'nine men and an officer' in London when Cross came into office in the summer of 1885. TNA HO 144/721.

6 In theory, there were to be forty-five Scotland Yard men around the ports and twenty-nine RIC men. Those CID men who reported to Williamson were listed with a W after their names and those who reported direct to Gosselin had a G. Melville reported to Williamson, who in turn was supposed to report to Gosselin anyway, TNA HO 144/133/A34848B, Jenkinson memorandum of 11 March 1884; also TNA MEPO 3/3070, Police at Ports.

7 21 May 1885, Edward Jenkinson to Earl Spencer. Spencer Papers, BL.

8 Christy Campbell, *Fenian Fire,* Harper Collins 2002 pp.157 and 167 concerning Burkham.

9 Minute of interview of 17 June 1885, TNA HO 144.721.

10 Memorandum, E. Jenkinson 22 June 1885, TNA HO 144.721.

11 Letter from Sir William Vernon Harcourt to James Monro, 22 June 1885, TNA HO 144.721.

12 Note from J. Monro 4 July 1885, TNA HO 144.721.

13 Campbell, ibid., see refs to Carroll-Tevis and Casey.

14 Campbell, ibid., p.177 concerning General Millen.

15 Memo from Edward Jenkinson, 26 September 1885, p.16, TNA 30/6/62.

16 BL MSS Add Gladstone Papers 44493 p.177.

17 Note on Relations between Mr Jenkinson and Metropolitan Police in connection with Fenian conspiracies, &c. Monro 28 May 1886, TNA HO 144/721.

18   Memo, Lushington to Childers, 14 March 1886, TNA HO 144/721.

19   Monro 28 May 1886, ibid.

20   Monro 28 May 1886, ibid.

21   Monro to Sir Charles Warren, Commissioner of Police, 24 September 1886,
     TNA HO 144/721.

22   Francis Elliot to FO, 10 July 1886, TNA FO 146/2844.

23   HM Consul Le Havre to FO, 26 July 1886, TNA FO 5/1975.

24   Campbell, ibid. see refs. to Maharajah Duleep Singh, Tevis.

25   HM Consul Le Havre to FO, 2 October 1886, TNA FO 5/1975.

26   Cypher communication from Sir R. Monier St Petersburg 4 August 1886.

27   Campbell, ibid., p.201.

28   Matthews to Jenkinson, 11 December 1886, TNA HO 144/157.

Chapter 4: A Very Dangerous Game

1   FO to Captain Surplice, HM Consul at Boulogne, 14 June 1887.

2   Monro report to Matthews marked 'Secret' 4 November 1887, TNA HO
     144/1537.

3   Monro report, ibid.

4   Monro report, ibid.

5   Campbell, ibid., p.251.

6   Memo from Monro headed 'secret', 4 November 1887, TNA HO144/1537.

7   This arises from Monro's remark (see final Monro quotation below) that
     Melville had at this time been 'formerly stationed' at Le Havre and that the
     Home Office as Monro said 'have an agent in Paris' who was Melville. It was
     Melville who called at the embassy.

8   See for instance Philip Magnus, King Edward VII, John Murray 1964. There
     were occasional assassination threats and a Tory Government, at least, was par-
     ticularly conscious of threats to political stability from royal blackmail, financial
     scandal, and all the other traps lying in wait for a prince out for a good time.
     The Ambassador in Paris was reasonably well informed about what was going
     on in HRH's life.

9   Campbell, ibid.

10   James Monro, April 1903.

11   Campbell, ibid.

12   James Monro, ibid.

13   James Monro, ibid. This account he could only have received from Melville.

14   George Dilnot, The Story of Scotland Yard, Geoffrey Bles 1930.

15   Christy Campbell, Fenian Fire, Harper Collins 2002, p.294.

16   The Pall Mall Gazette, 'The Criminals and Police of London: A Report of an
     Unofficial Commission', Tuesday 9 October 1888.

17   The Pall Mall Gazette, ibid.

18   The Pall Mall Gazette, ibid.

19   Quoted by George Dilnot, ibid., from Sir Robert Anderson KCB, The Lighter
     Side of my Official Life, Hodder and Stoughton 1910 .

20   The full story of Tumblety's arrest and flight, together with a copy of the
     Littlechild letter, is to be found in Stewart P. Evans and Paul Gainey, The Lodger,
     Century 1995.

21   Evans and Gainey, ibid., p.184.

22   Angust McLaren, A prescription for murder: the Victorian serial killings of Dr Thomas
     Neill Cream, University of Chicago Press 1993.

23 Evans and Gainey, ibid., p.xi.

24 Evans and Gainey, ibid., favour 22 Batty Street, off Commercial Road, as the site of his lodging.

25 Pearson to Home Under-Secretary, 20 November 1888, TNA HO 144/208/A49500M, sub. 3 (quoted by Bernard Porter).

26 Melville's eldest son, William, gave a number of talks on Radio Station 2YA, New Zealand, commencing 24 August 1937. Melville's involvement in the Ripper episode was one of his anecdotes.

27 Quoted in Evans and Gainey, ibid., p.xii.

28 See report from Montreal in the *St Louis Republican* of 22 December 1888, quoted by Evans and Gainey, ibid. p.227.

29 Quoted in Evans and Gainey, ibid., p.225.

30 Evans and Gainey, ibid., p.228 *et seq*.

31 Evans and Gainey, ibid.

Chapter 5: War on Terror

1   Michael Davitt, *Notes of an Amateur Detective*, Trinity College Dublin Library, TCD MS 9551.

2   Barry Hollingsworth, *The Society of Friends of Russian Freedom: English Liberals and Russian Socialists, 1890-1917*, Oxford Slavonic Papers n.s. vol 3 (1970).

3   Correspondence between Foreign Office, Home Office and Anderson, 14 January to 4 February 1890. HO 45/9816/B7734, subs 1-2 (cited by Porter).

4   Hollingsworth, ibid.

5   S. Stepniak, *The Dynamite Scares and Anarchy* in New Review vol. 6 (1892) p.533.

6   John Sweeney, *At Scotland Yard*, 1904.

7   Gosselin to Anderson, 12 January 1890, the story re-told that day in Anderson's letter to Balfour (Secretary of State for Ireland), PRO 30/60/13/2.

8   Bernard Porter, *The Origins of the Vigilant State*, Weidenfeld and Nicholson 1987.

9   Bernard Porter, ibid.

10 Bernard Porter, ibid., pp.105-106.

11 TNA FO 45/677.

12 Her maiden name was Allen.

13 Entry 88, Register of Marriages in the Registration District of the Isle of Wight, 8 August 1891.

14 Hsi-Huey Liang, *The Rise of Modern Police and the European State System from Metternich to the Second World War*, Cambridge 1992, and in particular E. Thomas Wood, *Wars on Terror: French and British Responses to the Anarchist Violence of the 1890s*, MPhil dissertation, 2002, Pembroke College, Cambridge.

15 *The Walsall Anarchists: Précis of the Case for the Convicts in Mitigation of Sentence*, Walsall Archives A53582/28. Melville said in court in April 1892 that he had known Coulon for two years.

16 Mathieu Deflem, *Bureaucratization and Social Control: Historical Foundations of International Police Co-operation*, Law and Society Review 34(3): pp.601-40, 2000.

17 'It doesn't matter. You are such and such?' – 'Yes.' – 'Where do you live?', J.A. Cole, *Prince of Spies; Henri Le Caron*, Faber and Faber 1984.

18 Joseph Conrad, *The Secret Agent*, (Methuen 1907) Folio Society 1999.

19 PhD dissertation by Lindsay Clutterbuck, 'The Methodology of Police Operations', pp.173 *et seq*.

20 *The Birmingham News*, Saturday 13 February 1892.

21 TNA HO 144/243/A53582C, Letter of 16 May 1892.

22 *The Walsall Anarchists*, ibid. The spelling of Battola here is incorrect – records show the correct spelling to be Battolla, as used in the main text.

23 TNA FO YS/10259, Memo no. X36450/1, 18 March 1892.

24 From an account (p45) in a supplement to *Freedom* of June 1892.

25 Zéro no.6, London 23 November 1893. Archives de la Préfecture de Police, Paris (APP). See note 22 above about spelling of Battola.

26 Patrick McIntyre in *Reynolds' Newspaper*, 14 April 1895.

27 Clutterbuck, ibid.

28 A homosexual brothel having been raided, titled patrons were named; one fled abroad and another sued the editor of a newspaper. The brothel-keeper was allowed to flee.

29 APP 21000-2-A, Zéro no.2 from London 11 February 1892.

30 APP 21000-2-A, Black from London 26 July 1892.

31 APP 2100-2-A, Black from London 6 April 1892.

32 APP 21000-2-A, Zéro no.2 from London 22 August 1892.

33 APP 21000-2-A, Zéro no.2 from London 3 September 1892.

34 APP 21000-2-A, Zero no.2 from London, 4 October 1892.

35 APP 21000-2-A, Zéro no.2 from London 16 November 1892.

36 Archive of the Imperial Russian Secret Police (Okhrana), Box #35 Index #Vc Folder 1 'Relations with Scotland Yard', Hoover Institution, Stanford, California

37 *L'Autorité,* 12 April 1892.

38 Williamson died at the end of 1889.

39 Typed report, unattributed, dated 3 May 1892, APP.

40 Confidential letter from Anderson at New Scotland Yard to the Under-Secretary of State at the Home Office, 24 May 1892, TNA HO B2840c.

41 Clutterbuck, ibid.: Williamson as quoted in Frederick Bussey, *Irish Conspiracies,* Everitt and Co (London) 1910.

Chapter 6: A Man to be Trusted

1 Article in *Paris,* 13 December 1892.

2 Note to M. l'Officier de Paix de la 1ère brigade dated 21 December 1892, from the Cabinet of the Préfecture's premier bureau. Lists official instructions about London clubs to be watched. APP 21000 2 A.

3 Report of agent R, 31 December 1892. APP 21000 2 A.

4 Patrick McIntyre, *Scotland Yard: its Mysteries and Methods,* in *Reynolds' Newspaper* 10 February 1895.

5 Angus McLaren, *A Prescription for Murder: the Victorian Serial Killings of Dr Thomas Neill Cream,* University of Chicago Press 1993.

6 Christy Campbell, *Fenian Fire,* Harper Collins 2002.

7 Campbell, ibid.

8 APP 21000 2 A, from Inspector Moser to M. Goron, London 26 April 1893.

9 From McLaren, ibid. p.112: 'At the end of the report on Haynes's interview the question was put forward whether Haynes could be relied on. An unidentified officer at Scotland Yard wrote in the margin "no".' Cites Scotland Yard 19 May 1892, TNA MEPO 3 144; and also J.B. Tunbridge report, 28 May 1892, TNA MEPO 3 144.

10 Excerpts from various reports, APP 21000 2 A, 1893 first half of year.

11 Memo from Melville at the CID, New Scotland Yard, 24 May 1893, TNA HO 45/9739/A54881.

12 TNA HO 45/9739/A54881.

13 Report from Y3 in Paris, 30 September 1893; APP.

14 Excerpts from various reports, APP. 21000 2 A, October and November 1893.

15 The story of congratulations is from a cutting, enclosed with an agent's report, from *Le 19e siècle*.

16 Extract from an unnamed French paper, report from London 3 December, APP.

17 Article translated back into English from an undated French paper. The *Daily Graphic* account would have appeared on Saturday 17 or Monday 19 February 1894, APP.

18 Later in the year, when an Italian anarchist assassinated President Carnot in Lyons, Fédée pointed out that he had passed on a warning to the Lyons police but it was evidently disregarded. See *l'Echo de Paris*, 20 June 1894.

19 George Dilnot, *Great Detectives and their Methods* Houghton Mifflin Co, NY 1928.

20 The *Standard*, 23 April 1894. Cutting in HO 144/259/ASS860.

21 'Anarchist leader at Bow Street' from the *Standard* of 24 April and the *Daily Chronicle* of 25 April 1894. Cuttings in TNA HO 144/259/ASS86022TNA B280c/42a.

Chapter 7: The Lodging House

1 The weekly *Illustrated London News* was first. The *Daily Mail* was using half-tone photographs by the end of the century.

2 *Police Review and Parade Gossip,* May 17 1895, citing the *Daily Chronicle*.

3 For instance, a letter from the Austro-Hungarian Embassy to Earl Kimberley, and Sweeney's reply, respecting a couple of Bohemian anarchists. Melville adds in a postscript that the only Bohemian anarchist paper is printed in America. January 1885. TNA HO/144/SP7 B2840C/54.

4 *Police Review and Parade Gossip,* 2 October and 9 October 1896.

5 Charles Kingston, *A Gallery of Rogues,* London 1924. Ch. XVIII, quoted in Kimball, *The Harassment of Russian Revolutionaries Abroad: the London Trial of Vladimir Burtsev in 1898.*

6 Barry Hollingsworth, *The Society of Friends of Russian Freedom: English Liberals and Russian Socialists, 1890-1917.* A paper read at the Anglo-Soviet Conference of Historians in London, September 1969.

7 Sigmund Rosenblum changed his name to Sidney Reilly in June 1899 and he joined the Secret Intelligence Service in 1918 under that name. Dubbed 'Britain's Master Spy' and the 'Ace of Spies', his exploits were serialised in the 1930s by the London *Evening Standard* and syndicated in the foreign press. Shortly after the publication of the first James Bond novel *Casino Royale* in April 1953, Ian Fleming told a contemporary at *The Sunday Times*, where he worked as Foreign Manager, that he had created James Bond as the result of reading about the exploits of Sidney Reilly in the archives of the British Secret Services during the Second World War. For a full account of Reilly, his life and associations, refer to Andrew Cook, *Ace of Spies – The True Story of Sidney Reilly,* Tempus Publishing (second edition) 2004.

8 Report by V. Rataev (Okhrana, Paris) to Department of Police, St Petersburg, 24 February 1903, Fond 102, Inventory 316, 1898, Article 1, Section 16, Paragraph A, pp.84-85, State Archive of the Russian Federation (GARF), Moscow.

9 Bernard Porter, *The Origins of the Vigilant State,* The Boydell Press 1991, Chapter 9.

10 Okhrana Archive, Box #35, Index #Vc, Folder 3, 'Relations with Scotland Yard', Hoover Institution, Stanford, California.

11 Hollingsworth, ibid.

12 Confidential Memorandum on the Publication in Russian enclosed in M. Lessar's *Note Verbale* of 6 September 1897, TNA FO 65/1544.

13 *Parliamentary Debates* IVth series, vol. 53 (Loodon 1898) cols. 879, 1209-10, cited in Kimball, ibid.

14 Unsigned letter to 'Cher Monsieur Melville', Okhrana Archive, Box #35 Index #Vc Folder 3 'Relations with Scotland Yard', Hoover Institution, Stanford, California.

15 Cook, ibid.

16 Entry 17, Register of Births in the Registration District of Belmullet, County Mayo, 1 February 1878.

17 E. Thomas Wood, *Wars on Terror: French and British responses to the anarchist violence of the 1890s*, MPhil dissertation, 2002, Pembroke College, Cambridge.

18 Written as 'Je n'ai pas besoin d'ajouter que tout individu soupconné d'avoir l'intention decommettre un des actes criminels précités en contravention de la loi anglaise est soumis à l'observation policière'. TNA HO 45/10254/X36450.

19 TNA FO YS 102SY.

20 Foreign Office minute initialled K.E.D. (Digby), 2 January 1899, TNA FO YS 102SY.

21 Robin Bruce Lockhart, *Ace of Spies*, Hodder and Stoughton 1967.

22 Cook, ibid, p.49ff.

23 The papers and recollections of Beatrice Houdini were published in *Houdini, His Life Story* by Harcourt, Brace and Company, New York, 1928.

24 Porter, ibid., makes this point.

25 The hated regulation boots were abandoned in 1897 in favour of a boot allowance for uniformed men.

26 An account of the Legitimation League affair is in Porter, ibid.

27 All biographies of Havelock Ellis tell the story. See also *The Times*, 1 November 1898.

28 Porter, ibid.

29 John Sweeney, *At Scotland Yard*, London 1904.

30 APP 310000-18-A, Letter from Euréka, London 4 October 1899.

31 Assistant Commissioner Henry's report to Home Office, 7 January 1902, TNA FO YS 102SY.

32 Harold Brust, *I Guarded Kings*, Hillman-Curl, Inc. New York, 1936, relates both the Prince of Wales's brush with death (pp48-50) and the murder of King Humbert (p80).

33 Copy Sanderson's Foreign Office response to H.E. Count Hartsfeldt, 9 August 1900. TNA HO 144/527/X7983/2.

34 Sanderson's response, ibid.

35 The story is told in his autobiography, *Steinhauer*, published in English by The Bodley Head in 1930. It was 'edited by' Sidney Felstead.

36 He was fifty-one years old.

37 At the inquest, held on 25 April 1901 by Edward N. Wood, Deputy Coroner for London, the unidentified body was said to be that of a twenty-four-year-old woman found in the afternoon of 23 April, Inquest ref. # DAZ 067009.

38 The one-armed anarchist was I. Blumenfeld, executed in Warsaw in January 1906 (source Politicheskie partii Rossii: istoriia i sovremennost, glava X, Anarkhisty, Rosspen, Moskva, 2000).

39 Assistant Commissioner Henry's reports to Home Office, ibid., 7 January 1902 and 28 April 1902. The April report is a response to a German query. All quotations here are from the January report.

40 Postponed from 1901, when he had appendicitis.

41 A detailed account of Rubini's time in England, signed by Melville, was sub-
    mitted on 3 December 1902, TNA HO 45/10482/X77377.

42 Memorandum (Immediate and Secret) from Sir Edward Bradford, 24 May 1902,
    TNA HO 144/545/A55176.

43 Memorandum of 24 May, ibid.

44 So is he said to have cried to the police who arrested him. Brust, ibid., p.48.
    See also pp.60-61.

45 Letter to 'Murdoch' from Sir E. Bradford, 21 November 1902, TNA HO
    144/668/X84164.

46 Report by W. Melville MVO, 25 November 1904, MI5 file PF NE 4570.

47 Ibid.

48 Ibid.

49 Ibid.

50 Ibid.

51 Ibid.

52 Ibid.

Chapter 8: W. Morgan, General Agent

1   Probably the Eagle Insurance Office, where James Melville later worked
    according to his *Who Was Who* entry.

2   From the will of William Melville, proven in April 1918: 'I bequeath to Bridget
    Moore (*née* Joyce) of Plymouth the sum of thirty pounds free of duty in recog-
    nition of her kindness and the excellent manner in which she looked after my
    children on the death of my first wife.' (Family Division of the High Court of
    Justice, Principal Probate Registry, 20 April 1918, No.864).

3   A thought which occurred to Bernard Porter as late as 1985 when 'One of the
    very few files from this period to which the Home Office still denies access is one
    which contained correspondence about the expenses he claimed… It is unfor-
    tunate for his memory that the available historical record is so incomplete, giving
    rise to what may be unworthy and are certainly uncorroborated qualms.' Bernard
    Porter, *The Origins of the Vigilant State,* Weidenfeld and Nicolson 1985. These docu-
    ments are now available and give evidence of payments to, for instance, Coulon.

4   Quoted in Michael Smith, *The Spying Game: The Secret History of British
    Espionage,* Politico's Publishing 2003.

5   Christopher Andrew, *Secret Service,* Heinemann 1985.

6   Smith, ibid.

7   Smith, ibid.

8   Smith, ibid., p.55.

9   Andrew, ibid.

10 Note of 30 November 1906 from Major George Cockerill at the War Office to
    Sir Charles Hardinge, who has recently taken over from Sir Thomas Sanderson
    at the Foreign Office: 'I promised to enquire whether we had any record here
    of the origin of the system under which we obtain Secret Service funds from
    the Foreign Office. I have ascertained that it dates from the early part of 1886
    and that the arrangement was initiated by Mr Sanderson (as he then was) and
    Sir Henry Brackenbury.' TNA HO 3/133.

11 Quoted in Andrew, ibid., p.31.

12 Memo from Sir Thomas Sanderson annotated by Lord Lansdowne, 16
    September 1903.

13 Sir Edward Henry to Sir Thomas Sanderson, 28 September 1903. The money discussion must by now have taken place. To a great extent arrangements were in place well before anything was put in writing by the parties concerned.

14 Memoir by William Melville MVO MBE, TNA KV1/8, p.3.

15 Vernon Kell's curriculum vitae, attached to letter dated 19 September 1909 to the War Office, TNA KV 1/5.

16 For a full account of this period in Reilly's life see Andrew Cook, *Ace of Spies – The True Story of Sidney Reilly*, Tempus Publishing 2004.

17 Anthony Wood, *Great Britain 1900-1965*, Longman 1978, p.49.

18 Wood, ibid., points out that this treaty was key to the eventual Entente (1904) between England and France. The French were already committed by treaty to come to the aid of Russia if required; any Japan *v.* Russia conflict might draw them into a war with England.

19 Armgaard K. Graves, *Secrets of the German War Office*, T. Werner Laurie 1914.

20 Graves, ibid., p.41.

21 Graves, ibid, p.45.

22 British intelligence reports to this effect from 1918 are listed in Cook, ibid., notes to Chapter 8.

23 Letter from E.G. Pretyman MP, Civil Lord of the Admiralty, to Sir Charles Greenway, 30 April 1919 (Record of the Anglo-Iranian Oil Company Ltd, Volume 1, (1901-18), pp.50-51, BP Archive, University of Warwick.

24 See Cook, ibid., in particular the chapter 'The Broker' in which his skills at misinformation on the one hand, and public relations on the other, are described.

25 'Lenin, Iskra and Clerkenwell', edited version of the lecture given by Tish Collins, (Librarian, Marx Memorial Library) at the 69th Marx Memorial Lecture (Marx Memorial Library, London); Lenin by Robert Service, p.169ff.

26 Herbert Fitch, *Traitors Within*, p.11ff.

27 MI5 file PF NE 4570.

28 Memoir by William Melville MVO MBE, TNA KV 1/8, p.8; Julian Marchlewski (1866–1925) alias Kujawiak and Karskii was the anarchist Melville met in Whitechapel. In 1893 he collaborated with Rosa Luxemburg to form a socialist underground movement in Russian Poland. A delegate to the Second International, he edited a socialist publication for several years in Poland and then went into exile. He was considered by other revolutionaries to be more committed to Polish independence than to the overall Marxist cause.

29 Report by V. Rataev (Okhrana, Paris) to Department of Police, St Petersburg, 24 February 1903. Fond 102, Inventory 316, 1898, Article 1, Section 16, Paragraph A, pp.84-85, State Archive of the Russian Federation (GARF), Moscow.

30 Akashi Motojiro, *Rakka ryusui, Colonel Akashi's Report on his Secret Co-operation with the Russian Revolutionary Parties during the Russo-Japanese War*, Finnish Historical Society, Helsinki, 1988, p.46.

31 Akashi, ibid., pp.32, 47, 52.

32 Memoir by William Melville, ibid., p.9 *et seq.*

33 Memoir by William Melville, ibid.

34 Memoir by William Melville, ibid.

35 Memoir by William Melville, ibid.

36 Memoir by William Melville, ibid.

37 Letter from Colonel Davies at War Office (Winchester House, St James's Square) to Sir Thomas Sanderson, 5 January 1905, TNA HD 130.

38 Sir Edward Henry refers to a claim for defamation by a man called Parmeggiani who claimed not to be the anarchist of that name referred to in Sweeney's memoir. The outcome, in October 1905, was unsuccessful for the plaintiff.

39 Sir Edward Henry to Colonel Davies, 21 January 1905, TNA HD 3/130.
40 From Colonel Davies to Sir Thomas Sanderson, 23 January 1905, TNA HD 3/130.
41 Note from Sir Thomas Sanderson initialled at end by L, 25 January 1905, TNA HD 3/130.
42 From Colonel Davies to Sir Thomas Sanderson, 31 January 1905, TNA HD 3/130.
43 Memoir by William Melville, ibid., p.9.
44 Sir Thomas Sanderson to 'Johnstone', 10 October 1905, TNA HD 3/131.
45 Sir George Clarke to M.D. Chalmers, 7 February 1905, TNA HD 317/43.
46 M.D. Chalmers to Sir George Clarke, 7 February 1905, TNA HD 317/43.
47 Report of 18 November 1905, TNA HD 3/131.
48 Under the Official Secrets Act of 1889.
49 Report of 21 November 1905, TNA HD 3/131.
50 Note scribbled on Sanderson's cover note of 29 November 1905: 'Yes: the suggestion at the end seems a reasonable one L'.
51 Letter from M.D. Chalmers in the office of the Secretary of State, Home Department, to Sir Thomas Sanderson, 30 November 1905, TNA HD 3/131.

Chapter 9: Shifting Sands

1 I am indebted to Dr Nicholas Hiley for the information that the article and the letter appeared in the *Daily Express* of 28 February 1906 (p2 col. 8) and 2 March 1906 (p5 col. 7) respectively.
2 From the outside, there is today only one clue to Melville's decade there: an unusually robust cast-iron garden gate, tall and ornate, with a design of Tudor roses. The black iron railings, no doubt removed during some munitions drive in the Second World War, remain as a row of stumps half-hidden by a hedge.
3 Memoirs of William Melville MVO MBE, p.15, PRO KV1/8.
4 Melville memoirs, ibid, p.16.
5 Armgaard K. Graves, *Secrets of the German War Office,* T. Werner Laurie 1914. His account is to be treated with circumspection. Steinhauer, who had not hired him and was probably miffed at the amount of money this man had got out of the War Office, says all Graves ever sent to Berlin was either worthless information or requests for money. See *Steinhauer,* below.
6 *Steinhauer, the Kaiser's Master Spy,* ed. Sidney Felstead, The Bodley Head, 1930.
7 Letter from Captain Repington to Sir Charles Hardinge, 21 March 1906, TNA HD 3/133.
8 Letter from Cleays to Captain Repington, 19 March 1906, TNA HD 3/133.
9 Sir Thomas Sanderson to Sir Charles Hardinge, 22 March 1906, TNA HD 3/133.
10 Lt-Col Charles A'Court Repington, *Vestigia,* Constable and Co., 1919.
11 Felstead, ibid., p.11.
12 Major Cockerill to Sir Charles Hardinge, 30 November 1906, TNA HD 3/133.
13 Melville memoirs, ibid.
14 Melville memoirs, ibid.
15 Michael Smith, *The Spying Game: the secret history of British espionage,* Politico's Publishing 2003.
16 Melville memoirs, ibid.
17 Melville memoirs, ibid.
18 Melville memoirs, ibid.

03

19 *History of the Development of Military Intelligence, The War Office 1855 to 1939,* Lt-Col William R.V. Isaac, TNA WO106/6083.

20 Details about the 1907 study are to be found in Nicholas P. Hiley, *The Failure of British Espionage against Germany 1907-1914,* Historical Journal 26, 4 (1983) pp.867-89.

21 *Steinhauer,* ibid.

22 *Steinhauer,* ibid.

23 Christopher Andrew, *Secret Service,* Heinemann 1985. Rué later became a double agent and was responsible for entrapping the inept British 'spy' Bertrand Stewart in 1911.

24 Hiley, ibid. Hiley says there was a man at Kiel but does not name him; but Hector C. Bywater and H.C. Ferraby, *Strange Intelligence: Memoirs of Naval Secret Service,* Constable 1931, strongly suggests Bywater.

25 Smith, ibid., p.63 says that this information appears in a series of articles about the Secret Service printed in the *Daily Telegraph* in September 1930. The author was almost certainly H.C. Bywater.

26 Hiley, ibid., mentions that mail could have been sent to another London office. According to the December 1908 Secret Service account (TNA HD3/138) E was already receiving £5 for 'rent' and a separate annual payment of £200 paid half-and-half by the Secret Service fund and the Admiralty; who E was and why rent was paid is unclear. The three offices known to have been clearing-houses for mail were at 24 Victoria Street (Melville until – almost certainly – December of 1908), Temple Avenue after that date (Melville again) and (from autumn of 1908) the 64 Victoria Street office of Edward Drew who was known as D.

27 Letter marked 'Private', Lord Fisher to Sir Charles Hardinge, 30 January 1909, TNA HD3/139.

28 Quoted in Hiley, ibid.

29 Letter from Sir Charles Hardinge to the British Ambassador at Constantinople, 12 January 1909, TNA HO 3/139.

30 Hiley, ibid.

31 Letter from Vernon Kell to the War Office, 19 September 1909, TNA KV 1/5.

32 Note prepared for DMO on 4 October 1908, almost certainly by James Edmonds. At this date Edmonds and his assistant were both writing briefing documents for the DMO in an attempt to get a reorganisation of the Secret Service. TNA KV 1/1.

33 Secret Service accounts for August 1909 submitted to General Staff, TNA HD 3/138.

34 Alan Judd, *The Quest for C: Mansfield Cumming and the Founding of the Secret Service,* Harper Collins 2000, p.144.

35 Judd, ibid., p.144.

Chapter 10: The Bureau

1 The affair of wide repercussions in which a French army officer called Dreyfus was vilified and exiled from causes rooted in anti-semitism in the French military establishment. Emil Zola's *J'Accuse* was the key document in the fight to clear his name.

2 Central Officer's Special Report, Enquiry re Kaulitz Farlow, signed P. Quinn Chief Inspector; MacNaghten's covering note dated 31 March 1902. PRO HO 45/1042/X77377.

3 See Andrew Cook, *Ace of Spies – The True Story of Sidney Reilly,* Tempus Publishing 2004, p.78ff.

4 Cook, ibid., for more about the St Petersburg paper, and the Ozone Preparations Company and its business in patent medicines. The location in Fleet Street is interesting but its significance in news-gathering or placing news remains a matter for speculation.

5 George Dilnot, *Great Detectives and their Methods,* Houghton Mifflin 1928.

6 Judd, *The Quest for C: Mansfield Cumming and the Founding of the Secret Service,* Harper Collins 1999, has details of this period.

7 For instance the nitpicking opposition to a claim for £2 p.a. from the Consul General in Genoa in return for news of ships coming and going from the port, TNA HO 3/139.

8 Judd, ibid., p.120.

9 Diary of Vernon Kell: 1910/1911, TNA KV 1/10. The order would be rescinded following a meeting held on 30 August.

10 Judd, *The Quest for C: Mansfield Cumming and the Founding of the Secret Service,* Harper Collins 1999.

11 Diary of Vernon Kell, ibid.

12 Hector C. Bywater and H.C. Ferraby, *Strange Intelligence: Memoirs of Naval Secret Service,* Constable 1931.

13 Judd, ibid., p.203.

14 They were caught spying while on leave in August 1910 and jailed. For reference to the internal naval enquiry that followed their release see Judd, ibid., p.237. They told Cumming they blamed Regnart for what happened to them (Judd, ibid., p.259). Kell's diary for 11 October reveals that one of them, before leaving England, had told his barber in Portsmouth that he was just off to do some spying in Germany.

15 She was possibly related to Major Wodehouse, Assistant Commissioner, Metropolitan Police, who instructed the Superintendent of Portsmouth Dockyard in October to communicate 'anything of importance' directly to Kell 'so as to lose no time'. See Diary of Vernon Kell, ibid., 12 October and 17 October 1910.

16 Diary of Vernon Kell, ibid., 6 September 1910.

17 *The Times* Thursday 8 September 1910 p.4 col. e.

18 Diary of Vernon Kell, ibid., 6 September 1910.

19 *The Times* 10 September 1910 p.5 col. e quotes both German papers.

20 *The Times* 16 September p.7 col. d, 21 September 1910 p.7 col. b, and 29 September 1910 p.9 col. e.

21 *The Times* 11 November 1910 p.4 col. d and 15 November 1910 p.5 col. e.

22 Mistakenly identified by the press at the time as 'Dr Phil Max Schultz' because he was a DPhil.

23 *The Times* 29 August 1911 p.4 col. c.

24 *The Times* 4 November 1911 p.9 col. g.

25 Inspector Herbert Fitch, a former Scotland Yard Special Branch officer, in *Traitors Within* published in 1933 by Doubleday Doran of New York, was able to take entire credit for investigating this case and several others. He joined Special Branch in 1903 and claims to have spoken four languages. It is certain that he sometimes made arrests in Melville's cases and was used by Melville on shadowing duty. He was demoted to the rank of sergeant on 6 December 1923 for 'rendering himself unfit for duty through drink while on duty' and resigned from the Metropolitan Police a month after his demotion on 8 January 1924, PRO, MEPO 4/347, 4/447, p.120.

26 Diary of Vernon Kell, ibid., 11 August 1910. Churchill was Home Secretary 1910-11.

27 MI5 file PF 363/1: Steinhauer, Gustav, TNA KV 4/112.

28 The 'chance remark on a train' version is also ascribed to Captain Eric Holt-Wilson, who replaced Stanley-Clarke as Kell's assistant several months after the event. It seems to this author that something is lacking, and that is the account of the further surveillance in London which comes from Bywater and Ferraby, below. Steinhauer, whose book is commended in his MI5 file as 'a very fair account of his organisation in this country' blames the carelessness of an unnamed German Admiralty official. Others have named the man as Captain von Rebeur-Paschwitz, who was connected with German naval intelligence.

29 Hector C. Bywater and H.C. Ferraby, ibid.

30 MI5 file PF 363/1: Steinhauer, Gustav, TNA KV4/112.

31 *Steinhauer,* ed. Sidney Felstead, The Bodley Head 1930.

32 This emerged at Ernst's trial in 1914.

33 Judd, ibid., p.95.

34 Diary of Vernon Kell, ibid., 13 October 1910.

35 Estimates vary between twenty and thirty thousand.

36 Michael Smith, *The Spying Game, the Secret History of British Espionage,* Politico's Publishing 2003.

37 Diary of Vernon Kell, ibid., 16 August 1910. The 'Stores' refers to the Army and Navy Stores in Victoria Street.

38 MI5's *Seniority List and Register of Past and Present Members* made up in 1919 shows that the service believed in keeping secrets within the family: the Chief Clerk, employed from March 1910, was J.R. Westmacott.

39 Judd, his biographer, ibid., (p121) refers to Ashley Gardens in the Vauxhall Bridge Road – it was actually Ashley Mansions.

40 Diary of Vernon Kell, ibid., 3 March 1911. Maybe this led to the flushing-out operation which took place in July, when the SSB placed a news item about wireless telegraphy experiments near Dorking and Kell and Melville went down there to see if any foreigners turned up to watch (ibid., 7 and 8 July 1911) Unfortunately they arrived a day late, when the Royal Engineers had demonstrated their skill and left.

41 Diary of Vernon Kell, ibid., 24 February 1911. Kell's friend is still so important that his name is blanked out of the records. Alfred Harmsworth, Lord Northcliffe, is a possible candidate; owner of the *Daily Mail,* he was convinced that Germany could and would attack.

42 *The Times* Wednesday 26 July 1911 p.12 col. a.

43 The Act quoted in *The Security Service 1908-1945: the Official History,* PRO Publications 1999, p.68.

44 *The Times* Wednesday 26 July as above.

Chapter 11: Drift to War

1 Correspondence between the police and MI5 concerning Jacob Peters began in 1920; he later became Vice Chairman of the Cheka, a forerunner of the KGB. His daughter, who years afterwards worked at the British Embassy in Moscow, was at one point scrutinised by MI5. (See TNA KV 3/1026). Correspondence about what happened to Peter the Painter, greatly illuminated by people who were part of the émigré political scene at the time, is in TNA KV 3/39 and includes material from after the Second World War. The conclusion was that Peter the Painter later returned to Britain after the First World War and worked

for ARCOS as Anton Miller (*maliar* is Russian for 'painter'). He may have been wrongly executed as a British spy in the mid-1920s. The Sidney Street file compiled by the Okhrana, State Archive of the Russian Federation (GARF), Moscow, Fond 102, Osobiy Otdel, 1910, article 359.

2   Harold Brust, *I Guarded Kings*, Hillman-Curl Inc., New York 1936.

3   *The Political Background of the Houndsditch murders and the Sidney Street Siege*, undated report with appendices, TNA KV3/39.

4   *The Times*, 9 May 1911.

5   Frederick Porter Wensley, *Detective Days*, Cassell and Co, 1931.

6   Appendix to *The Political Background of the Houndsditch Murders, &c*, ibid. Gardstein was the wounded man who died.

7   *Houndsditch 1910* in TNA KV 3/39.

8   He was hidden for four days at 24A, Dock Road, North Woolwich, before getting out of the country. See note 1 above.

9   Archie Potts's account of James Melville's life (Metropolitan Police Museum) cites *The Times* of 3 May 1911.

10 Private letter to Archie Potts from Mary Melville (James's daughter), 29 March 1988, Metropolitan Police Museum, ibid.

11 Anthony Wood, *Great Britain 1900-1965*, Longman 1968, p.72.

12 The Ilfracombe holiday is referred to in the diary of Vernon Kell, 3 and 5 September 1910, TNA KV 1/10 and in the *Ilfracombe Gazette and Observer*, 29 August 1910.

13 See *The Times* 18 March 1912 p.3 col. D, and 23 March 1912 p.7 col. a.

14 Christopher Andrew, *Secret Service*, Heinemann 1985, p.61.

15 *Steinhauer, the Kaiser's Master Spy*, ed. Sidney Felstead, The Bodley Head 1930.

16 *Hampshire Telegraph*, Friday 16 February 1912.

17 *The Times* Saturday 10 February 1912 p.7 col. a. He was released after hostilities began in 1914 and put on the 'watch' list rather than being interned. He died before the end of the war.

18 *Steinhauer*, ibid.

19 Dr Armgaard Karl Graves, *Secrets of the German War Office*, T. Werner Laurie 1914.

20 Graves, ibid.

21 *Steinhauer*, ibid., p.19.

22 Michael Smith in *The Spying Game*, Politico's Publishing 2003, cites (p73) Holt-Wilson for Melville's authorship of the list. However there was more than one, as later notes to this chapter confirm.

23 S.W. List XX: List of persons to be arrested in case of war, TNA KV 1/7.

24 *The Times*, Thursday 21 November 1912, p.4 col. c.

25 *Steinhauer*, ibid. pp.67 *et seq*. According to Steinhauer, Hentschel had been recruited in 1908, when he was a waiter in London.

26 *Steinhauer*, ibid.

27 *The Times* Thursday 21 November 1912, p.4 col. c.

28 Witnesses called to the hearing attested to his travel and also his bank payments. *The Times*, 4 December 1912, p.3 col. g.

29 *The Times*, Tuesday 19 November 1912, p.4 col. f.

30 *The Times*, Friday 17 January 1913, p.38 col. e.

31 Melville's detectives appear from TNA KV 1/44 f.57 (re Hagn) to have been known as the Special Staff; this would date from 1913-14 when their number began to increase.

32 *Steinhauer*, ibid.

33 *Steinhauer*, ibid., p.64.

34 MI5 Steinhauer file, ibid.
35 Losel was known to the authorities. He was on a list of persons to be jailed on the outbreak of war.
36 *Steinhauer*, ibid.
37 MI5 Steinhauer file, ibid.
38 TNA KV 1/7, ff45-7 'persons to be arrested in case of war' last amended on or after 30 July 1914; Daily Chronicle, 15 July 1915. I am indebted to Nick Hiley for his research and observations concerning the 1914 arrests on which I have relied in this chapter.
39 Hector C. Bywater and H.C. Ferraby, *Strange Intelligence: Memoirs of Naval Secret Service,* Constable 1931.
40 Hector C. Bywater and H.C. Ferraby, ibid.

Chapter 12: G Men

1 TNA DPP 1/29 Court Martial of Carl Hans Lody otherwise Charles A. Inglis, held at Westminster Guildhall 30 October to 2 November 1914.
2 Sidney T. Felstead, *German Spies at Bay,* Hutchinson and Co 1920; also John Fraser, then a Yeoman Warder of the Tower, whose sensitive account is reproduced in 'Stephen's Study Room' at www.stephen-stratford.co.uk/karl_lody.htm.
3 MI5 records (TNA KV 1/59 and TNA KV 1/69) list them as John Regan (joined 7 June 1911), Henry Fitzgerald (1 November 1912), William Burrell (5 May 1915), Arthur Hailstone (6 June 1915), C. Tartellin (17 December 1915), A. Regan *sic* (18 September 1916) and P. Whittome (1 November 1916). They were collectively known as the 'Special Staff'.
4 Chart marked 'Secret', *Directorate of Special Intelligence Showing Channels of Control,* Templewood Papers, II, 4a (3), Cambridge University Library.
5 See Stella Rimington, *Open Secret,* Hutchinson 2001, and Christopher Andrew, *Secret Service,* Heinemann 1985.
6 Felstead, ibid.
7 Bernard Porter, *Plots and Paranoia: the History of Political Espionage in Britain 1790-1988,* Routledge 1989, p.135. The information comes from a handwritten memoir that belongs to Professor John Dancy whose father, Dr Jack Dancy, wrote it half a century later (dancy Memoirs, pp.1132, 1460, 1481ff, 1690ff, 1912, 1937ff). Alan Judd, in *The Quest for C: Mansfield Cumming and the Founding of the Secret Service,* Harper Collins 2000, quite rightly casts doubt on the claim that Sidney Reilly was present at a lecture in 1915.
8 Michael Smith, *The Spying Game: the Secret History of British Espionage,* Politico's Publishing 2003.
9 Letter from John Ross, Specialist Crime Directorate, New Scotland Yard to the author, 18 December 2003.
10 Judd, ibid., p.377.
11 'They were given a history lesson by a cousin of the current Lord Chancellor, who taught them how espionage had a long, continuous and proud tradition in Britain, right back to the time of Walsingham.' – Bernard Porter, ibid., p.135. Porter's book was published in 1989. The Lord Chancellor until 1987 was Quintin Hogg, Lord Hailsham.
12 Felstead, ibid.
13 Felstead, ibid. The 'police' are detectives from Melville's section. (In Felstead's account, written with information supplied by Basil Thomon of Special Branch, they are referred to as police).

14   TNA KV 1/41 and 42, TNA KV 1/39-44, and TNA WO 141/2/2.
15   TNA KV 1/42 p.72 *et seq.*
16   General Court Martial of Willem Johannes Roos and Haicke Marinus Petrus Janssen held at Westminster Guildhall 17 July 1915. TNA WO 71/1312.
17   Fitch, ibid.
18   TNA KV1/42 para. 1251.
19   TNA KV1/42 para. 1258.
20   She died in Broadmoor, the asylum for the criminally insane, in 1921.
21   Roland Wild and Derek Curtis-Bennett, *Curtis,* Cassell and Co. 1937.
22   Herbert Fitch in *Traitors Within,* ibid., relates the case; it is among those of which Melville (who is not mentioned) had charge.
23   Information on George Vaux Bacon and associated cases is from TNA KV 1/42 series p.155.
24   TNA KV 1/44, f57, Felstead, in *German Spies at Bay,* ibid.
25   p.113 in the Folio Society edition of 1999.
26   Will of William Melville, Esq, ibid.

BIBLIOGRAPHY

Charles A'Court Repington, *Vestigia* (Constable, 1919)
Rupert Allason, *The Branch* (Secker and Warburg, 1983)
Sir Robert Anderson, *The Lighter Side of my Official Life* (Hodder and Stoughton, 1910)
Christopher Andrew, *Secret Service* (Heinemann, 1985)
Lady Susan Ardagh, *The Life of Sir John Ardagh* (John Murray, 1909)
Sir Henry Brackenbury, *Some Memories of my Spare Time* (Blackwood and Sons, 1909)
Harold Brust, *I Guarded Kings* (Hillman-Curl, 1931)
Hector Bywater and H.C. Ferraby, *Strange Intelligence* (Constable, 1931)
Christy Campbell, *Fenian Fire* (Harper Collins, 2002)
J.A. Cole, *Prince of Spies: Henri le Caron* (Faber and Faber, 1984)
Sir Arthur Conan Doyle, *Sherlock Holmes – The Complete Facsimile Edition* (Wordsworth, 1989)
Joseph Conrad, *The Secret Agent* (Heinemann, 1921)
Andrew Cook, *On His Majesty's Secret Service – Sidney Reilly ST1* (Tempus, 2002)
Andrew Cook, *Ace of Spies – The True Story of Sidney Reilly* (Tempus, 2004)
Derek Curtis-Bennett, *Curtis – The Life of Sir Henry Curtis-Bennett* (Cassell, 1937)
Richard Deacon, *A History of the Russian Secret Service* (Taplinger, 1972)
Richard Deacon, *A History of the British Secret Service* (Frederick Muller, 1969)
George Dilnot, *Great Detectives and their Methods* (Houghton Mifflin, 1928)
Stewart Evans and Paul Gainey, *The Lodger* (Century, 1995)
Sydney Felstead, *German Spies at Bay* (Hutchinson, 1920)
Herbert Fitch, *Traitors Within* (Doubleday, 1933)
Lord Edward Gleichen, *A Guardsman's Memories* (Blackwood, 1933)
Armgaard Karl Graves, *Secrets of the German War Office* (T. Werner Laurie, 1914)
S.H. Jeyes, *Life of Sir Howard Vincent* (George Allen, 1928)
Alan Judd, *The Quest for C* (Harper Collins, 1999)

Howard Kellock, *Houdini* (Harcourt, Brace and Co., 1928)

Henri Le Caron, *25 Years in the Secret Service: The Recollections of a Spy* (Heinemann, 1893)

John Littlechild, *The Reminiscences of Chief Inspector Littlechild* (Leadenhall Press, 1894)

Giles MacDonogh, *The Last Kaiser* (Weidenfeld and Nicolson, 2000)

Angus McLaren, *Prescription for Murder* (University of Chicago Press, 1993)

Donald McCormick, *Murder by Perfection* (John Long, 1970)

Akashi Motojiro, *Rakka Ryusui* (SHS, Helsinki, 1988)

Bernard Porter, *The Origins of the Vigilant State* (Weidenfeld and Nicolson 1987)

Bernard Porter, *Plots and Paranoia: A History of Political Espionage in Britain*
  (Routledge 1989)

Stella Rimington, *Open Secret* (Hutchinson, 2001)

Colin Rogers, *The Battle of Stepney* (Robert Hale, 1981)

Donald Rumbelow, *The Sidney Street Siege* (St Martin's Press, 1973)

J. Schneer, *Ben Tillett* (Croom Helm, 1982)

Robert Service, *Lenin* (Macmillan, 2000)

Kenneth Silverman, *Houdini!!! The Career of Erich Weiss* (Harper Collins, 1996)

Michael Smith, *New Cloak, Old Dagger* (Victor Gollancz, 1996)

Michael Smith, *The Spying Game* (Politico's, 2003)

Richard Spence, *Trust No One – The Secret World of Sidney Reilly* (Feral House, 2002)

Gustav Steinhauer, *The Kaiser's Master Spy* (Bodley Head, 1930)

T.E. Stoakley, *Sneem: The Knot in the Ring* (Sneem Tourist Association, 1986)

Frederick Porter Wensley, *Detective Days* (Cassell and Co, 1931)

Nigel West, *MI5: British Security Operations 1909-1945* (Bodley Head, 1981)

Nigel West, *MI6: British Secret Intelligence Operations 1909-1945* (Weidenfeld and
  Nicolson, 1983)

Anthony Wood, *Great Britain 1900-1965* (Longman, 1978)

The Security Service 1908-1945, The Official History (PRO, 1999)

LIST OF ILLUSTRATIONS

Nicholas of Russia, 1902 (Metropolitan Police)
13 William Melville 1903 (Melville Family)
14 Colonel Sir James Trotter (National Army Museum)
15 Winchester House, St James Square (Author)
16 Sir Francis Davies (National Army Museum)
17 Le Grand Hôtel, Cannes (Author)
18 William Knox D'Arcy (BP plc)
19 Sidney Reilly (Author)
20 William Melville 1906 (Melville Family)
21 25 Victoria Street, office of W Morgan General Agent (Author)
22 64 Victoria Street, first Headquarters of the SSB (Westminster City Archive)
23 Captain Sir Mansfield Cumming (Author)
24 Major Sir James Edmonds (National Army Museum)
25 Colonel Sir Vernon Kell (Hulton Getty)
26 Temple Chambers, Temple (Author)
27 3 Paper Buildings, Temple; Bureau Headquarters 1911-12 (Author)
28 Watergate House, York Buildings, Bureau Headquarters 1912 (Westminster City Archive)
29 MI5 G Branch (Security Service)
30 Gustav Steinhauer (Author)
31 Karl Muller (Author)
32 Willem Roos (Author)
33 George Vaux Bacon (Author)
34 Haicke Janssen (Author)
35 Sir James Melville (Melville Family)
36 Lieutenant Henry Curtis-Bennett (Author)
37 Melville's grave (Author)

Melville Documents

1 Melville's last year at school (School Register)
2 Melville joins the Metropolitan Police, 1872 (E Division Register)
3 Melville Report on anarchist suspect, 23 January 1895
4 Harry Houdini's signature in Scotland Yard visitors' book, June 1900
5 Melville 'retires' 1903 (*Times* hail him 'most celebrated detective of the day')
6 Business card of W. Morgan, General Agent (aka M)
7 Business card of H.D. Long (one of M's first agents)
8 M seeks a pay rise (letter 23 January 1905)
9 Report written by Melville, 8 April 1904 (re Long's mission to Germany)
10 Secret Service accounts for December 1908 showing agents' salaries
11 Service record of Col. Vernon Kell
12 Melville's farewell, December 1917
13 MO5's list of the twenty-one German spies arrested August 1914
14 MI5 Seniority List/Register, December 1919 (M is top of list)

INDEX

TEMPUS – REVEALING HISTORY

Quacks Fakers and Charlatans in Medicine
ROY PORTER

'A delightful book' *The Daily Telegraph*

'Hugely entertaining' *BBC History Magazine*

£12.99   0 7524 2590 0

The Tudors
RICHARD REX

'Up-to-date, readable and reliable. The best introduction to England's most important dynasty' *David Starkey*

'Vivid, entertaining... quite simply the best short introduction' *Eamon Duffy*

'Told with enviable narrative skill... a delight for any reader' *THES*

£9.99   0 7524 3333 4

The Kings & Queens of England
MARK ORMROD

'Of the numerous books on the kings and queens of England, this is the best' *Alison Weir*

£9.99   0 7524 2598 6

The Covent Garden Ladies
Pimp General Jack & the Extraordinary Story of Harris's List
HALLIE RUBENHOLD

'Sex toys, porn... forget Ann Summers, Miss Love was at it 250 years ago' *The Times*

'Compelling' *The Independent on Sunday*

'Marvellous' *Leonie Frieda*

'Filthy' *The Guardian*

£9.99   0 7524 3739 9

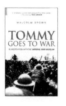

Okinawa 1945
GEORGE FEIFER

'A great book... Feifer's account of the three sides and their experiences far surpasses most books about war'
Stephen Ambrose

£17.99   0 7524 3324 5

Tommy Goes To War
MALCOLM BROWN

'A remarkably vivid and frank account of the British soldier in the trenches'
Max Arthur

'The fury, fear, mud, blood, boredom and bravery that made up life on the Western Front are vividly presented and illustrated'
The Sunday Telegraph

£12.99   0 7524 2980 4

Ace of Spies The True Story of Sidney Reilly
ANDREW COOK

'The most definitive biography of the spying ace yet written... both a compelling narrative and a myth-shattering *tour de force*'
Simon Sebag Montefiore

'The absolute last word on the subject' *Nigel West*

'Makes poor 007 look like a bit of a wuss'
The Mail on Sunday

£12.99   0 7524 2959 0

Sex Crimes
From Renaissance to Enlightenment
W.M. NAPHY

'Wonderfully scandalous'
Diarmaid MacCulloch

£10.99   0 7524 2977 9

If you are interested in purchasing other books published by Tempus, or in case you have difficulty finding any Tempus books in your local bookshop, you can also place orders directly through our website

www.tempus-publishing.com

TEMPUS – REVEALING HISTORY

D-Day The First 72 Hours
WILLIAM F. BUCKINGHAM

'A compelling narrative' *The Observer*
A *BBC History Magazine* Book of the Year 2004

£9.99   0 7524 2842 X

The London Monster
Terror on the Streets in 1790
JAN BONDESON

'Gripping' *The Guardian*
'Excellent... monster-mania brought a reign of terror to the ill-lit streets of the capital'
The Independent

£9.99   0 7524 3327 X

London
A Historical Companion
KENNETH PANTON

'A readable and reliable work of reference that deserves a place on every Londoner's bookshelf'
Stephen Inwood

£20   0 7524 3434 9

M: MI5's First Spymaster
ANDREW COOK

'Serious spook history' *Andrew Roberts*
'Groundbreaking' *The Sunday Telegraph*
'Brilliantly researched' *Dame Stella Rimington*

£20   0 7524 2896 9

Agincourt A New History
ANNE CURRY

'A highly distinguished and convincing account'
Christopher Hibbert
'A *tour de force*' *Alison Weir*
'*The* book on the battle' *Richard Holmes*
A *BBC History Magazine* Book of the Year 2005

£25   0 7524 2828 4

Battle of the Atlantic
MARC MILNER

'The most comprehensive short survey of the U-boat battles' *Sir John Keegan*
'Some events are fortunate in their historian, none more so than the Battle of the Atlantic. Marc Milner is *the* historian of the Atlantic campaign... a compelling narrative' *Andrew Lambert*

£12.99   0 7524 3332 6

The English Resistance
The Underground War Against the Normans
PETER REX

'An invaluable rehabilitation of an ignored resistance movement' *The Sunday Times*
'Peter Rex's scholarship is remarkable'
The Sunday Express

£12.99   0 7524 3733 X

Elizabeth Wydeville: The Slandered Queen
ARLENE OKERLUND

'A penetrating, thorough and wholly convincing vindication of this unlucky queen'
Sarah Gristwood
'A gripping tale of lust, loss and tragedy'
Alison Weir
A *BBC History Magazine* Book of the Year 2005

£18.99   0 7524 3384 9

If you are interested in purchasing other books published by Tempus, or in case you have difficulty finding any Tempus books in your local bookshop, you can also place orders directly through our website

www.tempus-publishing.com